Once a Priest

First Published 2015

Bretwalda Books, Unit 8, Fir Tree Close, Epsom, Surrey KT17 3LD
info@BretwaldaBooks.com
www.BretwaldaBooks.com
ISBN (978-1-910440-11-7)

Author Peter Mullen can be seen recounting anecdotes from his career on our
YouTube Channel:
"BretwaldaBooks"

Printed and bound in Great Britain by
Marston Book Services Ltd, Oxfordshire

Once a Priest

by
Peter Mullen

I: Inferno

I

"God is dead!" That was the slogan most shouted by the theological avant garde when I was ordained in 1970. And why not? We had just rocked and giggled our way through the swinging sixties, so why shouldn't God swing too – as it were from a gibbet? Death of God theology – that prize oxymoron – was a transatlantic infection of course, like Flower Power, LSD and the adenoidal idiot Bob Dylan. It was inspired by Californian luminaries with typically preposterous names: Thomas J.J. Altizer and T.W. Ogletree. I had just spent three years at right-on parties among the miniskirts at Liverpool University where I read the astringent philosophical analysts Wittgenstein, Ryle, Austin and Strawson, so my reaction to the West Coast Mystics and the announcement of God's funeral was, predictably enough I suppose, "You've gotta be kidding!"

I was in a minority, though, because all that cloven fantasy from the USA took quite a hold in Britain. There was a de rigueur lack of rigour among the students – surprisingly among the Advanced Aesthetics class who declared that The Beatles had surpassed Bach:

"All a matter of opinion."

That, in the debauched intellectual climate, had come to mean that every opinion was as good as any other. Luther had said, "Every man his own priest" and the egalitarian, secular, sixties echoed, "Everyone his or her own expert."

"Let it all hang out!"

"Do your own thing, man!"

The individualism expressed by doing your own thing was exhibited chiefly in everyone between the ages of sixteen and twenty-five dressing in the same infantilised gaudiness and playing the same handful of maudlin pop records: Massachusetts... the House of the Rising Sun... Sugar, Sugar and, oddest of all among such enlightened progressives, I believe in yesterday. Everyone looked as if they had fallen off the cover of Sergeant Pepper. Many spoke, in that mid-Atlantic twang, of "freaking out." Many more smoked cannabis, a drug which a medical pal of mine described as "a mild sedative" – though I never saw a hippie in need of sedation. "Laid back" was the thing to be. Everybody got laid. Lots. The coming of the contraceptive pill made sexual liberation obligatory. The counter culture was rapidly becoming the culture. On a rare visit to the university, my father, ex-RAF, said, unphilosophically, "To think what we sacrificed for such spoilt prats as these!"

The girls in the Modern Languages Department wore micro-skirts and dressed like Barbie dolls. They got shagged silly night and day, because the feminists had not yet arrived to warn them of the dangers of becoming mere sex-objects, nor the Greens to tell them that all the lacquer which turned their lovely hair to scented straw was destroying the ozone layer.

They were all in the concrete and trash Arts Faculty Building reading Timothy Leary and Hermann Hesse's psychedelic fantasy Steppenwolf. They were into alternative politics and anti-psychiatry: R.D. Laing and Thomas Szasz. They were into anti in a big way. They took their pills and their lower seconds. The most advanced of them were into the zombiefied cult of something called "progressive pop music". There was one record in particular which seemed to sum up the epoch and the women alike: it had a cow on the front and it was by a group calling themselves Pink Floyd. They would travel miles to hear Pink Floyd, to gape lugubriously into the middle distance and, enthralled by the technological mysticism of the electronic guitar – and Timothy Leary - they turned on, tuned in and dropped out. There were other forlorn quasi-musical gadgets of which god of all (and never so dead) was the Moog Synthesiser. On campus, as we had learnt to call it, strangers of either sex would occasionally saunter up to you and attempt to fondle your private parts.

All you need is love...

There were other flowerings. For instance, there was student politics. This chiefly consisted in students staying away from Politics lectures in order to organise sit-ins in the aptly named Administration Block, laughingly called the Senate. One day in March 1970, I left

The Cambridge pub and I was just crossing Abercrombie Square when I heard the voice of the Vice Chancellor addressing the lumpen intelligentsia by megaphone. They would not agree to leave the Administration Block and this meant the domestic staff could not get in to receive their wages. So negligible in the end were the ordinary needs of your actual working class to this elite league of pampered thugs. A transcript of what passed for conversational exchange between the head of the university and the more volatile of his indolent lodgers was eventually made public:

"Why do you refuse to leave the Senate Building?"

"It's an official sit-in." (An official sit in - from the proud-to-be-spontaneous generation)

"What's it for?"

"You are keeping secret files on us."

"Of course there are no such files. You are among the filing cabinets. Produce the files if you can find them!"

"That's just it. We can't find them – it's because they're secret!"

It was, after all, Leibnitz who had pointed out the notorious difficulty involved in trying to prove that something does not exist.

The Philosophy Department had an arrangement with the Psychology Department whereby each year the philosophers were invited to attend a keynote public lecture sponsored by the psychologists. Behaviourism was the – literally mindless – fashion in psychology, satirised by Arthur Koestler in his book The Ghost in the Machine:

"Now that we have lost our soul, gone out of our mind and seem about to lose all sense of consciousness, what is there left for psychologists to study? Professor B.F. Skinner answers, 'Rats!'"

(His initials really were B.F.)

Vigorous Professor Charlie Lloyd, Head of our Philosophy Department, led the charge across the square to the Psychology lecture theatre. All his Staff accompanied him: the brilliant and glamorous Oxford star, Paul Helm, the very ancient and very past-it lecturer in Ancient Philosophy, Pamela Huby and the visiting teaching scholar for that year, the engaging American John King Farlow who around that time awarded me the prize of a bottle of whisky for an essay I had written on the problem of induction.

This was the gist. Dirty Bertie Russell argues in his The Problems of Philosophy that, just because the sun has risen every morning in the past, gives us no reason to think that the sun will rise again tomorrow morning. I offered the opinion that, even if the sun had risen on only nine mornings out of every ten in the past, that would still give us good reason to believe it would rise tomorrow. To say that the fact the sun had risen every morning – never having missed one sunrise – gives us no reason to believe it will rise tomorrow is just a misuse of the word reason. If never-failing sunrise gives us no reason to believe in a future sunrise, what could possibly count as a reason for such a belief? Technically, this is an example of ignoratio elenchi – missing the fucking point – by high redefinition of the word reason.

It was a bottle of The Famous Grouse.

The crazy limits to which Hume and Russell took scepticism really undermines any sort of philosophical discussion before it can even get started. I produced a second reductio ad absurdum criticism of Dirty Bertie's argument: I mean if, as he suggests, we have to deny ourselves the rationality of any of our predictions concerning the future, then we must also deny the validity of all our recollections of the past – for, as believe that we have no reason to suppose the sun will rise tomorrow, we might as well believe that we have no reason to believe the sun has ever risen before, and that the whole world came into existence this morning, complete with memories and scientific laws.

Anyhow, we all arrived like wolves on the fold, sat on the front row and listened to the prestigious visiting lecturer – his offering punctuated by guffaws from Charlie Lloyd. The very second the speaker had finished, Lloyd was up on his feet:

"Thank you for your exposition of behaviourism, Professor. Am I to conclude from your argument that the only way a Behaviourist discovers he is hungry is when he observes himself running home for his lunch?"

Helm corpsed. Even Huby smiled a bleak and faraway smile. None of the psychologists got the joke.

I took my degree in a pair of morning trousers borrowed from a Jewish anthropologist. I remember they had to have the seam at the back let out because Alan Hyam was half my size. The ceremony – for the degree, not the snipping of the trousers – took place in the Royal Philharmonic Hall in Upper Parliament Street, the home of the Liverpool Phil. For the serenity of the Duchess who handed me my degree, I was glad that my bare arse was concealed by my coat tails. It was a sweaty July day. The gulls shrieked over the Liver Building and the Mersey stank of oil and sounded with the melancholy horns of the tugboats. Synthesisers blared and Barbie dolls with their rotted straw hair strutted up and down Bold Street among the trendy shops. Everything about Liverpool, from the waterfront to The Beatles' accent spoke of cataarh and phlegm.

That night the Phil played the Sinfonia Concertante in E-flat K.364 after which I walked among the litter of Upper Parliament Street towards the quay. The sun had fallen like a cricket ball behind three tall chimneys over Wallasey, and the Mersey looked like brown Windsor soup. There was a giddy swell on the crossing. The boat was one of two – The Royal Iris and The Royal Daffodil. Both had been at Dunkirk. A young man with tangled hair sat playing his sullen guitar on the open top-deck. Halfway through I've looked at life from both sides now he vomited with admirable precision into the hole in his instrument.

My landlady Florrie Wood was a saint. She had taken me in three years earlier when I had descended from Leeds looking for accommodation. She charged £2-7-6 per week – which, being translated, amounts to £2.37.5p - and for this I got a first floor flat overlooking leafy Shrewsbury Road, a small kitchen and a shared bathroom. Electricity was by means of a shilling-in-the-slot. She had a daughter Carol who had married a Scot and one, younger, not so unlucky, who performed handstands against the garden wall. Of such things dreams were made on. Florrie also had a son Chris who was not all there. He used to go off alone to watch horror films at The Essoldo. He would return and talk to himself in the lavatory:

"It's all right, Dracula. It's all right. Come on, let's get into the bath. O hell, it's not hot! It's not even cold. But that girl we strangled had great tits, didn't she?"

Late at night, he enjoyed frequent audible orgasms, the noise of them bursting like the cries of tropical birds into my attempted sleep.

From this regional outpost of cultural decadence, I went to be a Curate in Crossgates, a suburb on the east side of Leeds. I had been raised in Leeds in my grandfather's newsagent's - between the gas works and the prison -in the Armley slums. Crossgates was much smarter than Armley and its people thought well of themselves. Urbane, three-bedroom semis, people "keeping themselves to themselves" while living lives of quiet avariciousness which they attempted to pass off as praiseworthy thrift. There was also, adjacent Seacroft Hospital, the council estate: small, sad houses in grey concrete which they had tried to adorn and beautify a little with a burnt umbra decoration which looked like so many scabs.

Crossgates was a respectable place. Still, it shared Leeds' general ambience of surliness and monotone misery. If you were to take a Leeds bloke – but they all say "guy" now of course – for a slap up meal with Champagne, followed by a leg show, and then you phoned him the next day to ask if he had enjoyed himself, his Mogodon response would be, "It weren't bad." Leeds people behave as if they are always expecting someone to cheat them. There is a Leeds saying which describe its citizens:

"They allus look as if they've lost half a crown and found a tanner." That was before decimalisation and so it requires translation: "They always look as if they have lost twelve-and-a-half pence and found two-and-a-half-pee."

Leeds folk remind me of what Pound said of Housman:

"We'll all be dead soon – so let us behave as if we're dead already."

There is always that whine. How to describe the psychology of Leeds lads technically? They are miserable buggers. They have a football team which plays dour and dirty.

By 1970 most Crossgates people had a car and a colour telly. They were ambitious, if not for themselves, at least for their offspring whom they desired should "better themselves" – which meant make more money than their parents.

Was God dead, then?

Not in our parish. God was Howard Broadstairs, the rotund, avuncular, High Church freemason and Vicar of St James who had inherited a thriving concern from his predecessor, Walter Dillam, recently promoted to the uber-salubrious church of St Wilfred's,

Harrogate – pronounced "arrygut" by the Leeds oiks – where he had been able to spend £2000 on a lid for the font. Harrogate, a place so genteel, a place where the birds have the good manners to fall silent for a couple of hours every afternoon while the terminally-prosperous take their nap.

I was the junior of two curates at St James. The senior curate, poor sod, asthmatic, mildly epileptic who had originally been refused ordination by the Church bureaucracy which attends to these things but who had finally squeezed through on account of his father's, a cathedral canon, personal friendship with the diocesan bishop.

I was allotted a house banal as all the others looking out over the playing fields of the RC secondary school, and received £65 per month stipend plus £3 expenses borne by the parish. I began to brew my own beer.

Staff meetings were hilarious. Squinting Broadstairs would sit opposite me and the agitated senior curate. He would simply tell us what to do, whom to visit in the parish, what to preach about, all down to the last detail – especially about how much altar wine we should consecrate at the Parish Communion. The senior curate was, as the psychiatrists say, "disorientated for space and time." He would consecrate a flagon and a half where one chalice would have been enough. Priests are commanded to consume all that is left over from the administration to the people. So Broadstairs would approach me in the sanctuary and say,

"You'd better drink it, Peter. That bugger's giddy enough when he's sober."

Two –and-a- half pints of sweet sherry at 10.30am equips you in the face of all dangers. We ought to have sung:

"Junior curate, endless bliss,

On sanctified perpetual piss."

That fellow was lanky, fey, establishment, overworking, under-brained son of Cambridge University – all parrot fashion and no plumage. His voice was like an attack of tinnitus. He knew his Greek but not what it meant. A man who could easily put one and one together and make one and a half or, on a good day, one and five eighths. He had ginger hair, balding, and that silver spoon egalitarianism about him. Impeccably socialist – well, Harold

Wilson's Labour Party anyhow. He much resembled the mini-skirted pseudo-whores in the Modern Languages Department who affected rigorous independence of spirit but knew exactly how and when to shout for "Daddy!"

The senior curate supported Oxfam and thought it scandalous that Broadstairs – he called him "Well now, Mr Broadstairs..." – should be a freemason.

I could have felt guilty about mocking a man as unfortunate as the senior curate, were it not for his copious odiousness. He wanted to marry. The whole parish knew this. It was a truth universally acknowledged. Moreover, he used to ask spinsters in the parish embarrassing questions about female sexuality. We said Evening Prayer in the Lady Chapel at 5.15 every weekday. One Monday afternoon as we were strolling towards the lych-gate, I summoned up the solicitude to enquire about the state of his love life. I said,

"That nice girl Jill thinks the world of you."

He brushed the remnants of his ginger mop from his eyes: "Oh yes," he flapped and his ears flapped and he bent forwards and backwards so violently I thought he would fall over, "...I think Jill is a lovely girl, salt of the earth in fact. But then I remind myself who I am and that my grandfather was British Ambassador in Washington – and I think I deserve somebody rather better."

Mr Collins in Miss Austen's domestic comedy.

I told the story unabridged to Well now Mr Broadstairs who promptly departed for a fortnight's holiday, leaving me in charge of church and parish. This was difficult since I was, in my first year, only a deacon and so not qualified to celebrate the Holy Communion. There was a daily Holy Communion, sometimes early in the morning, and all these services would have to be conducted by the senior curate. So I had to make sure he was out of bed, in his vestments and in the Lady Chapel at the proper hour. It was not as easy as it sounds. Once, before a packed church, he had entered the pastoral green of a Trinity season sanctuary, clad in the violent red of Whitsun and martyrs. Devout old ladies, falling about, nearly dying of laughter. More jokes about parrots.

I visited as instructed. Ellie Firth who, like Florence Nightingale before her, had enjoyed a sickbed for sixty years. There was old Fred

Leckenby who sang the Agnus Dei to me in Latin the night before he died. And then there was Polly McNeil...

Polly lived in the row of houses behind the RC secondary school and by the bus stop on the main route to the city centre. She said, "Oh, you're the new one aren't you. Come in and have a drink."

She was lissome, perky, thirty-fivish, nerves strung up to concert pitch. She also had a nervous tic which made it look as if she was constantly winking at you. It took you a few minutes to realise she was. Long black hair and a dress as florid as Joseph's technicoloured dreamcoat. I recalled some American writer's description of the type: "She dressed as if she was on her way to an erotic funeral."

She had made a fruitcake and she offered me a slice. I took it. You always did. We were instructed in our pastoral training to accept everything offered. Between two and five in the afternoon you could easily eat and drink enough for a fortnight. It was not unusual to turn up for Evening Prayer and have to throw up in the graveyard before you entered church.

She said, "My husband's working away. I get very lonely. We've only moved into this house not long since."

I took another sip of dry sherry and said, "Would you like me to do a house blessing?"

She turned to the drinks cabinet and said, "Yes please. And then will you fuck me? We needn't go upstairs...." God knows what she thought I would be capable of if I couldn't manage the stairs! She added conspiratorially, "I keep a bed next door" – gesturing towards the heavy green curtain in the corner.

Standing up, putting my sherry glass down on the polished table: "Bless this house and home, O Lord and those who dwell here. May they live in love and peace together and always be in safety under thy protection..."

"Oh I'm not in love with him. He never comes near me these days. He's more interested in his foreign stamps collection."

She unbuttoned her blouse. No bra. Perkier than I'd thought.

"Really, Polly, I have to be going!"

I still don't know how I got out alive. As I trotted down the street I turned and there was her laughing face in the window. What did one do in these cases? Render an account to the vicar?

"Well now Mr Broadstairs yon housewife at number eighteen tried to fuck me..."

Report the woman to the Rural Dean? Her GP? The police? I decided to say nothing and hope that was an end of it. But a few weeks later she came to Sunday Choral Evensong. It was my turn to preach and as I got up to walk to the pulpit she rose from her seat and for a tempestuous half a minute I thought she was about to make a scene. Would she start to undo her dress again, or what? She merely turned and left the church. Karen Martin in the Young Wives approached me as I was saying Goodnight to everyone at the door:

"I saw you blushing, Peter. If you take my advice, I'd steer well clear of that one. She's....known for it" – twisting her mouth into a sort of lubricious contempt.

Deacons in the church have been disparagingly described as neither flesh, fish nor fowl on account of the fact that there is very little they are permitted to do in the sacramental services. He cannot celebrate the Holy Communion, of course, or solemnise matrimony or even give a blessing. But while Broadstairs was away, I had a thing to do which even deacons and trainees are supposed to be able to do: take a funeral. Only this was a baby, four months old....

They said they would bring the coffin at 11.15. I stood waiting at the top of the chancel steps. The west doors were open and I could see the straight gravel path, lined by cherry trees, as far as the lych-gate and the main road. Behind me, in late Victorian stained glass, the blond and gaudy Galilean suffered little children to come to his, as yet, unpierced palms, while black-bearded disciples sat nearby, chastened and glum.

Steadman arrived two minutes early, carrying the absurdly small pasteboard coffin. There were no mourners in our wide, clean parish church where the cheerful alleluiahs of Easter had recently rung out, and now the air was empty except for the mingled smells of burnt candles and brass polish. The undertaker approached slowly over the long red carpet until he stood just two feet in front of me. The church was altogether too large for that coffin – unlike the other week, a Tuesday, when we buried Willie Clement, eighty-six and sixteen stone, the bearers grunting in the teeming rain, pews filled with half the parish singing Abide With Me with more verve than you thought possible..

"Morning Peter. Bad job."

"It is."

We faced each other across the child's coffin which Steadman supported effortlessly on his forearms. Gillian Shotton, born the last day of January and, by the middle of May, found dead in her cot from what the medical experts, with admirable diagnostic precision, referred to as a cot-death. A piece of a Psalm then the Lord's Prayer.

We drove off through the streets and round the back of the housing estate on to the ring road which led to the Municipal Crematorium. I was hot under the cassock and surplice, the absurd box on my knee. Steadman smoked all the time. One or two flies buzzed in the spacious heavily-scented rear of the hearse where the steel catafalque with safety runners, unusually unused, reflected the bright sunlight. Steadman finished another cigarette and threw the end out of the window.

"How do you manage with these, Peter? I mean children?"

"It's the same for you though, isn't it? You have to visit the home and take the... do the necessary. I'd say it was worse for you."

"Ah but I have a sequence, you see. A patter. Forms to be filled in. Definite questions to be asked. I can hide behind the sequence of events."

"I have a sequence as well. The church has a sequence all its own."

We drove through the wide gates of the Crematorium. The Shotton family had not yet arrived. I got down from the car and handed the child's coffin to the verger. He stepped inside the chapel and placed it on the covered trestle by the reading desk where it looked more ridiculous still, as if there had been a shortage of full-size bodies and this miniature was the best anyone could do.

Two family saloon cars turned into the drive and a minute later they drew up outside the chapel. Charles and Anne Shotton sat in the front of the first car. She was young, about twenty-two, slim, pale-faced, the yellow hair falling over the collar of her black coat. She held a handkerchief to her eyes which were red and swollen. Two middle aged women with black veils climbed out of the other car and stood by the dead child's mother. There was a nervous economy of movement as people were unsure about what to do next, and in the sultry heat all sounds seemed muted, compounding the unreality of the scene. It was as if we were all on an old photograph.

Charles Shotton put an arm around his wife's shoulder and the two veiled sisters – cousins or aunts – stepped back a couple of paces. We walked up the short aisle silently as, from somewhere among the flowers, came the tin thin piping organ music: Jesu, Joy of Man's Desiring.

The mourners filled only the one pew at the front on the right hand side and there they looked uncomfortable, part sitting, part kneeling in an uneasy crouched position from which they glanced now and then, reluctantly, towards the miniature coffin. It drew their eyes. The music ended exactly as the verger closed the doors behind him and I was left to begin the short service of committal. It was all the family had asked for, the raw minimum, the most they could bring themselves to bear.

There was nothing, I said, that I could say, except that we committed Gillian to the Lord's safekeeping and prayed for God's comfort for her mother and father. Someone had placed a small teddy bear in a blue ribbon on the child's coffin. At the words of committal, Anne Shotton began to shake and sob silently. Her husband held her arm tightly. I pressed the button which signalled to the verger that it was time for him to come back. The same button also filled the hot chapel with more funereal musak. I moved to stand by the child's mother. She began an energetic, despairing cry which grew louder until she was turned to look me straight in the eye and shouting, "Why? Why?" And "I want Gillian back - that's all!"

The verger stepped, as he usually did, between the mourners and the coffin in case, as he always said, "Anyone decides to do anything silly."

By the powers of gentleness which must have been magical powers, Thomas Steadman – no doubt working to his own sequence of events – managed to lead the woman out into the fresh air where her sobbing took on such a fierce and deeply rhythmic pattern that she retched until she vomited. I told Charles Shotton I would call and see them soon and he apologised again and again for his wife's behaviour. "She's upset," he said, as if trying to persuade me. Poor Shotton, his face creased with embarrassment and guilt, like a tortured heretic leaping from the rack to say sorry to his inquisitors for making too much noise. Steadman delivered Anne, partly recovered, to her husband and they drove off in the back of one of the cars through the lines of posing angels.

I went back into the chapel which was empty, like a theatre between performances. The coffin had been removed from the trestle. I glanced through the triple-glazed window of the Garden of Peace, then turned through the narrow door towards the whirring furnaces. A young man stood by the machine used for grinding calcium remains. I looked at him. He nodded in the direction of the middle furnace of three. The lad held a pot of tea. On a small table near the calcium remains machine was one slim box file and a daily tabloid newspaper folded between the crossword and the racing tips.

"What shall I do with this then, Sir? D'you want to take it, or shall I hand it in at the office and let them send it on?"

"I'll take it."

I folded the small teddy bear under my arm and then stepped out down the drive towards the office to sign the register and collect my fee.

Was God dead? I called on Him, anyway. Then I went to join Steadman in the quiet and quality car.

II

Every Tuesday and Friday mornings there was a 6.30 celebration of Holy Communion in the Lady Chapel. Broadstairs ran the parish with military discipline. Holy Communion as follows: Tuesday 6.30. Wednesday 9.00. Thursday 7.15pm (for the Young Wives) Friday 6.30. Heaven defend the curate who neglected to enter the precise number of those attending in the register of services. Broadstairs was obsessed with numbers. Everything had a number. Religion by numbers – and about as creative as painting by numbers. The only other person who ever attended the early service was a superstitious Anglo-papist called Percy who required Mass at that ungodly hour only because he had to start work at 7.30. He called all the clergy Father and touched his cloth cap to us as often as he genuflected to the Reserved Sacrament. You could tell he drew religious satisfaction out of getting the clergy from their beds at the crack of dawn. With obsequious zeal he also rang the bells, which must have been a great encouragement for the whole parish, still abed.

But I am being unkind. Percy could be an irritation, but there are thousands like him for whom the church is the guarantee of reality – literally their salvation. And not just the formularies or the theology of the church, but its apparatus, paraphernalia and above all its personnel, the priests. All of us, shifty inadequate men shuffling from nave to sanctuary in our cassocks, we are, for such as Percy, the living proof of God and his heaven. The church calendar – Advent, Christmas, Epiphany, Easter, Ascension, Whit and Trinity – is the real clock for these people. They live in the church's shelter, within its rhythm. In better days, they used to be called the holy common folk of God. Priests despise them to the peril of their immortal souls

For my first year, before I was raised from deacon to priest, I could only watch as Broadstairs or the senior curate celebrated Holy Communion. It was the west-facing choreography – over the counter – and Broadstairs performed it immaculately, with a few added ultramontane gestures such as letting a bit of the priest's wafer drop into the consecrated wine as a symbol of the oneness of Christ's corporeality and sanguinity. This morsel had to be rescued before the administration of the chalice. In the High Church trade it was known as fishing. Broadstairs fished with aplomb – reminding me of Betty Clayton behind the counter in Whitkirk Road fish 'n' chip shop, scooping a special haddock out of the deep fry. The senior curate found this tricky manual act confounding – like the difficulty involved in trying to rub one's tummy and pat one's head at the same time - and he took so long over the job that sometimes he made Percy late for work. Between Holy Communion and Matins there was an interval during which the celebrant removed his vestments. During this meditative space I would often hear Broadstairs and the senior curate in a slanging match fifty yards away in the sacristy:

"What the hell were you doing with that chalice? Look here, I must have shown you how to do it a score of times!"

"Well now Mr Broadstairs, I don't think it's necessary to drop that bit of wafer in the cup. You only have to pull it out again."

Broadstairs gave him a glassy look:

"Not necessary? I sometimes wonder whether curates are necessary!"

Then Broadstairs would return to the Lady Chapel to say Matins, red in the face, his eyes watering, his voice cracking, his blood pressure off the top of the Richter scale – a condition only aggravated when the senior curate read the wrong lesson. Percy had gone by this time, leaving three parsons in that huge cavern, in what seemed like the middle of the night, poring over the more esoteric verses of The Book of Leviticus. Sometimes all three of us collapsed in giggles, as when, for example the reading ended with a line such as "...and behold they departed into Shittim." We read from The Revised Standard Bible. Where The Authorised Version rendered the verse in Isaiah, "...with twain he did fly" the RSV offered instead, "...with two he flew." So naturally we called it the Chinese Bible. Once the senior curate, in his scoopy voice, read, "Is the seer here?" We could hardly continue after that.

Disorientated for space and time. As with God, so with the senior curate: dark and light were both alike to him. One winter morning he locked me in church after Matins – because it was still dark at 7.30 and he thought it was evening – and I was released only after fifteen minutes of un-liturgical bell-ringing brought Mrs Sally Broadstairs, in her dressing gown, to my aid:

"Whatever's that silly boy done now!"

Broadstairs' ideas on man-management were straight out of the Teacher Training College Manual. Every minute of your day had to be accounted for, except when it was your day off – then you could bugger off to Iceland for all he cared. But don't go to see Leeds United on a Saturday afternoon if it means you'll be late for Evensong. The senior curate liked to go to symphony concerts at the town hall on Saturdays and he had to get the vicar's permission for this too. Broadstairs had his virtues but he turned small-mindedness into a fine art.

After early church, the weekday mornings were for study and writing sermons, but Broadstairs – no academic theologian - wouldn't raise objections if he called and found you playing with your train set. Afternoons were for parish visiting. This was obligatory and you had to list the names of all those you'd called on: fifty a week was the target. Religion by numbers again. Pastoral production line. The respectable burghers of Crossgates loved to organise themselves into groups and clubs: Brownies, Cubs, Men's Snooker (which one of the curates was asked to open with a prayer – what? Behold, O Lord, our balls of many colours), Scouts. Mothers' Union, Young Wives, the Choir, the Youth Club and half a dozen other cliques who hired the church hall.

So Broadstairs after Evensong: "What have you planned for tonight, Peter?"

"Going to the pub."

"Well, before you do, just go and look at the Girl Guides, will you?"

"You can get arrested for doing that!"

I liked to visit the choir practice which was conducted by an irascible, tobacco-stained and quite brilliant septuagenarian organist called W. Iles-Pulford – "Bill." He sat dignified as an aristocratic walrus at the console while the excitable baritone Gordon Wise shouted at the boys and flung his arms about like a drip dry shirt in a gale. Bill died and Broadstairs preached at his funeral:

"A young priest was offered his first parish. The night before he was to be inducted as Vicar of St Faithless, Littlehope, he visited an old rector for advice. 'Have you one word of guidance, Father?' The old man replied: 'Just the one: hate your organist!'"

The difference between an organist and a terrorist? You can negotiate with a terrorist.

Broadstairs did not hate Pulford. But he did have Van Gogh's ear for music which for him was simply to be used as the tiled floor is used - to get from one place to another during the service. As to hymns in general, Broadstairs would have sung Onward Christian Soldiers every week. Pulford's tastes were developed, refined: Orlando Gibbons, Bach, Tallis...

Struggling out of his surplice one morning, Broadstairs bawled across the choir vestry, "What the dickens was that thing you gave us for the offertory? I didn't know it."

"You didn't know Onward Christian Soldiers once - " And from his intonation you could tell there was meant to be the phrase, "Silly old sod!" added to his riposte.

Broadstairs the perfect musical philistine. Pulford brought in an amateur orchestra to sing Faure's Requiem and the next morning in the Lady Chapel the senior curate was playing a recording he'd made of the Pie Jesu, delicately sung by a local lad, when the vicar lumbered in: "What the devil's this – a concert?"

I think Harold Pinter must have learned his parsimonious, inconsequential dialogue from a suburban curate's account of his parish visiting: Mrs Morgan, number seven, a handsome lady with a moderate beard:

"I went out this morning. It must have been half past nine. I was back at a quarter past ten. My next door neighbour had lice. And her cat stank and clawed your nylon skirt..."

Such were the innards of social intercourse in Crossgates.

Mrs Morgan's words would usually degenerate into mute and malicious mouthings. And she would make a strange warbling, as if she was gargling with some unpleasant liquid behind those rubbery lips. You could not escape until you had drunk at least two cups of tepid tea from a cracked mug and complimented the leaden sponge cake. One day this was replaced by a red quiche that was pure biliousness. The Mrs Morgans of the parish – and there were hordes of them – never came to church. As you tried to leave the house they would seize you in an armlock and hint at sordid goings-on a generation ago which made them declare, "I'll never enter that place again as long as I live!"

There had been real life sordid goings-on in Crossgates. Long before the coming of the PTA and colour tellies, before Crossgates became A Nice Place to Live, the parish had been a coal-mining village. The locals were religious only in the English sense that they liked to know the nature and form of the church services they were staying away from. They attended St James only on major festivals, holding that other English maxim: there is no God and it is wise to pray to Him from time to time.

In 1919 the Church Authorities appointed a priest called Russell to the parish. He was a flamboyant Anglo-papist – as Ned Seagrove, retired bookie and local historian told me over a cup of Ovaltine:

"A bloody papal fifth columnist in the Church of England! Turned t'place into a medieval shrine."

He introduced confession, street processions with incense and a life-size statue of the Virgin Mary, twelve candles on the altar, lace, frilly cottas – the whole Anglocatholic daisy chain. This aroused the locals from their undogmatic slumbers. When he erected another, even bigger, statue of the Virgin in the south aisle, there were fights in church. A blacksmith, Stephen Dugdale, led the peasants' revolt:

"Take that bloody idol down or I'll smash it – and I'll smash you an' all while I'm at it!"

He did break the statue. And there are still scars on the stone pillar by the bell rope which in my day the senior curate would tug on to announce a service – usually when there was no service. In Crossgates in the 1920s the Reformation was fought all over again – and that in an industrial village which had just lost eighteen of its young men in the trenches.

There was brass as well as muck in Crossgates in those days and the disgruntled parishioners – unable to unseat the exotic Father Russell, despite the 1919 Enabling Act which had created Parochial Church Councils – built their own tin tabernacle and emblazoned it with the superscription of its accusation: FREE CHURCH OF ENGLAND.

Russell was left to his smells and bells and a congregation of four, which had included our own early morning Percy's dad

In 1925 Russell left. Ned told me: "They appointed a bloke called Cesar Romeo Taglisi and folks thought they'd got another incense-swinging fucker."

He turned out to be a huge, gentle man who spoke softly and loved children – a man with no doctrinal peculiarities.

"People loved him," said Ned "...thought Francis of Assisi had come back."

His name was anglicised to Taglis and he stayed, restoring the church and building up the congregation until 1950 when he died, serenely as he had lived. Dapper, upwardly-mobile bachelor Walter Dillam succeeded him and the suburban success story began.

One day early in 1971 I walked into the vicarage and heard Martin Hemsworth, the undertaker, relating a senior curate story to Broadstairs who was laughing and shaking so violently I thought he would have a seizure:

"Rita Whatmore's funeral and yon silly bugger curate suddenly comes running down the aisle shouting the bit you're supposed to say at the graveside. When he sees me, he stops the service and asks in that funny voice of his, 'Do I need a green ticket?'"

Hilarity threatened to crack the walls. At that moment the senior curate himself came in and actually joined in the merriment himself without knowing that he was the cause of it. All four of us in the vicar's study nearly wetting ourselves. At last Hemsworth, in his posh suit, slunk off to his posh car and Broadstairs made the senior curate and me sit down for the regular staff meeting, His Yorkshire cherub of a wife brought us cups of milky coffee. Then his mad sixteen year old daughter burst in, scarlet with anxiety and yelling, "My flies! Where are my flies?"

I mustered the will not to look. Broadstairs said, "I've put 'em in the garage." Much bitterness ensued. The mad girl screamed at him. Her beloved insects would die in the cold garage. It was all part of her biology course. She oozed forensic science and went on to train as a doctor and subsequently became a psychiatrist.

When Broadstairs had finished telling us when we were to preach, what we were to preach and for how long, he winked his good eye and shrank into the depths of his armchair. From this security, he asked his usual question, a rhetorical question – did we have anything we wanted to say?

"Well now Mr Broadstairs..," The senior curate began as usual, rocking backwards and forwards on the sofa as if he was testing the furniture to destruction. Broadstairs gave me a sly look and I was nearly sick with suppressed mirth.

"Have you got St Vitus' dance or what?"

"Well now Mr Broadstairs, I really do want to talk to you about the Youth Club Dance, but what I actually wanted to say..."

His movements became brisker. His manic lankiness made the vicar and me giddy. And, as he was on his way to the junior school to give his lesson, he was festooned with visual aids, teaching resources, rolled up paper, pencils, crayons, a metre ruler, coloured stickers, glue, gum, paint pots and a black witch's cap.

"...but I actually wanted to say that I'd like to organise the house to house collection for Christian Aid."

Broadstairs sat up and immediately enunciated his first principle of negotiations: "No."

There followed a sub-theological slanging match between the loopy genteel theoretical socialist from Cambridge University and the Reverend Yorkshire freemason who was certainly not going to allow his parishioners "...to be duped into giving money to terrorist organisations."

Moreover, he bridled at the prospect of another Youth Club Dance: "It's nowt but sex and broken windows!"

The senior curate shuffled off with his pique and parcel of pedagogical aids.

"Ichabod," said Broadstairs. "The glory hath departed."

He rounded on me, taking my record of pastoral visits in his hands and scowling at it as if it was a composite motion from the Trades Union Conference:

"You only visited fifty people last month. It's not enough. Yon fella -" a way he had of speaking of the senior curate while avoiding the pain that a mention of the man's name would cause him – "can visit two hundred."

Stung, I set out to put matters right the same afternoon. Betty, an aged aunt of mine, lived on the York Road at the northernmost edge of the parish. She answered the door with her right arm in a sling and her head bandaged:

"It was you pal, the other curate. He came to see me last week. I asked him if he wanted a piece of fruit cake. Well, I keep it on the cellar head. He would follow me – ever so close. I could feel his breath. He sways back and forth, doesn't he? Then he nodded so hard he head-butted me and I had to step back, like, to get clear of him. Well, I fell down the cellar steps and finished up in hospital."

I remembered Broadstairs' "two hundred."

One down and one hundred and ninety-nine to go.

Aunt Betty said, "He's ever so nice really. He took all the fruit cake. I said, while I was waiting for the ambulance, he could take it."

I discovered there was more to parish work than twenty-four church services each week – thirty-nine in Holy Week – Pinteresque visiting and servicing the Girl Guides. There was school and I was detailed to teach there every Thursday morning, ten and eleven year olds. The headmaster was on the verge of retirement. He had been there since 1944. His name was E. Smelt. No joking. I also had to lead a weekly assembly of the whole school.

There was a spacious hall with wide windows looking out over the schoolyard towards the houses and with the church in the background. The children sat on the floor on three sides of a square while I stood on the fourth side behind the lectern with the lions carved on it. Everyone in Crossgates was proud of the new school with its slim-line radiators and overhead projectors replacing the old school's dusty books, damp cupboards and rotting floorboards which thrust splinters into the children's backsides every time they sat down. The wondrous new school was also open plan which meant there were no dividing lines between the classrooms. So typically a class engrossed in arithmetic would have a singing class in their ears. The very progressive Miss Frankland assured me that this arrangement was "convenient for the flexible day." In fact it was chaos, all day bedlam.

I thought I would begin my teaching career by introducing them to The Lord's Prayer. It was a snowy winter and, as I stared over the heads of Class One, the children under the white glare of the wide windows looked like mere smudges on an overexposed photograph. The record player offered us Prokoviev: Lieutenant Kije – The Sleighride.

"Now then, what about this?"

I tried to sound arresting, but they were unimpressed. It was embarrassing when the children had to be shushed by the class teachers because one word from me and they did as they liked. When the murmuring had fallen to a barely tolerable level, I began again,

"We say 'Our Father, which art in heaven.' So what d'you think heaven is like?"

I rubbed my hands together as it were against an imagined chill. Jane Kelly in Class Two spoke as if reciting a nursery rhyme and swayed to and fro as she did so and I wondered if she had learnt this habit from the senior curate. She said heaven was like Christmas, "...because you get lots and lots of presents and lots of lovely things to eat." She was progressing very well towards perfecting the quiet avariciousness of the suburb. Before I had chance to respond to this theological insight, a child farted loudly and they all screamed with delight and shouted "Poo!"

After more interventions from the regular teachers, I was able to resume - after a fashion.

In junior schools surrealism rules. It is the childish version of the housewives' inconsequential banter on the visiting round. So Jeremy Walls broke in with, "We went to my Uncle Clifford's on Saturday and his cat got run over." This was too much for Louise Tanner who let out a great wail and had to be led away, much to the amusement of all the little sadists cross-legged on the floor.

Meanwhile Tina Martin raised her hand and asked, "Has Jeremy's cat gone to heaven?"

"It wasn't my cat. It was my Uncle Clifford's," shouted Jeremy, fixing her with a stare. He made it sound as if establishing ownership of the cat in this life had a bearing on its eternal destiny.

"It was squashed," he went on to whoops of delight. "The wheel ran right over it." His voice was pitched on a gloomy monotone, but he brightened as he explained, "Uncle Clifford had to scrape it off the road with a shovel."

The children were now in ecstasy. Only the staff looked pale and made mouths at one another. E. Smelt, clapping his hands, said,

"Now, now, Jeremy, I don't think Mr Mullen has come to our school to hear stories like that."

I seized inspiration: "I'm sure Jeremy's... I mean Jeremy's Uncle Clifford's cat has gone to heaven " - thus revealing a certainty about the afterlife of dumb beasts stronger than anything to be found in St Thomas Aquinas or even the Bible. A child's view of heaven is filled with so much livestock that they'd need a permit from the Common Agricultural Policy Office to shift it around the place. And when we read the story of Noah in Class Four, none of the children minded that every human creature save for eight persons was drowned in the deluge, but suggest that some animals perished and they would all be writing to Blue Peter to complain.

There was a shuffle and a scarcely audible muttering from the front row. Little Sarah Brocklebank was furiously mouthing a question. Her twisted, overemphatic expression reminded me of women lip-reading over the noise of the looms. "Speak up, Sarah – there's a good girl," said the highly fanciable Miss Frankland as she leaned over to restrain a big lad in Class Three who was attempting to perpetrate some barely recognisable sexual act on his neighbour. At last little Sarah with the long black hair had her turn:

"We had jelly yesterday. My Mum said we couldn't have jelly because Wayne – that's my brother..."

(Miss Frankland raised her eyes as if praying for a stay of execution)

"...was naughty and did a loud wee-wee in the biscuit tin."

Uproar.

"But then Auntie Jean came and we did have jelly."

"Well that was nice for you, Sarah" (I was catching the drift) "...and what flavour jelly did you have?"

But she only sat silently as if stunned. A dozen or more hands went up, however, all in a frenzy to let me know their favourite flavours. Cruelly, I brushed them all aside and made one last stab at getting back to The Lord's Prayer:

"So what d'you think – is there jelly in heaven?"

My words were met with utter silence. At once I knew what it must be like for an actor to dry on stage. Sarah's hand went up again. It was a lifeline.

"Well, Sarah, and what are you going to tell us about heaven?"

Her fingers went in her mouth and she shook shook her head slowly:

"Please, Sir, my Auntie has got a budgie and it's green."

No one seemed in the least surprised at merely one more non sequitur. There was nothing for it but to join in the plot: "And what's your Auntie's budgie called?"

"Her green budgie?"

"Has she got more than the one?"

The child's face took on an expression of the most dazed indifference and she said nothing. Tiny Philip McEvany put up his hand and announced in a piping voice that it was his birthday.

"That's nice, Philip. Right then everyone – let's sing Happy Birthday! How old are you Philip?"

"Five," he said "but I'm not four now."

They sang: "Happy birthday to you. Squashed tomatoes and stew."

And I couldn't help thinking of Jeremy's cat – I mean Jeremy's Uncle Clifford's cat. We said The Lord's Prayer and a prayer for old people who found it difficult to get about in the snow. We sang Little Drops of Water and I noticed a constant dripping of the melted snow overhanging the window. A pale sun half-appeared, racing through thin clouds. Someone rang a bell. In a minute we were drinking coffee in the Staff Room. Miss Frankland smiled. E. Smelt said I had done well.

I began to think I was in the wrong job. I could not see what I was for. The Crossgates middle class were nice enough in their own way and it was hard to imagine they felt as if they needed to be saved from anything. There was not so much as one candle-power of religion in the whole of the suburb. I was bored with the ice and lemon world of the PTA and even with looking at the Girl Guides. One day I was sitting in the pub reading the cricket report and about to take the first swallow of my third pint of Theakstons bitter when I was overtaken with what I can only term a fit of inspiration, that not uncommon feeling of sudden clarity which can accompany mild inebriation. I knew what I would do: if there was no religion in Crossgates, then I would import some. Or, if not religion exactly, then at least a frisson of mental activity, something to demonstrate that there was more to life than the Church Fabric Committee and hanging around Austhorpe Road on Saturday afternoon waiting for late bargains on Stevenson's meat stall

Of course, this innovation would have to await the Imprimateur and nihil obstat from the vicar. I raised it at the staff meeting and so, for once, it was the senior curate's turn to observe rather than suffer Broadstairs' benign, infinitely destructive negativity.

"A discussion group?"

"Yes."

"And what are you going to discuss?"

"The Christian faith."

"The Christian faith?" – as if this were the syllabus of some alien cult – "And where are you going to hold the group?"

"At my house."

"At your own house? At the curate's house."

"Well, yes. I am the curate and that's where I live. I can't think of anywhere else."

"You can't think of anywhere else! And who d'you reckon will come to this group then?"

He twisted his lips around the word group with the sort of revulsion you would have for dog shit on the carpet.

"I shall advertise it in the parish magazine."

"In the parish magazine?" More dog shit. "You might end up with atheists, folk with funny views...cause a lot of bother..."

"Well, what of it? Now look, I suppose an especially suspicious person could find something objectionable about a priest inviting his people, his friends, round to his own house to talk about God – but I can't for the life of me imagine what the objections might be."

"Now don't you come that sarcastic tone with me, lad!"

"I wasn't being sarcastic but you were being obtuse."

The senior curate wore the expression of someone who had just come under machine gun fire for the first time. He was scratching at the arm of the sofa and Broadstairs' ire was in competition with itself over which was the more infuriating, my outrageous proposal to talk to local Christians about God or the damage to the fabric of his furniture. Puce and sweating, the senior curate stood up:

"Well now Mr Broadstairs, I shall have to be going to the library before they close."

When we were alone:

"Vicar, it's not as if I'm planning an orgy."

He looked as if he would have preferred an orgy. It wasn't that he was unintelligent, but he just did not believe that the mind should concern itself with such a worthless activity as thinking . He was not deliberately cruel, but it was clear that the prospect of a discussion group – his people actually asking questions and perhaps even agreeing to disagree on a few matters here and there – filled him with terror. He could be a kind and helpful pastor, but his character and his methods cut off the small number of his parishioners who could not see the PTA Annual Dance or the Men's Group's trip to the ball-bearings factory as previews of the beatific vision.

"What night were you planning to hold the group?"

"I thought maybe Wednesday."

He stood up sharply and looked for a second as if he might faint.

"You can't have Wednesday – who's going to see to the Young Wives?"

I suppressed the remark that sprang to mind and said I'd ask the senior curate.

"I could easily swap him seeing to the Young Wives for looking at the Girl Guides."

His one good eye was squinting to discern facetiousness.

"All right then. Give it a try. But I'm not expecting any trouble!"

I wondered what his repertoire of responses would be if he ever did sense trouble on the agenda.

Among the folk with funny views who turned up on the first Wednesday evening were Jock Henderson, a slim, silver-haired accountant on the verge of retirement, John Foster, a mathematician, and his wife Anne with big eyes and a red hat, David Paget, an agreeably bolshy sixth former who looked exactly like Parsley the lion in the children's television series The Herbs and Dr Joan Abbot, a voluptuous sociologist who came to church occasionally and did not get on with the vicar who, learning of her profession, regarded her as worse than a communist and an atheist. The most interesting member of the group was Edward Cowie, a composer working with Alexander Goehr in the Music Department at Leeds University. This lot were probably the only half dozen in the parish who had read some Henry James but no Catherine Cookson.

III

Most afternoons I would set off to drown myself in an orgy of pastoral care. Mrs Jennie Johnson, toothless widow, Rosicrucian, owner of two parrots. The small 1960s bungalow stank of stale piss and bird droppings. You had to knock loudly and walk straight in as Jennie could not get up from her chair.

"Is that you?" she called.

"No, it's me!"

"Oh it's you."

And the parrots started squawking and talking – "It's you...It's me" – like a cricket commentary on an old wireless set that had wandered off the wavelength. Spindly Jennie with Gorgon's hair was seventy-eight that very day and there were cards over the fireplace to prove it. On the table in front of her, she had set out the Tarot cards.

"Still at your black magic eh? God knows what the vicar would say if he knew I was seeing you, Jennie: he's not over fond of Methodists, never mind old witches like you!"

And she cackled appropriately. Her laughter went into a cough and she shook and slavered like an old dog.

"I'll give you a reading."

I told her it was against my religion but her face took on a sort of absented mystical look and she said,

"There are some things you don't know. Some things even the Catholic church doesn't know."

At this pronouncement the parrots fell silent, as if waiting for the revelation of the Great Unknowns. The old lady raised her arm and pointed at the Kitsch pictures over the fireplace featuring shining white crosses festooned with garlands of roses. Rosicrucianism sounded as if it were an agreeable form of crucifixion – drugged in the florist's perhaps.

"Look, I've got a new picture. It's from a jumble sale at St Cuthbert's, down Hunslet. 'Course I couldn't go myself, but our Janet fetched it up."

Fetched it up – and it looked like it.

"It used to be on the wall in Rose Lodge at Belle Isle."

On the wall opposite was a life size portrait of her late husband, Harry dressed in the regalia of what looked like the Grand Wizard.

"Now my Harry, he took the Royal Arch degree, you know."

She renewed her benign cackling:

"You call yourself a philosopher, Peter. Well let me tell you, Des Carts was a Rosicrucian. And Leeb Nits. And Jacob Bum – he was another. Will you have a drink with me for my birthday? Go on – you know where it is."

It was on the sideboard. Draught sweet sherry in a Teachers whisky bottle, brought from Armitage's in Scholes by her next door neighbour. There were two cracked teacups containing a few flies apiece. She drained hers, smacking her lips:

"There, that's better – like a blood transfusion."

I shook the remaining flies out of the other cup and downed mine too.

"Happy Birthday, Jennie!"

"Ah, but what is happiness? Are you happy, Peter? Are you really – or do you just think you are?"

"I think, therefore I'm happy."

"What's that?"

"Des Carts."

"Look pour me some more of that wine and I'll tell you what's the trouble with you."

This time she gazed into the cracked cup as if in the act of divination, the aroma of the sherry blending sickeningly with the other malarias.

She said, "You think too much – that's what's the matter with you."

The parrots began again. "Look," she said "there's the tower struck by lightning. You're in for a rough time, Peter old love..."

She spoke the words so consolingly. Then:

"But the end will be glorious. Oh you just wait! You see, there's your main card. It's the sun."

We drank some more sherry then I kissed her goodbye and stepped out into the dizzy street. It had begun to rain. No sun after all. I could hardly wait for my glorious end. In the event, Jennie's came first. Next morning at 7.30 the neighbour Janet phoned me;

"I just went to take her milk in as usual and there she was, gone. At the bottom of the stairs. Dead. She was ever such a funny colour."

I took the funeral the following Monday at the Palace of Euphemisms called Lawnswood Crematorium. The artificial music piped The Old Rugged Cross and Rock of Ages. The procedure was enlivened by a spasm of Masonic twitches over the coffin before I pressed the button which sent Jennie on her way. I spent half an hour in conversation with the two cheerful necrophiles who operated the furnaces. As I walked down the drive, I saw her smoke rising out of the thin chimney stack. It seemed to blow in the shape of a question mark.

Indeed a curate is only half a parish priest. His vicar is king and he truly saith to this man, "Go!" and he goeth and "Come!" and behold he cometh. Every parish is bizarre in its own way and the priest more than anyone, more even than the family doctor, sees the insane side of people, the preposterousness, the greed, the dirt, the neurosis, the outrageous expectations, the anxiety, sickness, death. And all these things are ever-present, even at the christening, the wedding, the Sunday Mass. Crossgates seemed madder than most – but what did I know? This was the only place I'd seen. From the paranoid control-freakery of the vicar to the sheer looniness of the slapstick senior curate with his nauseating self-satisfaction – "I deserve somebody rather better" – to the many denizens of the bloody place who were like characters out of Grand Guignol, the parish was an amalgam of satanic pantomime and theatre of the absurd. The Inferno of Signor Dante is no exaggeration.

Never mind being locked in the church by a bloke who doesn't know day from night, just look at this:

Brian Smith died, age fifty-four. He was a dustman until he dropped dead on the cart - inconveniently only a couple of minutes before his scheduled lunch break – outside the Manston Hotel on Austhorpe Road. Mrs Smith took it very badly:

"We were supposed to be going to Benidorm next month an' all."

Brian was put in his coffin in his wedding suit with a large photo of the missus clasped across his chest, his mates walking behind the hearse, just as they daily trudged daily behind the muck cart. And in the crem? A recording of a song from the children's TV programme Chigley:

"We are the Corporation dustmen in the Corporation dustcart
And we clean up all the rubbish and the mess:
We're efficient, clean and thorough as we tidy up the borough,
We're the Corporation dustmen, we're the best."

At the staff meeting Broadstairs asked how the Discussion Group was going:

"Have you rewritten the Nicene Creed yet?"

I told him it was the highlight of the week. Light in the darkness. But even in the night the Pinteresque dialogue of my parish visits – one woman, a nurse for God's sake, had that very day said, "He got renal failure and then his kidneys packed up" – crowded into my sleep. Lusty old crones in dormer bungalows coming at me with fruit cakes and cups of tea. The séance of the Men's Group over their clattering dominoes. Women deriving more delight than was decent over a yard of fabric at the bring-and-buy.

Edward Cowie was the eminence of the Discussion Group. Accent all John Cleese. Height the same. Relentlessly alert. One evening just before we began, David Paget was reading Pendennis' column in The Observer which related how a young pianist had ascended the platform at the Queen Elizabeth Hall to play Liszt's B-minor sonata – a piece, as the columnist oozed,

"...of notorious difficulty. The young man broke down halfway and quit the platform in tears. With reserves of courage which must have been supernatural, he returned, as the audience gasped, and began again, bringing the whole thing to a triumphant conclusion amid gales of applause."

"Who writes this crap?" said Cowie before sitting at the upright and playing the sonata from start to finish, from memory.

The Discussion Group was a lifesaver. Certainly God was not dead. He wasn't even ill.

1971 was the year when church bureaucrats were trying to get the Anglican and Methodist churches to unite. Michael Ramsey, with the unruly white eyebrows and the look of Methuselah he had carried since the age of eighteen, was Archbishop of Canterbury. He wanted to go down in history as the man responsible for stitching the two churches together. Broadstairs was dead against. The senior curate wildly in favour. I didn't give a damn – because the issue was never theological but merely bureaucratic. Join two shambolic office elites together and they are only thereby made twice as unfit for purpose. It was a long-running talking shop, all expenses paid.

The Crossgates clergy used to meet at something called a Fraternal – though the atmosphere more often niffed of fratricide. We Anglicans were joined by Naylor the browbeaten Methodist Minister who had to hide the fact that he enjoyed the very occasional bottle of sweet cider from his misery guts congregation. He was a genial socialist of such mild veniality that he would take the cider bottle from its hiding place in his shirts' drawer only after having made sure that the last stragglers from his Bright Hour meeting of parsimonious sourpusses had departed to their hot chocolate and early bed. Also present were two soutaned chain-smoking RC priests from St Theresa's. There was some sublime nastiness since the RCs did not even credit Anglican and Methodist holy orders as valid. A Papal Bull Apostolicae Curae of 1896 declared that Anglican orders in particular were "absolutely null and utterly void."

Archbishop Ramsey had an overblown reputation as a theologian, largely created by sycophantic mediocrities looking for preferment. His books are un-extraordinary and platitudinous. His voice was that of a caricature parson. He favoured all the left-wing causes going – nuclear disarmament, abortion and homosexual law reform - and he was especially keen to give his backing to the World Council of Churches' favourite storm-troopers, the bandits making a guerrilla war in South Africa. During the dispute between the British Government and Ian Smith's regime in Southern Rhodesia, he wrote to Prime Minister Harold Wilson:

"If you should judge it necessary to use force..." (to bring down Smith) "...then I am sure a great body of Christian opinion would support you."

Onward Christian soldiers, shoot your kith and kin.

There was something called potty training – POT, Post Ordination Training. I had to attend the university Department of Theology every Friday morning to study Christology with Fr Sylvanus Berry a sharp little New Zealander who was a monk at the very High Church College of the Resurrection, Mirfield. He rose to become Father Superior but that was not in my day. Half a dozen newly-ordained men from around Leeds made up the seminar. My personal tutor was the intellectual Vicar of Shadwell, Frank Lindars. Good old Frank, a devotee of the Catholic Thomist theologian Bernard Lonergan who I kept confusing with Lonnie Donegan. Thoughtful Frank. A hypochondriac who thought for ages he was given to serial heart attacks, only to have his GP point out the chest pains were owing to overdoing the soy sauce:

"Monosodium glutamate, Frank. Cut down on the Chinky takeaways."

Friday being a Percy day, I was in church for the early Mass at just after 6am so, by the time I had boarded the nine o'clock bus to the university, I had been out of bed for three and a half hours. The smoke-filled bus rattled and squealed down the York Road until it joined the traffic jam about a mile from the city centre.

The bus was crowded with early shoppers. A little girl sat by herself holding a cardboard box marked Kittyproof.

"It's Fritz," she said to the conductor. He smiled and refused the fare. She fumbled, trying to put the coins back into her purse, and dropped the cardboard box. An ugly black cat sprang out and leapt into the road in the path of the heavy traffic. The little girl screamed:

"I was only taking him to the vet," she yelled tearfully.

"Where do you live, love?"

"There, there!"

"Don't cry, little love. 'Ere, look what I've got..."

"It's probably all for the best. You wouldn't have liked it if he had had to be put down, would you now?"

The little girl listened to this theodicy appertaining to felines, sniffed and shook her head before resuming her screaming.

A fat woman in a long coat, the colour of phlegm, nudged the conductor and mouthed something inaudibly. I could only think of Jeremy's uncle Clifford's cat.

Requies cat in pacem.

The fat woman and the little girl alighted together, the fat woman holding the empty Kittyproof box.

In the bus station everyone filed off, leaving the driver leaning across his steering wheel and describing by gesticulation and curses the errors of the bald cunt in the Maxi. I bought a copy of The Times

Literary Supplement from a stall near Kirkgate market, walked along Boar Lane and up Park Row towards the university, the Parkinson Building.

We met in an upper room in a new block beside the Parkinson. It was really a small skyscraper, an ersatz medley entirely suitable for a city which could not make up its mind whether it was an overgrown West Riding market town taken to Jewish tailoring or a thrusting cosmopolis. I did read George Bernard Shaw's opinion of Leeds: "It wants burning." But I also read John Osborne's opinion of George Bernard Shaw:

"He writes like a Pakistani who learnt English at the age of twelve in order to become a chartered accountant."

Likewise, modern theologians obsessively research every new academic tome, but give the impression they have never read the Bible.

"Have you looked into Wolfhart Pannenberg's Jesus: God and Man?"

"Have you looked into St Mark's Gospel?"

My colleague, a curate from the west side of Leeds, thought I was being facetious. He was right. This obsession with the latest books was really a fetish surrounding terminology: the modern types had to know the new buzz word in the way that small boys growing up just after the war had to have the newest Dinky car or aeroplane assembly kit. When it came to Pannenberg you were spoilt for choice as there were buzz words by the bucket-load. There was analogical truth and there was doxological truth. I asked why, when it came to the New Testament, we could not be content with the plain truth. And then there was Pannenburg's stupid phrase phrase vertically from above – which only made me think of a ton of bricks. Is there not more than enough to ponder over several lifetimes in a single chapter of St John's Gospel than in all these neologistic fatuities?

"The trouble with you, Peter, is that you distrust the intellect."

"Don't you?"

The sophisticated life of the university erupted all around, just like Liverpool. Only the flat, bored Leeds accent drawling Right on, man sounded sillier than it had done in Scouseland. There were two left wing bookshops opposite the Parkinson, pictures of the dead Che

Guevara – soon to be used in a Christmas advertising stunt by the Church of England – copies of Mao's Little Red Book and scores of illiterate political newspapers and magazines such as Socialist Worker and the catchilly-titled Revolutionary Marxist Current. My favourite was Spectre which carried an ominous slogan under the masthead:

"There is a spectre haunting Europe, the spectre of communism."

It was from The Communist Manifesto. They might as well have written "Vote for Boris Karloff." Spectre was written in a deadpan ideological style that would have made the British Rail timetable read like a racy novel. Whether the proletariat in the railway goods yard at Copley Hill were aware of the spectre's haunting can only be conjectured: every actual worker I met was either a Daily Mirror or a Sun man: tits and racing tips. The minuscule, loudmouthed political sects, the Trotskyists and the International Socialists seemed to loathe each other more than they loathed the Tories. As in the Christology seminar, correct terminology and doctrinal purity were the coveted virtues.

Back in the seminar I was beginning to fancy a pint of bitter when the enthusiastic curate from Holbeck blurted out;

"Jesus was on the side of the underprivileged."

"Interesting word under-privileged. Are we supposed to be neither under-privileged nor over-privileged, but just ordinarily privileged?"

"He expressed solidarity with the poor."

"The Gospels tell of plenty of times when he ate and drank with rich bastards."

Fr Sylvanus wore his cassock which was always covered in cigarette ash. He talked rapidly out of the side of his mouth in a fruity antipodean accent. The impression was slightly shifty, as of a man handing in a betting slip. Ladies from Crossgates Mothers' Union who visited Mirfield on its annual Commemoration Day thought him jolly. I went to "Commem" in July 1971. Outdoor Mass with incense and shuffling old priests in their tattered liturgical finery. Cans of lager and cucumber sandwiches. At four o'clock, Benediction and Exposure of the Blessed Sacrament. Camp young priests chain-smoking and swigging gin. Lacenick and old arse.

After the seminar I used to go with Bob Shaw, curate of St Mary's Hunslet – where my father was baptised in 1920 – to The King Charles pub where we sat among the aromatic typists in their lunch hour and the posses of shoppers from Schofields and Lewis'. My grandfather had sat in the same pub at the end of the 19th century and had seen,

"A great shoal of rats running through the middle of the city."

Grandad must have been impressed by the sight, for he regaled me with this story many times before I had reached the age of seven.

Frank Lindars was a tutor in theology merely because that was what the Bishop of Ripon had asked him to be. If he had asked him to open a Chinese restaurant, Frank would have done so next day. He was that sort of bloke. He was vicar of the ludicrously prosperous parish of Shadwell to the north of the Leeds ring road. He was bored past contempt. He desperately tried to inject some tangibility into the rarefied Shadwell Social Scene by preaching that he thought we were living in the Last Days and that the Second Coming of Christ was imminent. I don't think he believed it. He used his eschatology as a stripper uses her clothes. Frank was also master of the cryptic utterance. We used to spend half our tutorial on a country walk on the outskirts of the village, among the teenagers on their ponies, and he would suddenly ask,

"Have you ever wondered why Maher-Shal-Al-Hash-Bash's mother called him that?"

He liked to talk about the so-called "problem of evil" – you know how it goes: if God is all-knowing, all powerful and perfectly good, why does he allow evil?

Millions of presumptuous words have been written on the subject, as if the mind of God were as accessible as the local supermarket. The Freewill Defence. The Satisfaction Theory of the Atonement. The Christus Victor solution. All to answer the question of where evil comes from. The only honest answer must be:

"Fuck knows."

Anyhow, we were on this subject again one morning as we walked the country lanes. I told Frank of an affecting short story I had read by Georges Bernanos. It was about a man pondering the problem of evil as he walked along. He was just getting to the fuck knows stage when he saw a beautiful young man with yellow hair leading a pure white pony. The snag was that the lovely young fellow was the devil. Just as I reached that point in the tale, Frank said,

"You mean like that?"

And a beautiful young man with yellow hair and leading a pure white pony came round the corner. I am not making this up. But you can't ask Frank I'm afraid. He's not around any longer.

As part of Potty training I was sent on a conference at Lee Abbey on the north Devon coast, a country house on the high cliffs between Lynton and Ilfracombe: Lorna Doone country. It was run as a sort of holiday hotel and mission centre. The rabid evangelicals had taken the place over and they saw it as their religious duty to get everyone Born Again, whosoever set foot in the place. It was all guitars and daft fundamentalism, sexual frustration and flashing evangelical teeth. It was hard to understand the difference this being Born Again business actually made. They were comfortable, white middle class teenagers from the posh suburbs and pretty repressed before they got themselves, as they put it, saved. Then they got saved and behold they were the same comfortable, white middle class teenagers from the posh suburbs – only more repressed. The boys seemed young for their age and the girls were emotionally weightless and spent a lot of time blushing and looking at the floor.

There was plenty of hymn-singing of the jolly jiving for Jesus sort, rapid firing of biblical proof texts about hell, and you were constantly being asked if you had been saved yet – as if you were being asked at what age precisely had you gone into long trousers, and had you experienced an orgasm yet. But there was no drink in the place. So about nine o'clock one evening, I and two theological students from King's College, London set off to walk through the Valley of the Rocks to the nearest pub, three miles away in Lynton. At the top of the hill the road turned a sharp corner and away to our right loomed a huge black cliff, blacker than the black January sky. Raymond said,

"Christ – there's more of the fear of God in that bloody thing than the Bible-thumpers dream about!"

The Lynton pub was ordinary enough but, after the corseted world of Lee Abbey, it was like being let loose in a magic garden. It was after midnight when we arrived back at what Phil, the other King's lad, had christened 'Dunsinnin'. Three pints of beer apiece in the middle of a six mile walk: we were soberly cheerful. But at once we were accused of being drunk – by a couple of the ravenous saved who were staying up late the better to browbeat a female recalcitrant.

The lad whose teeth stuck out the furthest said,

"While you were drinking in a house of sin, we were watching the Lord being crucified."

"Did you enjoy it?"

Apparently, they had been putting on a Passion Play. The unsaved and incompletely browbeaten girl said,

"I don't think you should use the death of Christ to make people feel guilty. It's emotional blackmail."

The toothy one was foaming at the mouth. He held a Bible with key verses underlined in red and he punched it as he spoke: the original Bible-thumper:

"It's not a question of making anyone feel guilty. You are guilty, all of you, of the Blood of the Lamb!"

"And so are you mate, whether you choose to join us at the pub or to stay on here practising spiritual masturbation."

The toothy one's friend – a large but curiously evaporated sort in a woolly jumper three sizes too big – resumed his offensive directed at the girl. She was exotic, exquisite with dark hair and blue eyes. Clare from Penzance.

The teeth shouted, "Those who reject Christ will be cast into everlasting darkness!"

"Oh shut up and piss off!"

They pissed off. The rest of us sat with Clare and talked until past four o'clock. She told us how, after the Passion Play, the religious fanatics had ordered the whole audience to come forward and give their lives to the Lord. She was the only one to have refused to follow orders.

"So they began to shout at me, saying over and again that I was damned. I asked them to leave me alone but they wouldn't. They said they were trying to love me into the Kingdom of God. It was horrible!"

Ray and Phil went off to bed and I sat beside Clare for a few minutes, staring into the cold ashes.

"I must go too," she said. "Thanks."

She kissed me on the cheek. I told her she could love me into the Kingdom any time she liked. She grinned and ran up the staircase.

By breakfast next day, rumour of my profane treatment of the religious maniacs – sorry, Christian young men – had got about and for the rest of the week I was regarded very coolly by the smiling saved authorities at the Abbey. When I got back to Leeds, I went to see Frank Lindars in posh Shadwell and told him the tale. He stared out through the wide window and said,

"No matter how experienced we become, we never quite get used to gratuitous cruelty in the name of religion, do we?"

His chilly question warmed me. He had made me feel included in the profession, priestcraft or whatever it was we were supposed to be about

I am not given to visions of the supernatural or transports of heavenly delight. But then there is the next best thing. Louise Fawcett, "Louie", was eighty-six, frail, and housebound. But frail in the sense that she had the mental strength of ten men and the tenacity of a limpet. She was so small and thin, she was almost disembodied mind, but friends said she had been stout in middle age. She had served long as headmistress of a school in Otley.

Louie's idea of church was high Baroque, everything an ultramontane frenzy of lights, colours and bells and with the incense thicker than a London peculiar. Showy, but her faith was anything but. It was tangible, earthy. For Louie, the doctrines of the faith were not propositions to which you might give intellectual assent: they were as close to daily life as the morning milk and the grocery van. She seemed to be on nodding terms with angels and archangels and the whole company of heaven. Her whole life was a spiritual brocade woven out of good works. Her devoted service for fifty years had been the making and mending of the priests' vestments.

"Now," she complained over the driest glass of sherry ever "I can't see to sew."

She had never married but had a home help and friends coming in and out all day long. In the parish she was regarded with a respect bordering on holy terror. For she had a copious mind and she was in the habit of speaking it. Like the God she worshipped, she was no respecter of persons. Even – especially – the parish clergy were daunted by her fierce piety which seemed to reflect their own devotion as only Laodicean.

Broadstairs gave me the task of taking her Holy Communion every Wednesday and Red Letter Saint's day. She was particular about the way this should be carried out. Visit most homes with your little black box and the Blessed Sacrament inside, and you would be instantly offered tea or coffee and treated to an enthusiastic disquisition on the fortunes of Leeds United or the latest episode of Coronation Street. Passing pleasantries. Not with Louie you didn't. She would receive you in strict silence and there would be no words at all which did not belong to the liturgy.

Afterwards, her conversation was spiritual rather than religious. I mean, whereas the usual question from house communicants is, "Were there many in church on Sunday?" with Louie the subject was God – not in any oppressive sense, for her love of God took the form of a natural joy in his creation – which was down to earth and mirrored in her own – as in the fresh-baked bread and the arranging of Easter lilies, her blissful response to the voices of children passing under the window: and this after thirty years a headmistress.

She made jams and cakes religiously and, too blind to sew or not, she still had an eye for the birds which had visited her lawn that morning. There was no hint of the puritan in Louie. Unlike most people in that respectable suburb, she never pretended to be shocked by the sleazier goings on – the casual adulteries, the children born out of wedlock, the drunks, routinely drunk.

"Most of our sins," she said one Wednesday morning in February when the fog was so thick you couldn't see from her window even as far as the rugby posts at the end of Barwick Road Recreation Ground, "are the result of human folly rather than human wickedness. God will laugh at us on Judgement Day, and then what red faces we shall all have!"

That was how she talked in that voice of hers like silver spoons on china cups. She never spoke of herself.

Louie had written a history of the parish, and Broadstairs wanted to get this off to the printer promptly so that we might sell copies at the back of church and, not least, so that Louie would see her work in finished form. But when it came to declaring a piece of work completed, Louie was as diffident and difficult as Dr Casaubon brooding over the penultimate draft of his Key to All Mythologies:

"I just want to read through the 1940s chapter once more."

Broadstairs had asked me to hurry her up a bit.

During the winter of 1972 she had a bad attack of bronchitis and the doctor was coming to see her twice a day at one stage. Louie never complained about feeling unwell – only that her illness was a nuisance preventing her from doing all she wanted to do. The chest trouble didn't clear up, even after two courses of antibiotics, and one morning Louie was rushed off – protesting – to St James Hospital and kept in for a week.

She was back home by the end of the month and I went to see her as usual on the Wednesday. The illness had knocked her back and she looked so delicate, insubstantial, like a mere sketch of her former self. Nevertheless, she was very businesslike that day:

"I want you to look over the last few pages of my parish history with me, please. And then you can take it away with you and give it to Father Broadstairs, with my apologies for lateness."

The manuscript was beautifully written in her own small handwriting. It had her character all over it. Certainly, there was nothing that could be usefully added to it and nothing, I said, should now delay its publication.

"That's that then," she said, from her rocking chair in the corner. "I wanted to get that out of the way. I've got cancer, you know, and I shan't be here for very much longer."

She explained that they had wanted to keep her in hospital, but she had begged them to let her return home to put her affairs in order while she still had the strength. She was prepared to go back into hospital when the time came. In the weeks that followed, I persuaded her to talk about her past a little for, as I said,

"I feel as if I know you very well, Louie, but I hardly know anything about you at all."

So we sat in her window on many afternoons and observed the coming of spring: the slow greening of the bushes, the strengthening light and the daffodils shaking in the breeze, in rhythm, as it seemed, with the church bell ringing for Evensong.

Louie was born in 1886 in Kettlewell in the Yorkshire Dales:

"Right by the river Wharfe in its infancy. D'you know, there was never a night I didn't fall asleep without its babble the last thing I heard. My father worked the land for Major Hargreaves. My mother died when I was nine. That was when I first knew about the angels.

"I was in the parlour by mother's coffin. Oh, everything was so white, and I was crying. I didn't want to live without her, and father didn't seem to know what he was doing, poor man. Out of his mind with sorrow. And my mother so beautiful – I wanted to get into the coffin beside her.

"That was when I first saw the angels. There was no sound except the river, and the room was filled with sunshine. Then the angel appeared by the side of mother's coffin."

"What did it look like?"

"It was an angel – golden, with wings!"

She said it as you might speak of a saucepan to an idiot in the kitchen:

"It's big and round, with a handle and a lid!"

"Have you always seen angels?"

"I always knew they were there, of course. But I saw them – actually saw them as I'm seeing you now – only once more, and that was when..."

Her speech trailed off and she fumbled with an ornament as she looked away. She was going to talk about herself, and the prospect embarrassed her. Then she looked right at me, and I was unnerved:

"I was in love. He went off to the First War. A letter came. I was at his mother's house. 'missing, believed killed.'

"I had no need of that letter. I knew. That's why I'd gone round to his mother's. The previous night, the angel had appeared. Nothing was said....I mean, I didn't hear any words but, as if written into my brain, 'Charles has been killed – but it's all right'.

"It wasn't all right. Not for me. I loved him so. Never loved another!"

And she laughed.

"I knew I had to go to his Ma – he always called her Ma. So I went."

"Did you tell her about the angel?"

"I told her Charles was all right. Then I just found I was saying The Lord's Prayer and the Hail Mary out loud. I don't remember much else about that day."

"What do you think these visions were? What are angels?"

"You should know that, Father. They're what we were always taught – messengers from God. Why do people think there's a version of the faith we tell the children and another for adults? There isn't. It's all the same."

Louie was not at all soft, but she was gentle. A strict schoolmistress, renowned for her acuity, and sometimes her acerbity, she was loved even by the most unwilling pupils. There were so many of her old girls in the parish. One said to me:

"She simply had a way with people – girls, staff, everybody. You felt better when she came into the room. You knew you couldn't say anything against her – ever!"

I watched her dying. I was there on the very day. It was like watching someone being born. She made such a good job of it, such fun of it. That was one of her expressions:

"Dying will be fun!"

She was never maudlin. Never sentimental. Not half in love with easeful death or any of that syrupy stuff.

She had been taken back into hospital and put into a sideward with flowers and her own Crucifix. The window looked out over the expanse of summer garden towards the gatehouse under the willows. Louie was pleased with this situation:

"I like to be able to see people come and go."

On 29th June, St Peter's Day, I took her Holy Communion. She was having difficulty breathing but she was as cheerful as ever. Taking the Sacrament seemed to tire her and she lay back on the pillow with a great sigh. She began to wheeze and snore, so that I thought she had fallen asleep.

Suddenly, she gripped my hand and heaved herself up in bed. Her body was all lightness, as if she had stepped out of it. Her eyes moved from side to side and it appeared she was following the progress of something across her field of vision. She smiled and laughed and squeezed my hand tightly. Her face – I could think only of the exultation at the Sanctus in Mozart's C-minor Mass: two choirs hurling antiphonal ecstasy at each other across the vault:

Dominus Deus Sabbaoth...

"You see, Father, they've come for me!"

She lay back slowly and died.

About a week later I was at the hospital to see someone else, and I spent a few minutes talking to the night sister on Louie's ward:

"That woman!" she said. "That woman – she was an angel!"

IV

There was something like a cloud, but it was also sometimes like a light, lurking in the back of my mind. One day about this time I realised with a shock it was a near compulsion to set something down in verse. This had happened only once before, when I was in the middle of my finals at Liverpool. On that May day 1970, I was walking on Upper Parliament Street on my way to take the Advanced Ethics paper which was part of the philosophy degree. I was between the two cathedrals: Scott's magnificent Anglican 19th century Gothic edifice and the modern Roman Catholic erection which all the Scousers referred to as Paddy's Wigwam. Suddenly:

Corpus Christi came, cathedral haunted,
Under the auspices of an ethics course...

Now, sitting by the window at home – I think it was Wednesday in Holy Week, something that was more than a snippet. It rolled itself out slowly, like a procession. The experience bore no resemblance to the means or method by which I am writing this memoir, prose. It was not automatic writing exactly, but it was like something visited upon me. You had to think, of course you did; but it was a form of thinking like no other I had practised before:

"This April is all death,
The most real thing sin,
With wages in advance
And time to spend them in.
The willow tree is angered by the wind,
The church bell blown off key:
Howling iridescence
And the walk to Calvary.
God is infinitely bored
By this procession
Of seasonal necessities;
But he makes no digression.
He cannot do otherwise
For his property is extreme:

To be the bloody eternal God
With a passion to redeem."

It was years before I had clapped eyes on Charles Sisson's description of poetry:

"The surprising eruption of the reluctant deposit on the mind's floor."

The idea of becoming a poet is repulsive. The supposition that one could is wildly arrogant and hubristic. Nevertheless, many do fill notebooks with pieces of writing which they distinguish as poetry on the sole grounds that the words do not quite reach the margins. Most of the stuff that gets printed is both pretentious and risible. Self-expression in any of the arts is a vacuous, narcissistic nonsense. It is not a matter of trying to express oneself – what, in any case, could that possibly mean? The notion that anyone, however unschooled, can be asked to sit down and write a poem is ridiculous: though schoolteachers ask their classes of nine-year-olds to do just that. She might as well ask them to compose a string quartet. There are, of course, one or two prodigious nine-year-olds here and there who can compose string quartets – but this is because they have learnt music. Why should things be any different when it comes to the writing of poetry?

Poetry is in fact the most difficult and elusive of literary genres and so I was both puzzled and apprehensive when, aware of these things, I found my thoughts delivering themselves in verse from time to time. I have never sat down with the pure intention of inventing a poem: in fact invention is not at all the right word. Rather, a few words in a particular rhythm insinuate themselves and, under a sort of compression of attention, emerge in verse – verse which may be indifferent or bad, and even occasionally, given a following wind, not so bad. So one Sunday after we had read the story of Christ's baptism in the River Jordan:

What is the world doing while it waits on spring?
The earth itself, half open, aching
Trees sparse, assenting, murmuring;
And a bird, no more than an idiot,
Rummaging, predilecting
What?

To be part of the scheme of things.
The Nazarene gets up out of the cold water
After the Baptist's absurd appellations
And stands under only the devil's light
In the cracked wilderness of Judea.
The bird observes
Only what there is to see and hear:
"Thou art my Son in whom I am delighted."
And thinking his Creator speaks to him
Flutters away excited.

Holy Week in Crossgates was hell. Forty-eight services with the long Gospel readings which the senior curate stumbled through so slowly that I feared we'd be in the Lady Chapel until Whitsuntide. But the worst of it was the Ecumenical Procession of Witness around the parish on Good Friday. We all assembled outside church at 6.45pm in the encircling gloom. I carried the Cross, followed by the lumbering senior curate in his Fair Isle pullover and then Broadstairs shrivelled up under his clerical cloak. The two haughty Roman priests red-nosed in black suits and the Methodist minister looking distraught, as if he had lost his long phylactery.

A smattering of the more religious of our flock followed us through the streets to the Chapel for the hymn sandwich. Kids yelped and jeered at us. A few tagged along, only to be shouted at from doorsteps by unchurched parents embarrassed and bewildered. Most of the suburban pagans had the good grace to crawl back under their cars, pretend to be pruning the roses or otherwise avert their gaze from the dumb show. A naughty boy by the newsagent's called out, "Daft cunts!" You didn't know whether to laugh or cry. I kept wishing we were being led by the Sally Ann band: at least the oompahs would have drowned the catcalls. I thought of the Lee Abbey God Squad and how they would have loved all this "...suffering for the Lord's sake."

As the service was in the Chapel, it was the Methodist minister's turn to say the long prayers:

"O Lord we would praise thy holy name...and we would ask thee, thanking thee, that thou wouldst..."

And so on, etc.

What was all this with the Methodist Uriah Heepish style? We would...thou wouldst. Never mind would...wouldst. Just get on with it! And the prayers were extempore – but they were the same every year, such was the paucity of the religious imagination among Crossgates Methodists. The local bourgeoisie knew well enough that cleanliness is next to godliness and so the tradition was to spend all Holy Saturday sprucing the church for the Festival. Jack Rhodes, one of Broadstairs' Masonic cronies was there clad in something like Winston Churchill's siren suit:

"How much are you charging the Church Council for your labour, Peter? My time's worth £10 an hour."

He knew his own value did Jack. Genial, generous Jack Rhodes who often invited me to drink his Scotch and watch the snooker on one of the first colour tellies in Crossgates.

Verse happened again on Easter Day:

Fireflies in the dust
Under the crescent moon;
A star in the moon's arms
Like a boatman in his boat.
The Magdalene's cloak is
Night's blanket
Shielding beloved sleep.
On this night dust returns to life,
And Adam no longer y-bounden.
Early ripples on Galilee,
Fishes and loaves,
Bread and wine;
Christ with the Holy Ghost
Quickening the breath.

Just after Easter I was asked to give a talk to a new thing called PND – People Next Door. It was the latest in a long line of talkative gimmicks dreamed up by the bishops. Stuff like PND is out-of-date and past it before they hold the first meeting. Like dowdy cast-off clothes – the conversation, the people themselves behind the bloody door, laceratingly banal. Always some new initiative and usually given a set of initials: PND, or CTTN. CTTN? That was Call to the North, the Archbishop of York's wheeze to re-evangelise the north of England. He invented it on a train journey from some London committee to a church blessing in Newcastle. All those vast Victorian Gothic churches in the grimy northern towns – and all empty. They obviously needed a call from the Archbish. I imagined the reaction: a Geordie in the same train compartment thrusting up a hearty "V" sign and shouting into the Archbish's face,

"Why eye – bugger off man! This is the north calling back!"

The PND meeting took place in a large detached house in Austhorpe Road, all teak and potted plants. There was a grandfather clock in the hall and another in the sitting-room, slightly out of synch, so the chimes seemed to go on antiphonally forever. A Bluthner baby grand and a mirror, which filled the whole wall, with roses on it. Our hostess, retired senior civil servant, Molly Simons with hair like wire wool, a beak like a bird of prey – which is what she was. No one under forty. Teachers, assistant librarians, two local solicitors and a chartered accountant and the gigantic, horse-faced woman like Ottoline Morrell who ran the wool shop at the top of York Road.

Unnerving to have the Lady Ottoline lookalike in the room when they had asked me to talk about the original Lady O's lover, Bertrand Russell. I couldn't resist kicking off with a parody of Dirty Bertie himself:

"And, as I pedalled orf into the sunset, I realised I was no longer in love with Lady Ottoline Morrell ...

"Yes Russell, Moore, Strachey, E.M. Forster – people who described themselves as the sensitive, the considerate and the plucky, all China tea and pacifism behind the high walls of Garsington while their countrymen were being slaughtered in the trenches."

I had managed to work myself into a bit of a froth. The librarian in plaid pattern silk tights cried out like one at the extreme of sexual excitement:

"Oh but Russell took a very principled stand on nuclear disarmament."

"Well, he would. A conchie in World War One. An appeaser in the 1930s. And something like a traitor today"

One of the solicitors – with that saturated tone which people adopt when they speak of We Christians said,

"I thought we were meant to oppose war?"

"And generally I do. But giving up your nuclear deterrent unilaterally is no way to prevent a war."

The - now rather detumescent – librarian said,

"But surely if we surrender our nuclear bombs, we shall not be attacked by potential enemies. It makes sense."

"Ah surrender – he'd like that, would Bertie. But actually the only country to have suffered a nuclear attack was Japan – and they didn't have the bomb."

"We're supposed to turn the other cheek."

"I may turn my own cheek if I wish, but I'm not permitted to turn the cheeks of my neighbour and his wife and children."

The reincarnate Lady Morrell said, "Now look here, I'm not sure I approve of the direction this conversation is taking."

I could have listened to her all night. Not for anything she said but for the way she said it. Such a mellifluous, tinkling cymbal intonation. You didn't expect a voice like that to issue from the throat of such a horse-faced crone. Her objection was entirely in character with the refined ethos of PND. They talked not as if war were an evil – necessary or not – but merely an offence against etiquette and taste, dontchaknow: exactly the sort of objection that Russell, Moore, Forster and the rest of the aesthetic gang put up. It offended their finer feelings. As they would say, their sensitivity.

The other solicitor: "We worship the Prince of Peace."

"The same: who said, I come not to bring peace but a sword."

The conversation stuttered on, struggling like a small boat against the wind to change course. Naturally, the only way to redeem a situation which was becoming disagreeable was to ask who was for sweet sherry and who for dry. It was becoming clear that PND stood for Pretty Numb Discussion.

The plaid librarian drew me into a corner while people were mingling and filling their glasses. O God, sex again:

"Is it true that Russell believed in free love?"

Wherever would we be for diversion if it were not for wishful thinking?

"Yes, he wrote a book about it. And he was a rare old goat. Lady Ottoline, Eliot's first wife, anybody handy..."

"It's disgusting!" she said with more than a hint of relish.

"Most of the bishops and the modern clergy would agree with him."

I told her about the radical theology that was in vogue in the seminaries.

"They call it situation ethics. No need for moral rules. You do what seems right in any given situation, according to the demands of love. All you need is love. It's the New Morality."

Molly Simons said, "It sounds like the old immorality to me."

Then, with the suddenness of someone chucking herself over the side of the ship, she gasped, "And what's the apophatic way?"

The sort of question you feel like beginning to answer with the phrase, "Well, I wouldn't start from here!"

"It is the view that we can talk about God only in terms of what he is not. So God appeared to Moses in the burning bush – but he was neither the bush nor the burning, so in what sense can it be said that he appeared? St Paul talks about the unknown God. In modern times Karl Barth uses the apophatic method and comes close to saying we can say nothing about God at all. Of course, all this raises the question of how to differentiate between a God you can't talk about and there being no God at all."

She took on a remote and haunted look. There was no sign of her climbing back on board. In fact:

"Thank you very much Peter. You've just completely destroyed my faith!"

Ask a silly question...

The first of the grandfather clocks began to strike

A couple of days later I was in the staff meeting with Broadstairs and the senior curate. The vicar had received another complaint about him:

"It's from Denis and Susan Cooper. You went to visit them rather late one evening – apparently. About a quarter past ten?"

"Well now Mr Broadstairs, you see I'd promised them I'd go and see them about their daughter's christening."

"At going on for midnight!"

Broadstairs was hoarse, anguished. His good eye moved off so waywardly to the left that I thought it was about to leave the room altogether. Still he managed to press his complaint with forensic thoroughness:

"You banged on the door. Susan says you hammered on it till she thought it was going to fall through."

"I thought they might not hear me – they might be upstairs."

"They were upstairs you idiot. They were so far up the bloody stairs, they were in bed!"

Long silence.

Broadstairs retrieved his eye and fixed the senior curate with it:

"But it's what you did next that takes the biscuit. When you couldn't get any answer from the door, you tried the window, didn't you? Now what made you do a damn silly thing like that?"

"I wasn't getting any answer from the door, Mr Broadstairs."

"When I say you tried the window, I mean you actually opened the window and climbed in!"

The senior curate's face turned as red as his hair. He threw himself violently back in his chair and his extensive legs flew forward and kicked over the coffee table. I was biting hard on my fountain pen but I was shaking hysterically, like a Parkinsons case suffering an attack of malaria. When I caught Broadstairs' eye, I was finished. But the vicar wasn't. He picked up the coffee table and for a moment I thought he was going to throw it at him.

"You knocked the Coopers' furniture about as well!"

"It was dark and I couldn't find the light switch. Then the baby started to cry..."

"What did you do then?"

"I thought I'd better leave."

"Oh yes – so you started to climb back out of the window."

"I couldn't find the door in the dark."

"Denis came down..."

"He was in his pyjamas."

Broadstairs was confounded by this piece of inconsequentiality. He went very quiet. Defeated. The senior curate looked distraught;

"I must say, Mr Broadstairs, I was very upset when Denis said he had a mind to call the police."

"You deserve to be locked up! Look, just make yourself scarce, will you, before I say something I shouldn't"

I thought I'd make a break for it.

"You just sit where you are, Peter Mullen. I've something to say to you as well."

The senior curate lumbered out of the room, clutching his briefcase in one hand and a huge multicoloured carrier bag in the other. Broadstairs eyed the bag as if it might contain high explosive:

"And what have you got there?"

"It's my swimming things and towel – I'm off to the baths."

Enough baggage for Polyphemus to take for a dip in the Adriatic.

The housebreaking incident was all behind him and he beamed a wide smile of rapturous geniality as his parting shot to the vicar who muttered:

"Mind you don't drown yourself!"

Normally after such a fandango, Broadstairs would usually let off a few expostulations of the What the hell can I do with him? sort. But not today. He was silent and he wore the look of a man in deepest mourning.

"What have I done to deserve you two? Yon fella careers around the parish like a one-man Brian Rix farce. And now what's this I hear? I'm told you've been upsetting people. Preaching violence, free love and atheism."

"Molly Simons?"

"Yes, Molly Simons. But she's not the only one. She wrote me a letter and there were several phone calls. You'd better see the letter."

Good quality paper, thick as parchment:

"Dear Vicar,

"I feel I must write to say a word about your curate Peter Mullen who has upset more than a few people in PND with his insensitive remarks and his general attitude. He began by criticising conscientious objectors – of whom my father was one – and went on to say most of the bishops are in favour of free love. These things were distressing enough but the last straw was when he seemed to suggest it was a matter of no importance whether God exists or not.

"I am sure he did not intend to unsettle us, but that is what he achieved. Our group consists entirely of people who are very loyal to St James' church and we are not quick to take offence. But if we are to be regaled with much more of this sort of thing, we shall have to consider whether we might find an alternative place of worship more to our liking. The east side of Leeds is not lacking for historic, hospitable churches.

Yours sincerely

Molly Simons"

"What, for goodness sake, did you say about conscientious objectors?"

"I was poking fun at Bertrand Russell and the Garsington crowd fancying themselves plucky and sensitive while true Englishmen were dying in the trenches. I didn't know – I didn't think – Molly's father had been a pacifist."

"That's just it, isn't it Peter, you don't think!"

"I feel strongly about that whole aesthetic of cowardice, Russell..."

"You should take that back, apologise! You've no cause to call people cowards just because you don't like their opinions."

He was in his cassock, pacing furiously. It was like being in a room in a black mist.

"People who refuse to fight are the last sort you need when the country's threatened with destruction."

"You will apologise to Molly Simons."

The vicar's wife stuck her head round the door to say she was going to the supermarket. When she noticed his savage demeanour she said,

"Whatever's got into you? Sit down before you give yourself a stroke!"

He did sit down, the very picture of a priest whose parish was falling apart. But at least he spoke more softly now:

"What's this free love business? What were you telling them? I know you've just come out of the university where they might do things differently for all I know, but all Molly's crowd are respectable middle class folk. They don't expect the curate of all people to talk dirty to them."

"Oh come off it! I wasn't talking dirty. I was asked about Russell's advocacy of free love and I told them that what he believed was preached now by leading clergymen. The new morality. You know that's the truth as well as I do. I've heard you complain about it many a time."

"You caused the most trouble – and not just with Molly – by what you said about God. Just what did you say exactly."

"I was asked a theological question and I said that the answer to it gave rise to problems about our idea of God."

"Look lad, your place is not to give people ideas about God. Your job is to comfort and reassure people."

It was my turn to be wound up:

"I don't mean problem as in toothache. I mean an interesting puzzle. Something we can actually enjoy grappling with. It was meant to be a bloody discussion group when all is said and done."

"You've got to go gently. You can't afford to put doubts in ordinary people's minds."

"Oh so they're ordinary now, are they? Well in my book it's quite ordinary for ordinary people to enjoy thinking about what, for God's sake, they're supposed to be thinking about in a theological discussion group. If we talked to our people a bit more as St Paul talked to the Corinthians and bit less like the presenter of Blue Peter, the church wouldn't be in the state it is these days. Or are we so full of soft soap and fake tan that we can't face a little reality when it comes up and bites us on the arse."

"There's no need to be crude."

"Well being subtle hasn't got me very far, has it!"

"Come on through to the kitchen and we'll have a cup of tea. Or you might fancy a beer eh?

"I won't if you don't mind. But I'll tell you what: I will apologise to Molly and to the rest of them at the next meeting. But then I'm not going to another PND session – ever. You can ask the senior curate to go if you like. He might like to try his nocturnal entry by the window method on them. The Local Education Authority have asked me to take a Wednesday night philosophy class for adults at John Smeaton school. We might even be able to discuss God there!"

"Wednesday night you say?"

As if I had uttered some unspeakable curse.

"Wednesday night."

The meaning of the phrase seemed to be more elusive to him than apophatic theology.

"Wednesday night. But who's going to look at the Young Wives?"

"You can look at them yourself if you like."

V

Wedding interviews were scheduled for Wednesday and Friday evenings, 7pm until 9 in the parish room, part of the vicarage and leading out into the garden. The clergy took turns. One Friday I sat there reading my book, occasionally strolling into the Maytime garden. If no one turned up it was not an unpleasant job. Ten to nine and I was just packing up when a startlingly beautiful woman in a white dress wafted through the door. She had not come to arrange a marriage:

"It's my son, Jeremy. He's seventeen. Started playing with the Ouija board. He's out of control. Goes into rages. Shouts. Screams. Growls in a low voice that's more like an animal. He steals from me and he's been caught shoplifting. Then sometimes he calms down and he's his old self again..."

She began to weep silently.

"...and in this mood he tells me he's possessed by the devil and he asks me to fetch a priest. And there's an awful smell about him and his room, anywhere he goes really. Not a natural smell. Something...oh I can't describe it. Like rotting flesh."

"What does his father say?"

"There is no father – was – I mean I'm divorced. Two years now."

This was a couple of notches above routine menopausal Angst. It was hard to concentrate. Emily Shawcross was the most exotic creature I had ever seen. Like something out of a fairytale or some Jungian anima fantasy. Das Ewig-weibliche. Lorelei or Rhine-maiden. All that long yellow hair. I said I would call and see her son. She appeared soothed, thanked me and left. A wraith gliding over the lawn and out of the iron gate.

I would go and see him, but what then? Bell, book and candle? I had no idea. Get the psychiatrist? Instead I went round to the front door and apologised for disturbing Broadstairs and his wife who were watching TV: Heaven Knows Mr Allison with Robert Mitchum and Deborah Kerr.

"There's a special man for jobs like this. Fancy title: Priest Responsible for the Ministry of Deliverance. Diocesan Exorcist in other words. I'll find his number for you. You'd better get in touch with him before you leap into action."

And back to watch Bob Mitchum trying to keep his hands off the glamorous nun.

I phoned Fr Hatton from the vicar's study. He said he would meet me at 9.30am the next day. Then I rang Emily Shawcross who was, she said, very relieved to know I would call on her so promptly.

At twenty-five to ten next morning my doorbell rang and I let in Fr Tom Hatton. About fifty years old. Thin to the point of attenuation. Like a pipe-cleaner. A black Roman cassock and cape and a biretta. A large briefcase big enough to carry a bomb – certainly capable of storing bell, book and several candles. His eyes were the remotest blue, dreamlike, strangely out of character with his sparse black costume and his lean, ascetic look – that of a man who had fasted for many more than forty days and forty nights.

"We'd better start straight away."

He entered my little front room and eyed it up as if he was checking for electronic bugs.

"Put your cassock on, Peter, will you."

He took out a rosary, knelt and began The Lord's Prayer, then Hail Mary.

"We'll say our Confession."

He pronounced the Absolution with such authority he might have been the Archangel Michael himself.

It was a short walk down Church Lane and across Austhorpe Road to the terrace house beside the rail track where Emily and Jeremy lived.

"Deliverance...leap into action. My boss made it sound like warfare."

"It is."

"How long have you been doing this job?"

"Peter, look, if you don't mind, we'll have time to talk afterwards."

So the rest of the distance in silence, except for the hiss of the car tyres on the wet road and a noisy interlude as a crocodile of kids ran in front of us on their way to the swimming baths.

There was no need to hammer on the door, senior curate style. Emily must have been watching out for us. She let us in before we'd had chance to knock. My God, she was right about the stink – like old cheese and fresh shit. The house seemed to be stuck in the 1950s. An old wooden wireless set and that thick, flowery wallpaper – what was it? Lincrusta. An ornate mirror over the tiled fireplace and some family photographs. On our way in we had disturbed the bell-chimes.

"Jeremy is just getting up."

No one said anything. Just the noises from above: the lavatory, the bathroom door, the lad clattering down the stairs.

He wore jeans and a polo neck shirt. Hair as yellow as his mother's. Around six feet tall but with a pinched, anaemic look. Spotty.

"Hello, Jeremy. Now, what's the trouble?"

At once hideous changes that came over the lad's face were as if his features were being ferociously moulded and pulled out of shape by a third party. He growled, making a very good impersonation of a possessed person in a horror film. But then – and more shocking, this – he sang – not words, but syllables, phonemes, almost tonic sol fa – in an exquisite tone. As if he, and not his mother, were the Lorelei. The Rhinemaiden. Such a smile. A blasphemous beatific vision. I had never been so frightened. No, not afraid exactly. More disgusted, sickened. I thought I was going to throw up.

Then he was quiet. His features contorted again and he drew back, nearly crouching, like a cornered cat in a nasty temper. Suddenly he leapt up and spat very productively at Fr Tom and then at me.

"Fuck off priests! I'll have you killed!"

With unnatural speed and ferocity, he launched into us, forcing us to the ground. Then he was out of the door and away. The bell chimes ringing for what seemed an age.

We gathered ourselves and Tom opened his box of tricks. No bell. No candle. But a book, certainly. The Rituale Romanum. Salt and Holy Water which he began to hurl at the wall, commanding the evil presence in Latin to depart and to go back to God, its Creator. Emily collapsed into an ample armchair. She looked not so much frightened as relieved.

The Exorcist and I went from room to room, upstairs into Jeremy's vile sleeping quarters, all black and lurid posters, the emblems of magic and necromancy all over the place. I was nearly sick with the stench. More salt. More Holy Water. A great deal more Latin. I felt suddenly intensely weary as if all the blood had been drained out of me. It was an effort to walk downstairs and say prayers with Emily. Then we sat around drinking coffee like any old church gang in the vestry after Matins.

She said, "I know where he's gone. The others – the group, sect or whatever you call them – they live on the far side of the ring road in Moortown. Some of them have been here. Well off, all of them. Business people."

"Have you somewhere to go. Can you lock this place up and leave for a while?"

"I'll stay."

I got details of Jeremy's probation officer, phoned to tell him what had happened. Tom reported the whole incident to the police and told them Mrs Shawcross had decided to stay in the house alone. They said they would send someone round.

Fr Tom caught his bus and I dawdled home, dragging my footsteps. I was thoroughly whacked and went straight to bed. I did not wake up until 5pm. The Yorkshire Evening Post was lying on the mat. Across the top of the front page was the headline LEEDS PRIESTS IN LOCAL EXORCISM. The most startling aspect was the photographs of Fr Tom and me and a summary report of the morning's events.

The Jeremy Shawcross affair was not the only demonstration to me that truly nasty things do happen in the most benign and boring communities. I recalled what Aquinas said about the banality of evil – yes, that saying which the lefties always attribute to Hannah Arendt. But it wasn't hers: she picked it up from St Thomas. I have mentioned already that I had been reading the short stories of George Bernanos. He also wrote some mighty novels, among them The Diary of A Country Priest. He begins the diary with the words, My parish is bored stiff. There was no better description of Crossgates. But when the Shawcross episode relieved the boredom, I wished heartily it had not. Maybe there is a lot to be said for boredom after all. Bernanos says somewhere else: You must learn to be mildly bored.

First Mrs Shawcross, then Mr Carrick. Neil Carrick was a man in his forties who lived across the road from me. Divorced – his wife had left him for her boss. Unstable. Manic depression they called it in those unenlightened days. Now they have changed their euphemism and call it bipolar disorder. What's the difference? The fact is when Neil was up, he was very, very up, but when he was down, he was buried. He was tall, angular, very athletic in his day, now greying, his face with more lines than Stanningly Junction.

The day after the Shawcross fiasco, I was walking towards the newsagents when I noticed seven bottles of milk on Neil's doorstep. He was doing his Rip Van Winkle act again. I bet he had taken to his bed and stayed there for – how long? – three days, a week perhaps, judging by the number of bottles. Was I the first to notice these? Very likely, the way the bored burghers of Crossgates kept themselves to themselves. It's rather difficult to practise charity if you're a solipsist.

He was not answering the door and the windows were fastened – so I couldn't get in even if I had fancied emulating the nocturnal practices of the senior curate. I shouted through the letterbox:

"Neil, I'm going to get the police to help me open this door!"

Immediately the sound of bolts being drawn. Neil appeared in his striped dressing gown, wildly unshaven, very niffy. He looked like a long-neglected inmate in a Third World jail. He frowned guiltily at the milk bottles.

"Shall we take pot luck on which one's the freshest and make a cup of tea? That's if you'll deign to let me in."

In the kitchen he clasped me in a tight and very smelly embrace and sobbed rhythmically. I managed to get him into the dusty sitting room.

"Nobody understands. Nobody understands how dark it is. One day I'm all right – well, I'm getting by anyway. Then I can feel everything slipping. Down into the mud. It's so dark. And I think the darkness will clear as long as I don't move. And that's it, I'm stuck."

"You moved smartly enough when I said I'd call the police."

"I've got a bit of history."

"Have you had anything to eat?"

"Last year – it was when I went the other way – you know – overactive, hyper. I'd gone a week without sleep and I was out of my head. You don't know what it's like when things are spinning as fast as that. I couldn't stand it a minute longer..."

The bread in the fridge had turned green at the edges and the slices of cooked meat might have been fossils.

"...so I got on the bike and went to Roundhay Park. I took the carving knife. I'd had enough."

"We'll have to empty that fridge and scrub it out. There's enough shit in there to start a cholera epidemic."

"That was when the copper nabbed me – by the little lake. There were kids everywhere, messing about in the water. He thought I was going to stab one. He thought I was a child-molester. I handed over the knife. He told me to lie face down on the grass and he put the cuffs on. I could hear him on his radio calling for help..."

"You know what you are, Neil. You're a silly bugger."

"They put me in the cells. I was there two nights. If it hadn't been for Mr Broadstairs I'd be there still. Or God knows where I'd be!"

Broadstairs had got in touch with Neil's GP and together they explained everything to the police. While Neil was drinking his tea and smoking his third cigarette, I phoned the same GP who promised to come round after surgery. So I made more tea and found an unopened packet of chocolate biscuits. I knew the GP – Geoff Prentiss – and once I'd let him in I left. Only a hundred yards or so to my own house. Long enough for me to conjecture that the sum of human misery is not finite.

I soon received confirmation of this conclusion. I was half asleep in front of some witless comedy show on ITV when the doorbell rang – not once, but over and over, as if someone were signalling Abandon Ship. There stood the ample Amelia in her Girl Guide uniform and floods of tears.

"I don't know where to turn, Peter! It's him again!"

Amelia, age seventeen, was the one upon whom the senior curate had laid the burden of his amorous ambition after he had forsaken the nurse who doted on him but was not quite up to the standard required by a descendant of the British Ambassador to Washington. He was making his ambition so grotesquely plain that, as Amelia said,

"The girls are laughing at me all the time."

"Do you..."

I didn't know how to put this, quite. But I didn't have to:

"Love him? Do I heck!"

"Then you should tell him straight that it's not on and you'd be pleased if he would stop pestering you. Get him when he's on his own – just after one of the weekday Masses would be a good time."

"I don't want to hurt his feelings."

"You don't want to spend the rest of your life with him either, do you?"

There was no answer but a shudder.

"You have a boyfriend anyway." I knew him, Carl, a nice lad who was all football and motorbikes.

"Yes, but the senior curate said I should look a little higher than Carl."

"Oh did he now! I'll say this for him: he's not wanting when it comes to sorting out the social pecking order!"

She was taking some of the Guides and Brownies to climb Mount Ingleborough in the Dales and Carl was going with them. The senior curate had told her that he thought he would join the outing too.

"Bloody hell! – sorry. The cheek of it! When is it, this trip?"

"A week on Saturday."

"Then you must see the senior curate and tell him to...leave him in no uncertainty about your feelings before then."

She lightened after that and we had a cup of tea.

"I was going to take the girls down Gaping Gill – you know, the deep pothole by the side of Ingleborough – but my dad said it wasn't safe."

Five minutes more of that sort of thing and she was off.

"Thanks ever so much." A lovely smile. She pedalled off up Manston Drive.

Towards the end of the summer, Broadstairs came back from holiday:

"Is my parish still in one piece then?"

"It is as you left it, Father."

"Much to do?"

"Three new weddings booked. A lot of twittering about the Autumn Fayre. Oh, and Mrs Clayton wants to see you."

He recoiled:

"I know what it'll be about."

So did I. There had been the misidentification of a grave a few weeks before – and I don't need to tell you the name of the author of this balls-up. Old George the sexton had come bounding out of The Travellers' Rest and accosted Broadstairs by the fire station:

"You've gone and shoved one down t'wrong 'ole, so I 'ears tell!"

The deceased was to have been buried in the family grave belonging to the Browns, but there were two family graves in the same row and both in the name of Brown. The wrong Brown family soon noticed the error and they kicked up a rumpus. In these matters the Home Office has to be officially involved. The exhumation must take place at night. Enter Broadstairs at midnight with his lantern on a long lead from the vicarage and two of Martin Hemsworth's hefty men with shovels. Nellie Clayton's house overlooked the churchyard and so, even if Mr Brown was eventually laid in his rightful resting place, Nellie would take no rest until she had let the vicar know she had observed the whole gruesome spectacle. Nellie had not had much fun recently. She had been in hospital for most of the summer and then the vicar had gone on holiday. This was her first opportunity to give him a bit of misery.

I had survived my probationary year as a deacon and now I was to be ordained priest in September in Ripon Cathedral. Before a deacon is ordained priest, he must be interviewed by the diocesan bishop. The bishop had an office in the middle of Leeds, in premises given the worthy title of The Church Institute. A 19th century municipal establishment with the flavour of Mayor and Corporation. Pale yellow walls vanishing into high dusty ceilings and the lavatories marked For the Use of the Public. You felt you ought to be wearing a watch chain before entering.

The Rt Rev'd John Richard Humpage Moorman was a scholar. His main work was the standard tome on the Franciscans but he had also written a book about St Luke's Gospel and another one called A History of the Church in England. That in instead of of was to let you know that the bishop was an anglocatholic who traced his Episcopal authority back to before the aberration of Henry VIII to the time of the Apostles themselves. He was tiny, austere, refined as pure silk, beady-eyed, his person at one with his status. If there had been two of him, you could have stuck one at each end of your mantelpiece.

"How are you getting on with Father Broadstairs?"

"Oh we shoved one down t'wrong 'ole a few weeks since."

"And with the senior curate?"

"Never a dull moment, bishop. You should see him stuffing his sit-up-and-beg through the sunshine roof of his Fiat 500. Did I tell you the one about his ex-girlfriend the nurse? And of course his grandfather was Ambassador to Washington."

Of course I said none of this. The conversation was all routine. He asked me if I was finding time for prayer and study. I said,

"Father Broadstairs helps us keep the mornings free for study." I thought he would appreciate the Father bit.

"It is a great privilege to celebrate the Eucharist." – a statement about as informative as "it's a great privilege to meet the Queen."

He asked me to kneel for his Blessing. At the door he smiled and I looked into his porcelain complexion and smiled nervously in return. A couple of pints in The King Charles and home on the bus.

VI

I stopped looking at the Young Wives and began my philosophy course at the John Smeaton school on Barwick Road. Concrete and glass: the building seemed to incarnate the ideology of 1960s educational theory. All shall run and all shall win prizes – and even unto them that do not run shall the prizes be awarded. My lot were the middle classes once again. Where had all the wonderful institutions which taught stuff to the workers disappeared to? – the Workers Educational Association, to name but one, had saved many a young branch from the burning.

There was Carol from the library and Steve the maths teacher at this very school. Paul in PR and Sheila the manageress – as lady managers used to be called in the days before our enlightenment. Jeanette, the very fanciable blonde from Wilton's bakery...in the office of course. A few others from roundabout and I got to remember their names in pretty quick time. The room we were allocated was spacious enough but I could have done without the constant humming of the fluorescent light fittings. There was a bilious Gauguin on the wall.

"Any questions then?"

"I don't get this ontological argument thing. Would you mind going over it again?"

Steve the maths teacher. It was a least a couple of notches up from the Young Wives.

"Anselm. There must be that the greater than which there cannot be conceived. Now which is greater: that which is greatest but does not exist or that which is greatest and does exist? Clearly the greatest is that which does exist. And this Anselm called God. Or as Descartes put it in Meditation Five, 'Existence belongs to God as three angles and three sides belong to a triangle.'"

"Ah but look man..." Echoes of Scouseland – "you can't just define God into existence like that. Who was it said that existence is not a predicate?"

"G.E. Moore – but what did he know!"

"That's no proof of the existence of God. It's just words."

"And that, Steve, is rather like saying that a wall is just bricks."

"No but it's a trick isn't it? Just because I can imagine there's a God doesn't mean God exists."

"What else does God do if he doesn't exist?"

I was glad to see that they laughed a bit.

"The point of the argument is that God necessarily exists."

"But nothing can necessarily exist. Things just either exist or they don't."

"Really? Well, try this: God could not just happen to exist. That is to say his existence – if he exists that is – cannot be contingent. Because the existence of anything contingent depends on the existence of something else. It follows that God's existence is either necessary or it is impossible. Since it is clearly not impossible – logically impossible – because I can affirm God's existence without contradicting myself – then God's existence must be necessary. Therefore God exists. Quod erat demonstrandum."

"That's settled then. Anyone for the pub?"

That was the very fanciable Jeanette.

In the pub the philosophy still poured out and frothed up, only now it moved informally, slackening its corsets, into general culture. What bucked me up like a course of steroids was their vivacious interest in things of the mind and the heart: books, music, paintings – and what was being said about these things. They all shared the contemporary view of artistic creativity – how could they not? – the romantic-sentimental notion of the original genius who produces masterpieces effortlessly out of thin air. Carol from the library adored Mozart, she said. But she had a vision of him as producing music as a slot machine dispenses coins.

"But he was twenty-five before he heard any Bach. What did he do? He composed little of his own for nearly a whole year, but went and copied out Bach's manuscripts to teach himself the art of fugue."

There is that other fashionable fallacy according to which artistic and creative people are almost bound to be left wing. Manageress Sheila – "I'm not really a drinker" but could down six Tia Marias within the hour – was deeply into Jean Paul Sartre from which cesspit she had progressed to the unreadable French structuralist novels by such as Michel Butor. It needed someone to notice that all the profoundest and most innovative writers of the 20th century were traditionalists, conservatives, men denounced by the lumpen intelligentsia as facists – and yes, with the word spelt wrongly just like that. Henry James, Eliot. Pound. Wyndham Lewis. Joyce. Sisson...

Those writers were the antidote to fashionable bullshit such as Deconstruction, which claimed that texts do not have meanings. In the gents I scribbled a few lines on the inside cover of Sisson's Poems Selected:

"D'y wanna know the creeda
Jacques Derrida?
Dere ain't no reada,
Dere ain't no wreida
Eida"

"Anyhow," I said "It was Schoenberg himself who said, 'Bach was the first to compose with twelve tones.'"

Even after three pints I could focus clearly on Jeanette's tight grey skirt easing towards the bar for more drinks. At last there seemed to be a twitch or two of life in this parish priest lark.

Moreover there is such a thing as objective truth – not only in the propositions of the valid syllogism but in the fact of God's existence and the reality of Christ's Presence in the Sacrament. Modern theology – I mean since the 18th century – is based on a mistake. The Enlightenment made man the measure of all things and theology was studied from that anthropocentric position. Theologians ceased to take the existence of God as the central given of their discipline. What they studied instead was their own methodology. Theology thus degenerated into a social science. God was reduced to a metaphor and miracles to the realm of mythology.

The greatest theologian of the 20th century, Karl Barth, owed his greatness precisely to the vehemence with which he rejected such relativism. He said,

"One of the temptations implicit in the secular study of religion, evident in its origins from the Enlightenment onwards, has been the tendency for it to become the mouthpiece for the post-Christian intelligentsia of European society, a kind of quasi-religion for scholarly non-believers."

What a paragraph! Never has a particular nail been more squarely bashed in the middle of its thick head. He also said that the liberal theologian looks into the deep pit of God's being and sees only his own face reflected. Only an idiot would claim that mathematics can be studied by other than mathematical means, or music by what is unmusical, or geography, history likewise. Theology, of all subjects, must be studied theologically. As numbers are the given of maths and notes that of music, so God is the root of all theology. Why should that be thought so strange an idea?

And so with the Sacrament of the Altar. It is not a symbol of anything. It is the bread we all break and the cup we all share, but that does not mean it is a mere metaphor for social integration. To be a Christian is to be one who takes Christ at his word: This is my Body....this is my Blood. Of course you can't understand how. The truth is transcendental. The old word is mystery. You can't explain it. You can only accept it. But once you accept it, you know for certain that it is true. As Augustine said, we do not understand so that we may believe, but we believe and understanding follows. Nothing here that would prove too difficult for an intelligent ten year old.

The ordination retreat was held at Barrowby, a country house on a hill not far from the village of Kirby Overblow in Wharfedale. The view was made in heaven. The beds were made in Sparta. Eight candidates arrived in time for dinner on the Friday. Those to be ordained deacon in their dog collars for the first time, grinning queasily. The four of us for priesting – with our vast experience of a whole year's parish work apiece - affected a practised nonchalance. After dinner, Compline and the first of the bishop's spiritual addresses, speckled with bits of Latin and in-jokes, odium of the trade. At Saturday lunch, we were read to from The Cloud of Unknowing – which could have been a reflection on the stew. In between admonitions, we were encouraged to go on long walks. Bob Shaw and I dawdled through the scabrous autumn woods to find pints of Guinness in The Shoulder of Mutton. Bob went off on his own to the bookshop in Harrogate and I sat over my second pint. That movement again – a few words in a particular rhythm.

71

The light varies in an ancient bar
Made gaudy by the lesions of this age;
Real oak beams and noise machines,
Mechanical chat to fill the chasm of time:
The epoch is askew like a broken arm.
"By the window a woman with a broken necklace
Frowns at the menu and sucks a cigarette.
The sunlit smoke betokens death;
Dona nobis pacem
I drink beer and pray to sleep.

On Sunday morning the soon-to-be-deacons were still struggling with their dog collars, as if they were mimicking Harry Houdini's acts of escapology. Talking was allowed in public rooms again. At 9.30 we set off in private cars for Ripon Cathedral. All ancient glass and stone, refracting the cold light, the organ rumbling through a Bach prelude. The echoes of ladies' heels in the aisles. Vergers with tapers lighting the tall candles.

In came the bobbing procession led by the dazzling Cross. O Praise Ye the Lord. The choir all gusto. The line, Loud organs his glory forth tell in deep tone gave the Master of the Music chance to let us hear his scarcely-tamed instrument growl. Immediately before the ordination the ancient hymn Veni Creator Spiritus. What you felt when you knelt before the bishop, among all those other priests, was the weight of their hands on your head. It really was an imposition. To the sound of the bells we were all photographed outside the west door. The elusiveness of great occasions. You think to yourself,

"This is truly tremendous. I shall always remember this!"

...and the next thing you know, you're sitting in front of a steak and kidney pie and your neighbour looks up and says,

"It was cold where we were sitting. Was Vera Ricketts there? I didn't see her."

On the Monday evening, about sixty people turned up for my first Mass. Standing celebrating at the Altar is a bit like being wicketkeeper to a fast bowler: you are the one everyone else is depending on. I suppose, whatever his doctrine of Christ's presence in the Eucharist, no priest can ever completely persuade himself that the awesome act is valid when he is performing it.

Every year the bishop entertained all the diocesan clergy for breakfast in an olde worlde restaurant in the market square in Ripon after the Eucharist in the cathedral. As we sauntered, at least a hundred and fifty of us, across the square, I heard a little girl ask her mother,

"What are they?"

So many parsons. The spectacle must have made the denizens of the little market town ponder what they had done to earn such a generous benediction. I recalled the words of a monk who once preached for us at college:

"Clergy are like manure. Spread thinly over a wide area they do much good. All lumped together in one place, they stink to highest heaven."

Our species was present in all its varieties. Bluff country parsons in tweeds, a surprise they had omitted to bring their shotguns, for there was always the off chance they would see something to kill. Delicate, mincing high churchmen all in black, a fair dusting of dandruff over their capes. Jesus freaks with purple cords and matted hairstyles, wildly excited about the rock musical Hair which had just opened at The Grand Theatre in Leeds. It failed. For exuberant lust was not a prominent feature of the Leeds character:

"How did the audience react to all that nude dancing?"

"Morosely. It fell like a B-minor Mass on Batley."

The great majority of my brethren were unostentatious, middle-of-the-road Anglicans in lounge suits. No extremes. Over the bacon and eggs the conversation was muffled, predictable. About the latest revision of the liturgy. Funeral fees. Rules for the erection of graveyard monuments. And a hundred enquiries of the style:

"Where's old Painswick-Martin these days? He was at Little Sodbury with Twitching for more years than was good for him."

All this punctuated now and again by a loud laugh, a stylised laugh, a clerical laugh.

The autumn PTA dance at Crossgates was an education. Gins and tonics galore. Martinis. I recalled that Ed Cowie had written the music for the advert for Martini: ...the right one, the bright one, Martini. Not many bright ones in the church hall that night. Broadstairs disapproved. I think he found the tepid lust embarrassing, so he had buggered off to his Lodge Night and left me to

"...have a look in at the dance."

The saxophones blared and the deodorants were, on the whole, efficient. At the start euphoria hung about the church hall like a miasma of cheap perfume but by ten-thirty most of the participants had managed to lose even the negligible amount of consciousness with which they had begun. The air was thick with cigarette smoke. You saw everything through a glass darkly. After a few drinks, the sensation was of being partially anaesthetised.

This annual dance usually threw up, so to speak, opportunities for the exercise of pastoral care. At least the aftermath did. Many a middle aged reveller from among the Nice People would defy paunch, dyspepsia and halitosis to protest undying tipsy lust for another man's wife. New liaisons blossomed in unlikely parts of the churchyard. Other trysts followed and desertions of the matrimonial home. Sometimes the unlikely lovers would fly away for seven nights on Ibiza. And, when you visited them in the long afternoons, forsaken wives, schooled by their younger friends in the burgeoning sisterhood, would declare:

"I'm glad to be rid of him. I never realised how much I lived in his shadow. I'm going to be me from now on."

But these disturbances usually settled themselves fairly quickly with the help of tears and Valium. In a few weeks, he had resumed his place at the dominoes table in The Travellers' Rest. And for her, being me extended only so far as enrolling in a weekly yoga class, leaving him to do the babysitting. And now when you looked in on them you found true love had been wonderfully restored:

"Well, it's come home to us at last: marriage is a partnership, isn't it love – give and take!"

That winter I began sneaking into the Brotherton Library at the university, sheepishly, as a reformed drunk slips into the four ale bar, hoping not to be noticed. There I met the Chaplain, Alan Overell. Another Chaplain, Geoff Allen at my theological college, had done his national service with Alan. In Geoff's view, Alan was

"...too good for this world."

Apparently, Geoff had phoned Alan and mentioned me:

"He said you were malcontent and useful."

Typical Geoff remark, that! Geoff who got a First at Durham, in spite of inventing footnotes in his dissertation:

"Guttersnipe and Weig (1947 ibid)"

Geoff doubled as ethics tutor and he used to like to tease and twit the more conservatively religious types. He would push them to the edge. His favourite ploy was just to keep asking Why? Why? Why? until the religiose chaps frothed with frustration. On one occasion the topic had been homosexuality – at just the time when the new law decriminalising it was about to be passed. One of the evangelical fundamentalists, Clive Farquasson, was outraged by Geoff's tolerant attitude towards the shirt-lifters. There was a certain irony because Clive himself was generally regarded as being closely attached to that persuasion – a suspicion not removed by the sweet and lisping way he had sung Play Misty for Me at the Christmas revue. And then there were his almost completely white curls and his light contralto. Clive snapped:

"The Bible says it's an abomination. Anyhow, it's against natural law."

Geoff laughed:

"How can it be against natural law? If God hadn't meant us to be queer, he wouldn't have given us arseholes. In the same way that he gave us ears for holding our pencils behind!"

It was too much for Clive and he rushed out of the room, followed by three of his co-religionists.

Angular Alan Overell, kind and refined, ran the university church – a 19th century building in black stone among all the white brick modernism of the academic departments. There was a large poster on his notice board listing half a dozen philosophers I had heard of, coming to preach in the spring term. My mind began to salivate. Alan asked me about Crossgates, and I told him. He was naturally sympathetic and quite unsentimental:

"Well, you're allowed out of your first curacy after a couple of years. Where would you like to go next?"

"Leeds University Chaplaincy?"

He laughed, put an arm on my shoulder and led me away for coffee. He spoke of poetry – David Jones and his Anathemata and the long prose description of his years in the trenches which Eliot had thought so much of. It became a habit to have a drink with Alan whenever I was at the Brotherton. One Friday he came out to Crossgates for lunch and said,

"I'm going to need an assistant. John White is leaving in the summer. I can't offer you a semi like this, but there's a very big flat. Why don't you come and have a look?"

Before I could look, the arrangement fell through. The curse of the senior curate struck again. It turned out that his father, being a close friend of the bishop, had got him to agree to ensure that his son would fill the next vacancy at the chaplaincy. Alan didn't want him. But it was of course impossible for Alan, having rejected him, to prefer a man who was his junior.

VII

Broadstairs was turning into Luchino Visconti. I was conducting a funeral when he bobbed up from behind a bush in the churchyard and began snapping his camera at me – as well as at the coffin, mourners, floral tributes and all. For the next month he turned up – like Mr Toad in the grip of a new craze - for everything: weddings, Parish Eucharists, Young Wives, Girl Guides, Men's Group – we all became part of his fantasy epic. The Church and Parish of Crossgates: A Photographic Record.

After a particularly arduous evening in the vicarage reviewing the lot:

"Well, what do you think of it, Peter?"

"All right so far as it goes, but there are a few things missing."

He looked as if I'd pissed on his strawberries:

"Such as?"

"You might have included the senior curate advancing upon my Aunt Betty until she falls down the cellar steps, or climbing in or out – take your pick – of that window on Austhorpe Road. Or a special view of him doing his parrot-in-the-wrong-colour act in out of season vestments. Or, if you wanted to go in for something really controversial, how about me talking about God at the parish discussion group?"

If he'd handed me the camera at that juncture, I could have got a lovely snap and called it The Vicar's Lofty Disdain.

Next day there was great excitement. The senior curate announced his resignation. The atmosphere in the vicarage was like VE Day.

"Where's he going? Should we phone and warn them, d'you think??"

Broadstairs simply shambled from room to room, happy beyond speech or language. He had this dirty chuckle, like lumps of coal being shaken around in a scuttle.

"Well you might ask. He's going to be Chaplain of a teacher training college for ladies!"

He didn't say another word. But watery-eyed, hoarse, almost delirious with joy, his eyes had taken on a look of fixed concentration, as if he were seeing a film preview of his senior curate's first week among the fleshpots of St Mary's Training College. Stumbling into their washrooms and knocking over whole clothes horses of underwear. Announcing his credentials as grandson of our man in Washington. Threatening them with trips to The History of Coal exhibition at Jesmond:

"I've got free tickets. They come with my membership of The Cambridge Industrial Society."

I made to leave. On my way to my class in the junior school. I asked Broadstairs if he had a bit of Sellotape for something I wanted to do in the lesson.

"Nay lad, don't you start. You've brought back a very nasty experience to my recollection, young man. When yon fella first came he asked if I'd anywhere he could park his bike. He was lodging with us you see for the first few weeks. Well, we had this outside lavatory in those days – you know, the old brick building stood by itself that we had pulled down. I said he could put it there if he liked.

"Anyhow, I went away for a few days. When I got back Jack Flash was standing on the doorstep. 'Well now Mr Broadstairs,' he said 'I wonder if you have a bit of Bostik?'

"I asked him what was the matter and he said there'd been a small accident in the lavatory while he was putting his bike in – but with a bit of Bostik he could put it right...."

Here the vicar began to roll about like an amalgamation of the Laughing Policeman and the Fat Man of the Fair.

"Well, we got to the lavatory and I opened the door. Never mind a bit of Bostik – I tell you the Royal Engineers couldn't have put it right. Total destruction. The cistern off the wall and the bowl broken away from the pipe and lying there in the corner. And yon fella nodding at it, with that look on his face..."

And his hysteria increased, infected me of course, and we were both a couple of daft girls helpless on laughing gas when Mrs Broadstairs came in to see what was the matter.

"What's so funny, boys?"

And it started us off all over again: Mrs Broadstairs joining in.

11th June was the senior curate's last Sunday in the parish. I can't remember what they gave him as a sending off present – a map and compass and a life's supply of Stemetil and phenobarbitone would have been best. Broadstairs went off for the whole of August leaving me in sole charge. Humid dawns celebrated with Percy in the Lady Chapel. Round and round the hot ringroad to a dozen funerals at the crem. All the Sunday services and three hideously trendy weddings, at one of which the bride chose Phil Collins' A Groovy Kind of Love which Pulford played immaculately and with towering disdain. At least in August the evening groups took a break and the Crossgates doctrine of Salvation by Parish Organisations lapsed. I had given firm notice that I was to leave the parish on 24th September.

I had a job to go to. An old college friend, Neil Handley, had called on me on his way back from a trip to some sort of ecclesiastical junket in York. Neil was the complete extravert: all manic consciousness and no self-consciousness. The true recipe for everlasting bliss, perhaps? He was bluff, broad and he barked. Bright as psychedelic wallpaper. He had some fathomless medical trouble with his brain and once or twice at college he had fallen completely comatose and had to be carted off to the intensive care while we all gathered in chapel to pray for him – only for him to pop up like the Jack-in-a-Box and suggest a trip to the pub.

Neil was all optimism and belly laughs. He played revivalist hymns on the out-of-tune piano in the common room, drowning the botched notes by his raucous singing. He made Heavenly Sunshine sound like hell on earth.

A Holy Fool. In the middle ages he might have been a saint or an innkeeper - or both. He was no scholar. I remember in the General Ordination Examinations – GOE, God's Own Exams – there was a question on the doctrine of the Double Procession. This is the bit in the Creed which says that the Holy Ghost proceedeth from the Father and the Son.

"What did you put for that, Neil?"

He looked vacant: "Oh I said it's when the vicar takes the choir procession around the church twice."

He detested all pomposity. He told me once how he was seated next to the Principal's thirteen year old son David at Friday Family Lunch,

"Now then young David, and d'you like playing football?"

"No."

"Cricket then?"

"No."

"And what do you like?"

"I like walking around the cricket field with my father and reciting Greek verbs."

"Oh I'm so glad you're a normal boy!"

On another legendary occasion in college chapel he was listed to read the lesson from The Book of Daniel about Nebuchadnezzar's feast. It is a very repetitive passage making mention several times of "...cornet, flute, harp, sackbut, psaltery and dulcimer and all kinds of musick."

Neil tired of the list and instead gave them, "...the same band as before."

Miraculously, he squeezed past the examiners and was appointed to a curacy in Ashton-under-Lyme where he endured two dismal years unappreciated by a vicar whom Neil described as "constipation with clothes on." From there he was rescued by the Rev'd Dr James Bentley, extraordinary vicar of Stretford, just a mile from the Manchester United football ground. James was looking for a second curate. Would I like to be considered for the job?

"I know for a fact James is coming to Leeds in a week or two. I'll mention you to him. You could ask him to lunch."

I packed. I went on a last trudge round the parish saying goodbye, trying without any success to place the last two years meaningfully in the chronology of my life. They had been a crash course in practical surrealism and in general disillusionment. The inconsequentiality of kids' questions in assembly. Old ladies dishing out gargantuan doses of lethal homemade wine in the middle of hot afternoons. The exotic lady in white, the stink and the exorcism. I can still see that frightening headline in the Yorkshire Evening Post when I close my eyes. E. Smelt had retired after twenty-seven years as headmaster. And then Polly McNeil:

"Yes please, and then will you fuck me?" She had come to a terrible end and surrealism prevailed even in death.

Margaret Blair told me:

"She got so depressed. She was out of her mind really at the finish. She went across Leeds and threw herself under a number fourteen bus to Stanningly Park. I don't know why ever she did such a thing – when the number sixteen runs right past her front door."

The last funeral I conducted in Leeds was that of my Uncle Bill – Willy Priestley – who went all through the war and rose to become Regimental Sergeant Major. Not bad for the son of a newsagent in the west Leeds slums. He was tall, suavely arrogant, a linguist. Everything for him was anticlimax after the army, especially after the Italian campaign...

When I was very young, he told me his stories, sprinkled with the delightful Eyetie lingo so mellifluous, so thrilling. Such an elegant, gallant, romantic man – slipping easily from one of his eight languages to another – did not belong where he ended up. Working for his father in the newsagent's shop. Counting the morning papers in sixes into the paper-boys' bags. Fleeing to the pub at midday. Returning to count out the evening papers just the same. He was no drunkard. He drank only beer. But he smoked himself to death and died of lung cancer aged fifty-eight. I cried at his funeral.

James Bentley arrived like a crash landing the following week, suave and brisk with a permanently ironical look. Why as he came through the door did I seem to hear the opening chords of Don Giovanni? I'm sure I would have smelt the sulphur if the smell of whisky had not got there first. His first words to me were,

"Do you get bored? I do."

"Crossgates is pretty boring, James."

"Life is a whirlpool of delight, but wheresoe'er the rabble drinketh, there the water is poisoned. Zarathustra."

He was thirty-five, nearly bald, a Lancastrian who had gone up to Oxford and distinguished himself as Postmaster of Merton. His mind was like a forest fire and that furtive look could be terrifying. You felt he might do simply anything next. He seemed to preset his eyes to look at something indiscernible a few feet in front of him, as if he were about to turn it to stone.

"When I'm bored I think of sex."

In time I got to recognise his aura of cultivated decadence. He once told me he saw himself as a mixture of Jonathan Swift, Oscar Wilde and Noel Coward – oh and Humphrey Bogart, about whom I heard him preach convincingly on at least five occasions. He could do Brando as well. His cultural milieu was the Weimar republic. He was into Weill and Dietrich and he had seen Bob Fosse's Cabaret five times – "Twice," as he said "in one day."

"Come and work with me," he said – just like Jesus talking to the fishermen. "We can buy you a house," he added, in between making fond noises about my home brew.

"I've no money to buy houses, James."

He looked stricken, melodramatically heart-sick:

"I'll get you a loan. Then when you leave you can sell it and make a profit. I don't smoke, do you?"

On the following Friday I hired a car and drove across the Pennines. The first impression of Stretford was of a miasma. It was oily and damp and, punching pungently through the damp, came the sweet sickly aroma from the Kelloggs factory – the sort of atmosphere you associate with funeral parlours. I entered Stretford via the Barton bridge section of the M63 which curved over the suburb like a colourless Valhalla rainbow and deposited you among the high rise flats and detritus that was the southern end of the Trafford Park Industrial Estate. I wondered what the children of the borough used for a playground:

What constitution have these children
Of Storey Street, recently demolished
And raised again on fifteen floors of
glass and stone?
A hell of aerials and broken lifts,
Desperate slogans and piss-soaked stairs.
Other concrete coffins litter the city.

"It's a grid system," said James, affecting a lusty pride in the place, "like Westinghouse's plan for New York."

Like Old Mother Riley was like Helen of Troy.

The locals – or at least those of them who aspired to semis like the denizens of Crossgates - liked to think of themselves as inhabitants of a select outer suburb, next to upmarket Sale on the Lancashire-Cheshire border. This was difficult, as every week the din reminded them of the proximity of Man U's Stretford end. They said yew for you; her for hair, Buzz for bus and cur for car. The overriding impression was of a community straining night and day not to vomit. With Kelloggs where it was, this could be difficult.

The vicarage on Barton Road was a small detached house. James, in his black cloak, ushered me inside, nodding theatrically and promising strong drink. Every wall lined with books. In the corner the TV set on with the sound down kept us up to date on the progress of the hijacking of Jewish athletes at the Munich Olympics.

The phone rang half a dozen times and James ignored it flamboyantly. When it rang again it pleased him to pick it up and, in a voice like warm oil,

"Hello! Hello! James Bentley. Yes, yes, of course! But later. I have at this moment a distinguished clergyman from Yorkshire as my guest. May I have the pleasure of stroking your bottom this evening, about seven?"

The grin never slipped. Then for my information: "That was the Hooded Claw. Miss Playboy 1953. Parish Verger."

Neil came in eating, singing Jesus wants me for a sunbeam.

"A nice lad, Neil is. Very religious."

The three of us climbed into James' red car – "I'm like a cosmodemonic Noddy" – and he gave us a tour of the parish. A bald man with a red face and a huge moustache, the very picture of the British colonel, nearly drove into us at a junction by the church. Evading him only by mounting the kerb, James wound down the window and shouted,

"Get back to where you came from - black bastard!"

We called at the church which was dedicated to All Saints. A whitewashed shack with stackable chairs rather than pews and contemporary starship commander style altar frontal and vestments. An electric organ like the one in the crem. The sort of place which gives vulgarity a bad name. Between All Saints and the corn flakes factory ran Raglan Road, a narrow street of shabby semis and parked curs. Neil lived at number 34 and he had painted the door and the window frame purple – as if to suggest the dwelling might be the home of a shirt-lifting bishop. Round the corner was a windswept car park beside a supermarket and an all night garage. Despite the absence of a cathedral, the locals called this place the precinct.

We called on James' bank manager who gave us whisky, offered me £500 towards the deposit on a house and £500 to buy a car. James and the bank manager like the Don and Leperello. There was a house for sale not far from Neil's and so we went straight there – after more whisky. A tiny woman of extraordinary curvaceousness opened the door and immediately blushed like the setting sun. James scooped her up and under his cloak:

"Noreen's a friend of mine."

The house smelt of bleach. There was a tiled fireplace and a huge bookcase without books but stuffed full of seaside novelties, a nest of glass tables with chromium legs and two foam-filled avant garde chairs. Here too was an electric organ, larger than the one in church.

"That's Noreen's organ. She plays with it a lot. I never touch it myself but I'm afraid I haven't been able to keep my hands off her."

He threw himself into a chair and unfastened his cloak.

"Come and play with me, dearest!"

"James!" Then by way of explanation: He's always like this..."

"How much are you asking, my pretty one?"

"£4750"

"I think Peter might offer £4250."

He stuck out an arm, palm upwards and nodded his head in a gesture of ostentatious honesty.

"Well, I'll have to think about it. You are good to me, James."

She kissed him juicily on the lips and leaned forward, revealing no visible means of support for her opulent breasts. We left in a whirl. Back at the vicarage James said,

"I'll have to leave you. There's a meeting of the Boundary Commission."

He spoke the words voluptuously, making the meeting of the Boundary Commission sound like a late night at the Kit Kat Club. This was confusing: a dissolute playboy, one could imagine - but a dissolute bureaucrat!

By six o'clock I had sobered up enough to drive back to Leeds. What was I letting myself in for? How long before I would be arrested as an accomplice after what combination of disgraceful facts? Still, I determined I would go and work with James. At least I wouldn't be bored to death, and the prospect of getting out of Crossgates was like the promise of a month in the Alps after two years in an iron lung. Embarking on a round of Goodbyes, then. Silver-haired Tom Clegg and Vikki his wife, who looked like Audrey Hepburn and talked like Marti Caine, took me for a vindaloo in Harrogate. These two lived only a couple of doors from me and I'd got to know them well once Joan Abbot had shoved them on to the PCC. I was sad to leave the philosophy class, but it was nice when Alan Overell offered to take it over.

Burning bridges and burning my boats. I felt as if I was starting a game of Russian Roulette. So what? Life is a whirlpool of delight.... Perhaps.

I had the unnerving experience of meeting my successor: Douglas Jones, a small Australian with a face like a shiny apple. He had been a missionary in Papua New Guinea for ten years – no doubt looking at the head-hunters. His wife had – as Broadstairs put it – "some mental trouble." The prospect of a loony clergy wife didn't faze the vicar. As he said,

"The senior curate was preparation for anything!"

Douglas had two violent and uncontrollable sons – typical parson's kids, as a member of the Mothers' Union had described them to me as I was on my way to give my very last talk to the ladies of the Methodist Bright Hour – that oxymoron.

On my last Sunday, Broadstairs made a bon voyage speech about me in the parish hall over the usual disgusting cups of instant coffee after the Parish Eucharist:

"Let me remind you of the Collect for the Day, the Seventeenth Sunday after Trinity: 'Lord, we pray thee that thy grace may always prevent and follow us...' And so it is our wish and our prayer for Peter: Prevent him, O Lord."

Nicely done and said with a smile. The bourgoisie strikes back. Ironically, the only members of the gathering who saw the joke were those who had been in my much-disapproved discussion group. I answered blandly enough. If I had been nerved to answer what I liked, what would I have said? That Broadstairs was a prig, a moron, a stultifying bastard and the mortal enemy of all delight. But, if I had been writing that speech some five years later, or indeed if I were writing it now, I would have said differently.

He also set me in the middle of the traditional ways which alone sustain us. It was Broadstairs' daily routine with all its tedious unalterability which showed me the value of repetition: the daily offices - I had come to know the Psalms off by heart through their daily recitation at Matins and Evensong. And I can recommend them as the stuff to get you though many a bad night. He had taught me how to celebrate Mass meaningfully and without the sickening intrusion of personality which is the nauseating practice of so many clerics. He had shown me the varieties of expertise and detail in performing the occasional offices of Baptism, Matrimony and The Burial of the Dead. Thanks were due even for his bluff anti-intellectualism and earthy Yorkshireness – which things made it not only impossible and unnatural but absolutely unavoidable to refer to him as anything other than Broadstairs. And, after all, to do so with affection.

VIII

Neil moved in with James and I was lodged temporarily behind the purple woodwork of 34 Raglan Road. On my first Saturday in the parish James asked me round for coffee:

"Well, guess what's happened to me! I've been appointed to the parish of St Mary, Oldham. Of course, even a man of my humble instincts couldn't possibly turn it down. It's the best church in the Manchester diocese. The civic church. And..." here he began to salivate – "it's the church patronised by the Oldham Rep. Imagine what theatrical delights we can produce there, Peter!"

"We?"

"Well naturally you'll be coming as my curate."

He was all broad gestures and over-inflected innocence.

"But the bishop has just installed me here!"

"Oh I can square everything with him. If you will be so kind as to look after Stretford for a few months while they find my successor, then you can come out and help me establish world domination in Oldham. I'm seeing the bishop on Monday, as it happens. He's got a very nice secretary. He should. If I had a secretary, I'd be fucking her."

"And will I be going into the property market in Oldham as well as here?"

"Leave it to me. I'll tell Noreen the deal's off. No need to buy her place now."

"And what about the bank loan?"

He threw up his hands like a Leeds Jewish tailor showing off a nice piece of worsted:

"Keep it my boy! Use it for something else. Why don't you take a holiday?"

He spent the next five minutes discoursing on the well-known fact that the prospect of war makes women frisky and free with their favours. At last I got a word in edgeways:

"I haven't even started work here yet, James!"

"...It's a well-known social phenomenon. Whenever there's a world crisis, women get easier. God, is that the time. I must get off to London. I'm seeing Dykes-Bower, the Queen's architect this afternoon."

I asked him for a week to make up my mind, though there was never any doubt that I would follow him. The more I saw of Stretford, the sooner I wanted to leave it forever. Kelloggs defined the atmosphere. You couldn't walk in that sickly stink for five minutes and still pretend you were living on the border of fashionable Cheshire. Then there was the local pub, The Melville, where the beer was so bad they said it was poured away and the customers drank the caustic fluid they used for cleaning the pipes. It was ill-lit so that everyone looked as if they were on a sepia photograph. Broken furniture. It smelt of burning rags. A 1930s doss house frequented by characters who might have been extras in The Night of the Living Dead. No one laughed there. Why should they?

The best pub in Stretford was the All Saints Church and Social Club, its name on the front in red lights, like a go-ahead saloon in a frontier outpost. This had been set up by James and Neil and licensed, as it said, for the sale of intoxicating liquor and tobacco. The clergy were in there every night, exercising pastoral care - chiefly by calling the Bingo numbers.

This was Neil: "Two fat ladies – 39"

Shrieks of protest. Was it not a well-known fact that two fat ladies were designated by the number 88?

"You're all Bingo fundamentalists – that's your bloody trouble. I make it more interesting!"

Howls of delight as he sat up on the stage and hurled his coloured balls into the wind machine. The Church Social Club was to Stretford what all those organisations were to Crossgates. You had, similarly, to go and look at them. You might say that Stretford was more interesting than Crossgates in the way that Purgatory is more interesting than Limbo.

One of my first assignments was to lead a church service for about a hundred and fifty disabled and mentally subnormal – now we would have to say people with learning difficulties – gathered from all over the parish and the lands beyond – Irlam, Trafford Park, Urmston and Salford. Few of them could keep quiet or sit still. Many had to visit the lavatory times without number. Others relieved themselves where they sat. It was like a scene from Hogarth. Raucous shouts, macabre laughter – and other noises. Evil farts bred by shitty institutional food. James gloried in its squalor. Grinning like a Toytown bear, he came to meet me at the end. He kissed and hugged many of the congregation as they limped, staggered or were wheeled from the church:

"I love ya, baby! God bless! Goodbye then! Tat Ta! God's good!"

And later in The Melville:

"Did you see me, Peter? Just like Francis of Assisi!"

It rained constantly. It seemed barely to get light. One day James whisked me off to meet a member of the Stretford Ecumenical Team. She was the Lutheran Pastorin Heidi Haller. First we called in the vestry and I was introduced to the Hooded Claw. This was Betty Taylor, the Sacristan, fifty-fivish, permanently bent double, all in black, with a black cap to cover her baldness. She had hollow cheeks and eyes like ball-bearings. She wore a pectoral crucifix of a size that would have been the envy of a cardinal archbishop.

"Come here darling. Don't let me have to chase you all round the room before I get to give your arse a squeeze!"

"James, there's the name of a best man here for Saturday's wedding and I can't make it out."

He slipped his arm around her waist and kissed her noisily:

"Now that is a difficult intellectual problem, my concubine! Tell you what, my dearest one: when the best man comes on Saturday, ask him his name and perhaps he will be kind enough to tell you what it is."

She looked at him as if he were speaking in a Syrian dialect.

"Now my love, I've solved your problem, and my beloved new curate – give him a kiss – and I must be away to visit Fraulein Pastorin Heidi Haller because she has kindly shipped over some duty free Pilsner for the relief of the clergy in Stretford."

And we were off before Betty had exercised her option to kiss me. James crashed the gears and drove through a red light. He was full of apologies:

"She's shy. She'll kiss you next time."

The Lutheran Church was a modern brick building with thick carpets and efficient central heating – tributes to German prosperity and German engineering. The Lutheran clergy were paid by the West

German state and Heidi was on about £13,000 a year – at a time when an English parish priest's stipend was £2600. Heidi was slim, angular, charming, refined and sitting with the Anglican Industrial Missioner for the Manchester Diocese, Brian Swales. He was not a missionary of the old imperial kind but one who had mastered the dialect of the tribe to whom he was bearing witness – full of convenors, workshop practice, composite resolutions and something called The Bridlington Agreement which seemed to be to trades unionists like Brian what the Chalcedonian Definition was to the Catholic Church.

Brian, genial, glasses, wearing a donkey jacket , was the first person I'd met that morning who was not in a cassock. Heidi poured some strong coffee and asked,

"Are we going to have that discussion about industrial alienation?"

"We've got the Eucharist first," said Brian who knocked out his pipe and blessed a half slice of Hovis and the dregs of a bottle of Marsala. It was all over inside three minutes.

James said, "I think we should take Peter to the film theatre."

He caressed the leggy Heidi, stroking her long black hair:

"Look at my beautiful Heidi! She speaks almost perfect English as well. Only I caught her out the other day, didn't I Liebling? That big headed vicar of Rusholme, what did you say of him?"

He affected both her voice and her expression remarkably:

"She said, 'He is so conceited, he thinks he is the bee's legs'!"

We sped off to the Manchester Film Theatre in James' red car. He talked to Heidi all the way in fluent German with a profound Lancashire accent. Imagine George Formby playing Hitler. Meanwhile Brian Swales named-dropped half a dozen German theologians who were said to have a social conscience. James interrupted his cooing at Heidi and said,

"But only Karl Barth opposed the Nazis."

The film was a camp, cultic affair: WR: The Mysteries of the Organism, a fantasy based on the erotic Marxism of Wilhelm Reich which argued there can be no political revolution without a sexual revolution. This doctrine was making inroads in the universities, naturally. The film featured the so called orgone boxes which were a combination of confessional, private massage parlour and padded cell. Really, people went to to see the film because it was packed full of the sort of filth not available in the regular cinemas. The scene that drew the lewdest gasp was that of the ideological nurses fondling the party apparatchik's spectacular member. There were long debates about whether this instrument was the actor's own or largely, so to speak, an augmentation courtesy of the make-up department.

WR; The Mysteries of the Organism was only marginally more surreal than everyday life in Stretford. From the sepia local to the Church Club a go-go, with Bingo featuring irrational numbers, the cackling ministrations of the Hooded Claw, to the service for the crippled and the lunatics which would have been more suitably accommodated in a medieval hospice. Manchester seemed to have given up Lowry and turned to Bosch.

I met another member of the Ecumenical team, the non-drinking Methodist minister Dr Rudge He went on a lot about the need for scholarship. James was squeezed up between Neil and Heidi. He said,

"Scholarship? Scholarship's being at your desk at half past five every morning, drunk or sober."

James was completing his own doctorate on The Public Worship and Regulation Act of 1875. In anyone else's hands this would have been tedious as painting double yellow lines. James wrote up the historical data with all the verve of an action thriller: the street fights over such issues as the clergyman's attire at the Altar, the arson attacks on ultramontane churches and naturally the sex. He didn't know about the goings on in Crossgates in Russell's and Taglis' day.

Beyond all the swearing and drinking and womanising, the obsessive politicking, boundary reports, trades union meetings, industrial alienation and the Urmston Council of Churches, James was a parish priest who faithfully visited his people and was tender as a mother hen with the sick and the dying. All December he chased through the mist and rain to Oldham, planning his own advent

In Crossgates, Christmas had meant lanterns at Midnight Eucharist. Children to church next morning with their presents and – once – with snow on their boots. Then the whole suburb sank into a ghostly twilight wherein the good burghers ate and drank themselves insensible. It lasted until the New Year when the PTA came out to play again at the Hogmanay Dance. In Stretford Christmas was Turkey Bingo Night in the Church Club and carols in the shopping precinct with accompaniment by the Sally Ann band. Christmas morning I went early to church to find only the Hooded Claw bent over the sacristy desk like Bob Cratchitt. Somehow a smile escaped from under all that blackness and she brought forth glasses of sherry and pieces of Christmas cake. It was like being fed by ravens:

"'ere yew air, Peter. Compliments of the season!"

She talked as they do on Coronation Street.

"When James was 'ere 'e would always give me a Christmas kiss..."

Why not? She tasted better than she looked.

At ten o'clock the service began with the scoopy electronic organ sounding just like the one on Opportunity Knocks. About a hundred turned up and three families asked me to have lunch with them. Instead, I went home and tried to sleep off the wear and tear of having run the parish by myself since the middle of November. The days following the Festival were a haze of red wine, imported Pilsner and farewells. Goodbye was said in church to Heidi and many Germans came – James having dropped in from Oldham and speaking to them in something like their own tongue. Heidi departed for a new post in the Fatherland. Neil was inducted by the bishop to his cure of souls and new Bingo crowd at the parish of Breightmet in Bolton. I was trying to do some philosophy again, as much to apply an astringent to all the loose, flabby living: comparing William James' pragmatism with things in the later philosophy of Wittgenstein. I felt very wooden.

On Friday 12th January I drove to Oldham in my second-hand Ford Cortina - courtesy of James' bank manager's loan. St Mary's was a huge, impressive building, a citadel on a hill built during an interlude of prosperity. Oldham was set at the greatest height above sea level of all the Lancashire cotton towns. The churchwarden Harry Heap – yes, his real name – described him exactly – told me:

"Oldham were allus first to close in't slump and last t'oppen in't good times."

The Mayor of Oldham was at the service, front right with his voluptuously geriatric wife, prompting thoughts of necrophilia. Her costume outshone the bishop. James grinned throughout like a schoolboy. The bun-fight, vol au vent and beer scramble afterwards gave the bishop opportunity to tell me he would licence me to the Oldham curacy on 13th March:

"Come early and have a cup of tea in my rooms."

Meanwhile, Stretford had to be swept up and put away. Half the time was taken up listening to wrangles over money at the Church Club: the bar takings were down since James and Neil had left. Well, well! Who'd have thought it? Then I was racing all over Manchester taking funerals and House Communion to predatory spinsters such as Miss Saunders and Miss Bell.

The Hooded Claw grew quite clingy too and she was forever telling me what she imagined to be dark secrets about James. But she always added:

"And he did love me – I'm sure of it."

She would meet me in the vestry to do the work of parish clerk at what was called Weekly Surgery. Why do MPs and the clergy describe their interviewing evenings as surgeries? It implies their constituents and parishioners are sick.

On my last Sunday in Stretford I had a pint with a local clergyman I had not met before. This was the Marxist, Howard Gray. He was the active, leaflet-dropping sort of Marxist. He had dropped leaflets in the General Synod. He had even dropped leaflets in the House of Commons, for all the good it did him. I didn't ask him what the leaflets were about, for I was afraid he might tell me. Howard gave me an Ancient Mariner stare and pointed his cigarette at me:

"You should beware of James. Make sure you don't get taken for a ride. He says he's left wing but that he needs a power-base before he can become politically active. Well, he couldn't wish for a better power base than Oldham, could he? But you'll see – he won't act."

"My experience is that James is forever acting."

In the early hours long after my induction party, I found myself on the floor, slowly sobering up in Oldham vicarage while nearby James sat fondling an ample twenty-something who helped in the church office. James said,

"I'm going to put Oldham on the map. I've commissioned Dykes-Bower, architect of Westminster Abbey, to reappoint the interior of St Mary's. We'll make people notice this town."

The young woman gazed into his eyes as if he had been singing the Liebstod.

The vicarage was like a plush bomb shelter, below the level of the inner ring road and the new estate. Triple glazing kept out the din of the lorries. I was to be ensconced in a Council flat, almost as salubrious as the vicarage, on what was called the Shaw Road Estate, on the leeward side of the mountain known as Oldham Edge. The Council had thoughtfully re-housed all the pensioners dislodged from their demolished Victorian terrace dwellings on this part of the Estate – thus separating them by a long one-in-four gradient from Tommy Fields market and the rest of the shops in Oldham town centre. When it snowed they either got social services to bring them victuals – or they starved.

The new estate was the first circle of hell. Not particularly high-rise, five or six storeys, but designed by sadistic architects with a mania for confusion. For instance, the inhabitants found it almost impossible to get to know their neighbours, or even to know who their neighbours were. This was because the flats had been so constructed that adjacent doors did not belong to adjacent dwellings: so your next door neighbour might live two doors to your right and on the floor above. The old stone built houses in their ribbon-like streets were in need of repair, but repaired they would have been serviceable for a further hundred years. At least those who dwelt therein knew that next door neighbour meant next door neighbour.

And how about play areas for the thousands of children of the Oldham artisans? The satanic planning department had indeed made generous provision by building the blocks of flats as a quadrangle with a green space in its interior on which were placed swings and roundabouts. This was workable for the families who lived on the ground floor, but what parents on the third or fifth floor could rest easy while their children were out of earshot, down there? None in fact. So you never saw children playing on the swings and roundabouts. What you did see plenty of was restless, disaffected youth turned bored and ugly, swigging beer and then smashing the empty bottles and leaving broken glass all over the playground. And there were no shops. Cut off from one another and with no natural meeting place, such as the corner shop had provided among the old streets, people – many of them old and crippled with rickets – kept themselves to themselves and slowly declined in front of their television sets.

There were concrete public stairways, and always the stench of piss. There were no dustbins but corporate rubbish shoots which were frequently set alight by the yobs and oiks. The stairways echoed and clanged every time anyone walked up or down. Rubbish fell out of the inadequate chutes and there was filth everywhere. Graffiti. People came to feel that their old town had been disembowelled. Youngsters, having known nothing better, grew up in the Lancashire version of the vicious landscape of Anthony Burgess's A Clockwork Orange. The film of the book was being screened in Oldham at the time.

I lived on the third floor at 157 St Stephen's House. God knows what it had to do with St Stephen. The only St Stephen's House I had ever heard of was the theological college by that name in Oxford, the preferred seminary for delicate aesthetes with the taste for frilly cottas and sodomy. My St Stephen's flat was the biggest house I had ever lived in, with four large bedrooms, a bathroom and separate lavatory, a fitted kitchen and a spacious sitting room with a panoramic view over the deserted playground. There was a thermostatically-controlled warm air central heating system which was roundly cursed by everyone because it usually blew only cold air and quantities of dust. The flats should have been an earthly paradise: instead, they were an instant slum. When I had occasion to drive through Oldham a mere twelve years later, the whole estate was derelict, vandalised and about to be demolished.

Eight hundred feet up in the Pennines and the views were magnificent. A bleak and bitter beauty. It was said that if you could see into Yorkshire, it was going to rain. And, if you couldn't see into Yorkshire, it was raining already. And in the hills, ancestral villages such as Delph and Denshaw. Working villages in the service of King Cotton. Out to the east, Saddleworth Moor, playground for Messrs Brady and Hindley. There was only one mill still operating in the town. I was invited to visit. No wonder hell is called pandemonium. The mill girls learnt to lip-read. It was a melancholy sight to see them minding their flying shuttles while clouds of dust from the fabric whirled all about. They sang, but you could not hear their songs for the noise of the looms. The dust settled on their lungs and all the old mill workers developed an exotic form of chronic bronchitis. Everyone smoked. In the tea break the old girls told me about initiation rites for young male apprentices:

"We'd get them in the toilets and black their balls with boot polish." Said with great affection and much coughing.

In the crypt at St Mary's there were lead coffins containing the bodies of dozens of schoolchildren who had died in a cholera outbreak in the 19th century. The church itself was all faded civic pride and a handful of somnolent old men. About forty people turned out for Evensong on a Sunday – a good number, but in that vastness looking like a very few pebbles on a broad beach. The lighting was ancient. The four churchwardens, after the fashion of more glorious days, sat in their own places at the back, half hidden by a font, big and ugly as the Albert Memorial. They were ensconced in opulent pews that resembled boxes at the theatre. It has been said that the parson in his pulpit is six feet above criticism. These churchwardens were fifty feet beyond earshot. Moreover, at the beginning of the sermon they turned out all the lights to save expense – all but the little lamp over the pulpit by which the parson was meant to read his notes. The sensation was of being in deep space, preaching into outer darkness.

A couple of centuries of bad diet among the mill workers had also produced a population which was considerably below average height. Oldham – I told 'em Oldham in the music hall joke – was second only to Wigan in the league table of antique provinciality:

""Can you tell me the way to Oldham?"

"Some 'old 'em this way and some 'old 'em that way. I just let mine flop about!"

(Best said with gestures)

The old charlatan George Bernard Shaw had proposed a new English alphabet which would be more rational than the twenty-six letters that Shakespeare had had to make do with. This from a man once described as being like a Pakistani who learnt English as a twelve year old in order to become a chartered accountant. Shaw's proposal became the basis for the Initial Teaching Alphabet (ITA) a crazy compilation with extra letters, dipthongs and other phonetic embellishments. The local education department rivalled the town planners in the spreading of pain and destruction: they instigated teaching ITA in the primary and junior schools. Truly, you might say, English as a foreign language. The kids were meant to learn their mother tongue by first learning the excrescence of ITA – an alien language. It was a dogma. Parents protested but the commissars for literacy insisted and there were no exceptions made.

I used to go into the church school to take a weekly assembly and I asked the headmistress whether any of the classic texts of English literature had been translated into ITA.

"No."

"Is it proposed to do so?"

"No."

"So one effect of this nonsense is that children learning to read will read only the rubbishy books composed in ITA."

"I don't think you should be so dismissive."

"Why not?"

"What's worth reading and what's not worth reading is a matter of personal opinion Mr Mullen."

"No it isn't. I should prefer the children to be given the chance to read Alice in Wonderland and A Christmas Carol in English. Oldham kids are deprived enough already and don't need the schools to add to their deprivation."

Miss Bailey wore a large flowery dress and when she stormed out, as now she did, she reminded me of that horror film in which great mounds of vegetation start to trundle about.

Oldham St Mary's Church of England Juniors was not the only school in the parish. There was the stylish Bluecoat School, an ancient charitable foundation adopted by the state system. I taught the fifth form every Friday afternoon and I had a few "A" level religious studies pupils from the sixth. It was a delight. The children were benign and teachable. They had manners. This school was an emblem of Oldham itself, the whole town. Despite the rickets, it was more robust and healthy than the Stretford agglomeration. The people were not as well off as the Stretfordians, but they were possessed of more reality. They had confidence and pride in their sense of place. I think it had something to do with the hilliness. It was fresher up there, a relief from the Kelloggian swamp of direst Manchester. Oldham did not merge muddily into adjacent suburbs. It was a place with a beginning, a middle and an end. There was the theatre, the busy high street with real shops: butchers, bakers, fruit stalls and fresh fish. Tommy Fields open market, next to the church, loud with the banter of the stallholders – that was before it was burnt down in a rash of arson attacks which torched a number of northern markets, including the legendary Kirkgate back in Leeds. Nevertheless, improvements were on the way. The planners had thought to construct an urban motorway which divided the town from its best park, and then they built the precinct, a soulless , windy expanse, the living proof that it was possible to get nothing out of nothing. New offices in the concrete mausoleum style and a dazzling white edifice – you might as well say elephant – brashly labelled Oldham College of Technology which, I suppose, sounded grander than Oldham Tech, though the lettering took up more space. Here you could indeed acquire new techniques: Beauty Therapy, Tourism and Golf Studies.

I set about visiting on the new estate like Theseus in the labyrinth: no Minotaur but plenty of old dragons just like the ones in Crossgates or Stretford but with different names. Horsfall, Stankard and Snape. Kenearly, Pratt and Higginbottom. There were a few of the old terraced houses still standing as if the developers, like some off-course German bomber, had missed their target. Modest cottages certainly, but by the side of the dismal new flats they looked aristocratic. Old ladies came out and stained their doorsteps with yellow stone and scrubbed the pavements – known as flags. Inside were gleaming Victorian kitchen ranges, polished every week with black lead.

In these streets overlooked by thrusting modernity, you knew who your neighbour was. You knew the fads and foibles of everyone in the street, and in the next street. Decent working class people. The proud deserving poor. You knew which members of which households were mucky or picaresque – the bloke who had been known to steal cigarettes from the newsagents, the feckless, filthy family who couldn't keep their house clean. And the man with bulging eyes at number 17 who was messing about with his daughters.

These old houses could have done with some money spending on them, and bathrooms would have been gratefully accepted by the residents. There were defects and dilapidations but basically the dwellings were soundly constructed both in their physical properties and consequently in their social cohesiveness. – everything that could not be said of the failed utopia of the planners' Shaw Road Estate.

I met the church organist only once before he withdrew to hospital with a chronic illness. His deputy agreed to play for the Sunday service but refused to attend the choir practice. So I volunteered. They were a jovial bunch of sadists, the choirmen, and there was a sprinkling of talkative old ladies. These old girls were hardly any trouble because most of them were deaf and so couldn't hear my instructions, still less disobey them – unlike the men. It was Hate your organist all over again, except I never let my sticky fingers near that noble instrument. We practised with the aid of – I mean despite – the old out-of-tune piano in the nave.

Donald Mearns, the real organist and choirmaster, had tried to knock a bit of music into them but now that he had retired sick, they lapsed. Victoriana was breaking out everywhere like a rash. All amateur choirs love the 19th century musical warhorses – just as the middle classes love the strangulated hernia sounds of Italian opera. No more Bach or Orlando Gibbons then. I tried the lovely hymn O Thou Who at Thy Eucharist Didst Pray on them:

"We used to have that with Dr Mearns," one bleated.

And that was enough to kill it. Their favourites were sentimental ballads with rows of diminished chords like wall-bars. And chromatic harmonies: The Old Rugged Cross which they used to belt out with feeling as if they were roaring Nellie Dean. Their saturated emotions would often have them hypnotising themselves into tears. They liked Love Divine All Loves Excelling, not to the thoughtful Stainer tune in Ancient and Modern Revised but to the thuggish, howling version in The Methodist Hymnbook. Worst of all they adored the lugubrious Twentieth Century Hymn Tunes - stuff that was cracked up to be modern but was really only sham antique. Imagine singing the glorious Trinitarian march Holy, Holy, Holy to a maudlin banality – with a beat – fit only to accompany the Palais Glide. And Lord of the Fucking Dance – to a tune cribbed by the odious Sidney Carter from an old Shaker melody. The St Mary's choir thought all this stuff wonderfully relevant. The deaf ladies wore their pointed caps even to rehearsals and the men sniggered at them behind their Psalters and pondered aloud whether they had as many wrinkles on their fannies as they had on their faces. The men's bawling and screaming suffused the nave with the evocative aroma of stale tobacco smoke. They always wanted to be away to the pub by half past nine and that was the best part:

"It's our tradition, Peter. Pints after hymn practice. Thirsting after righteousness, eh?"

There were other layfolk on the staff of St Mary's. One day James said,

"Let's go and look at the bell-ringers"

I seemed to see a spectre of Broadstairs rising over the Pennines – but Broadstairs without the salaciousness of James' leer. The scene in the belfry was eroticism off the top of the Richter scale. All the ringers were teenagers and they came dressed for strenuous work. Boys in jeans and t-shirts. Girls in skimpy dresses which rose way above their best intentions every time they pulled on the ropes. James simply sat and stared unabashed, his face lit up by a great banana split grin. They knew the effect they were having, those girls. White knickers. Red knickers. Pink knickers. The voluptuous Oldham lasses, James and me.

Young folk, old folk, everybody come:

Join St Mary's belfry sit and ogle under the dome.

Even today when I hear church bells there is that intrusive whiff of Pavlovian lubriciousness

Crossgates had been an enclave of clubbable churchy folk sheltered from the naughty world by a multitude of stultifyingly boring voluntary groups. Oldham was much more rough and tumble, politically aware. At Synod the debate was always about a social issue: this week industrial mission, next week the boundary changes. The earnest ecclesiastical politicos seemed to belief that the Kingdom of God, when it dawned, would be by an alliance of the local Labour Club and the Fabian Society. The grace of God would be administered by the welfare state. Putting the correct structures in place was a phrase you heard often over the brown ale and Lancashire black peas. Eliot's Men dreaming of systems so perfect that no one will need to be good came frequently to mind. Even in those days Michael Meacher was the MP and he was regularly in the back of James' car on his way to some political wrangle. Give me the lady bell-ringers any day. Meacher was known locally as Tony Benn's Vicar on Earth. He once looked severely at me and declared,

"Politics is about power, Peter." – as if I had thought it was about knicker elastic .

There was one hilarious apocalypse at Oldham crematorium – one of the most rickety burn-up sites in the land. I was warned that when you pushed the button at the end of the service there would be a nasty surprise. The mechanism was old and crabby. I pushed the button for the coffin to start its mechanical journey through the curtains and into the beyond. There was a great CHUNG! And everyone looked up, startled. That was nothing.

The coffin was supposed to pass through the curtains and onto a trolley placed in the anteroom by the two cheerful necrophiles who acted as vergers. Supposed to. Only this time they had forgotten.

So off goes Uncle Fred through the crack of doom. And suddenly there's an almighty CRASH! Followed by the loud utterance of two words from what I suppose we must call the other side – the second word was hell! The congregation were paralysed, no doubt thinking that those two words were Uncle Fred's first impressions of the life of the world to come. I went behind. What a scene: imagine the dead Scrooge in his nightshirt, the vergers' copy of The Sun having fallen across his face.

IX

Lancashire is a strongly Catholic county for historical reasons and when I lived there, Oldham was teeming with religious processions. The festivals of the Blessed Virgin mainly. Young girls in their white dresses and golden headbands. Old ladies in black and veiled. The priests in gorgeous copes. The thrurifer, altar boys, servers. Incense and Ave's. Numinously evocative. The Catholic kids loved it and the Protestant kids were envious as hell despite the best attempts of their parents to get them to regard these festivities as pagan superstition, the very mark of the beast. Faced with their children's disgruntlement, the Oldham Protestant parents turned fancifully to what they regarded as the colourful pagan past of Merrie England and invented Rose Queen Day.

So now, in addition to the Catholic pageants, there was a Protestant pageant, garlands, a procession and music – led not by the monsignor but by the mayor. Instead of the monstrance, the mace. No Ave's but the Hargreaves Mill brass band. Protestant grandmothers, though eschewing their Catholic sisters' exquisite black veils – the very emblem of geriatric sexuality, according to James - showed they could weep just as sentimentally as the left-footers. The clergy were obliged to join in somehow but, prayers having been deemed inappropriate by the protty organisers, we had nothing specific to do. So James and I joined all the other local vicars, put on scarf and hood and marched from Tommy Fields market to the bunfight in the Town Hall. Hargreaves' band played John Peel, The Yellow Rose of Texas and Colonel Bogey – a few of the boys turned out as the Rose Queen's guardsmen were reprimanded for murmuring the naughty words featuring the condition of genitalia among various Nazi leaders.

On the Monday after Rose Queen Day, I drove James out to visit Canon Kirkman, now retired, who had been James' predecessor at St Mary's. He lived on a ledge above the high moors of Todmorden in a village called Mankinholes – a word which, in James' mouth, did not always receive its proper pronunciation. The landscape around

Todmorden has a savage, windswept and rain-lashed beauty. Like Bronte country, a sort of industrial Transylvania. It required scant imagination to think you heard the gale in the sparse trees howling, Catherine Earnshaw! Catherine Earnshaw!

Canon Kirkman was tall and lean. He had the northerner's mournful intonation, more musical to be sure that the melancholy celebration of being hard done by that I heard in Leeds, but still a begrudging testimony of a whole life spent in making the best of a bad job. Of being passed over when it came to preferment:

"I could have been a bishop – more than once."

There was a mist over the moors that day, like the incoming tide. Kirkman's cottage was cavernous and dark and it had all the atmosphere of a last refuge. There was nothing meagre about the place though. The furniture was reassuringly ancient and sturdy and the lunch generous:

"I know you two boys are drinkers, so here's a bottle of Bull's Blood for you to share. I'll take none myself."

The fine line between hospitality and disapproval. I looked at him as he set the bottle down on the table and saw just the hint of John Knox coming with sullen oars from the Isle of Crail to bring the Scots the good news of their damnation.

"If ever you're under the weather, James, take a small glass before you go to bed."

He spoke with all the cheerfulness of a redundant apothecary. After a long Grace he sliced into a baked potato and said,

"Poor James and Peter! You'll find dear old Oldham a millstone. I was vicar for twenty-one years, you know."

James had drained his glass and was all alacrity, gesturing, witty, amusing. The impression was of a stand up comedian in a funeral parlour.

"Not a millstone Canon, but a milestone."

"You'll be writing Christmas card verses next, James," I whispered behind my napkin. We watched in wonderment as the old Canon drew a small bottle from his waistcoat pocket and shook a quantity of white powder all over his vegetables, with an expression of such distaste that i thought he was about to be sick.

"Snuff!" said James, and I got the giggles.

The Canon all unheeding, unhearing. He scowled at his food as if he were daring it to taste of something. He pushed it around his plate with the back of his fork and made little grunts between each mouthful. He was giving a very good impression of a man trying desperately not to enjoy his lunch:

"Poor James and Peter! That old church – I'll tell you something now...." And we waited while he treated a large piece of mutton to a lengthy chew.

"...it's too big..."

(The church or the piece of mutton?)

"...that's what's wrong with it. You'll never fill it. It's too big. I could never fill it."

"We will fill it, Canon – and in four weeks' time!"

"James, you do romance!"

He wiped his mouth and laid his big, damp hand over mine and said:

"He's a lovely man, is James, but he does romance. He does romance."

He turned to James: "You're a romancer, James!"

And I was glad of my Crossgates schooling in Pinteresque dialogue. James emptied his glass again and looked hopelessly to see whether another bottle might be forthcoming.

"I'm getting Danny Las Rue in, Canon. That's romance for you. Danny will fill the place."

The name Danny La Rue fell on Canon Kirkman like that of Marilyn Monroe on a High Court judge:

"Which diocese does he come from, then? Well, all I can say is he'll have to be a good preacher – but not many bishops are - whoever he is – if he's going to fill St Mary's. I never managed to fill it, you know – no, not in twenty-one years. And when I was a curate I got William Temple to come and preach..." adding, a la Alan Bennett, "...before he died."

"He's not a bishop, Harold. He's a female impersonator."

"Now then James, you will have your little joke!"

We said no to coffee. James collected the parish papers which the Canon had promised to hand over and we drove off into the mist. It was raining now, the relentless, steely Pennine rain that strikes into your face like knives:

"A man of God is Canon Kirkman," said James. "A man of God. God help us!"

The church was full for Danny La Rue of course and the gallery – not opened in half a century – was packed. I met the exquisite Mr La Rue before the service... I am here using the word service eccentrically... and he extended to me a hand that was damper than Canon Kirkman's and much more highly-perfumed. He stood on the stage which James' friends from the Oldham Rep had built and lisped a few camp jokes and – the religious bit – got in a plug for his personal charity, the Sunshine Coaches. The Rep were currently presenting Jesus Christ Superstar and a huge scoopy songstress came on and sang, I Don't Know How to Love Him. If she'd tried, he would have buckled under her weight. There was also a theatrical interlude, the retribution scene out of The Winslow Boy.

The tallow-faced, emaciated director of the Oldham Rep was there and I knew that he and James were fond of each other. He died soon after and James was quite overcome at the funeral, tossing flowers into the grave and saying,

"Sweets to the sweet."

Parish life was like perpetual motion under James:

"Have ideas, Peter. Enjoy your ideas. Visit your ten old ladies a week and see to what's got to be done around the parish – then do as you like. Love God and do as you like."

"There's an MA in theology at Lancaster. I thought I might take a look?"

"OK. It could be fun."

Lancaster was only an hour's drive up the M6 I arrived in the middle of the exam season. The university buildings were all white concrete and the site was windier than Oldham Edge. Gaudy modern. The sensation was like walking through a toothpaste advertisement. In the centre stood the infamous Bowling Tower, a favourite place among undergraduates for chucking themselves off. Another had done it the week before the exams. The chapel was like a public lavatory designed by Walt Disney. "Ecumenical" of course. I didn't go in.

I was interviewed by a member of the theology faculty, Dr Adrian Cunningham – genial and smart. The professor, who was in America at the moment, was actually called Smart – Ninian Smart who had for a long time made honest mileage out of what used to be known as comparative religion. This was now coming under pressure from the all-conquering progressive forces and being renamed Interfaith Dialogue. This was the label which excused professor and student alike from the interesting, though admittedly difficult, questions about the truth of religious propositions. The new fad declared that truth value in religion – where it existed at all – referred only to the psychological make-up of particular sets of believers, and so what might formerly have been adjudged objective theology was now only about personal dispositions, inclinations and preferences. In other words, don't study the beliefs, study the believers.

The related fad was for the multicultural society. Which meant that you must not be judgemental about other faiths. It was no use, as I discovered painfully, to suggest that the purpose of a university education was to enable its recipients to make judgements. Anyway, I thought, culture, like charity, is something that should begin at home. There was something fatuous about preferring a shallow acquaintance with Zen Buddhism and the Upanishads to a profound engagement with one's own sacred writings. Professors such as Ninian Smart would at any moment and in similar toothpaste adverts all over Europe and North America be warning their students to respect difference and embrace pluralism. It seemed odd that this enthusiasm for difference should be advocated in so many places where not only the syllabus was exactly the same but which looked alike. White concrete. A silly tower. A comical chapel. The thin gruel of personal opinion. It also seemed strange that the strongest advocates of multiculturalism, with its emphasis on the separation of cultures, condemned the same phenomenon, when it appeared in South Africa, as Apartheid. Dapper, amiable, mobile Dr Adrian said he felt sure I would enjoy the course. No thanks.

I began to dig in for the hard Pennine winter. Just to make life more interesting, in November the Arabs quadrupled the price of oil, British coalminers went on strike and Edward Heath, our most incompetent prime minister since Donald Duck, put the nation's factories and offices on a three day week. The lights were going out all over the country. Perpetual frost and snow. But if we thought it grim in Oldham, God knows what it must have been like out on the moors. I pictured Canon Kirkman delivering bottles of Bull's Blood to the lost sheep over Mankinholes.

James took himself off to the Dordogne for a week or two to finish his book on Karl Barth. I filled in my time with some bizarre pastoralia which included helping Steve Pimlott overcome his agoraphobia – and that on the edge of Saddleworth Moor! Might as well develop cheese-phobia then go and live in a mousetrap. We began the cure gingerly with a daily shuffle around the churchyard, extended after practice to a trip as far the market and graduating to visiting the new mock Tudor pub on the top of Oldham Edge. Pimlott explained:

"My psychiatrist prescribed the technique. Its proper name is operant conditioning by successive approximation. It means a bit at a time, gently do it, like."

"Really?"

There is a famous monologue by a Lancashire comedian about a lad called Albert who goes to visit Blackpool tower zoo with his parents and gets eaten by a lion. This came to mind when I took some Oldham schoolkids to Knowsley Road Safari Park and Jeanette Crosby was still missing half an hour after we were due to leave. She turned up at last. She said she had been stuck – I think she meant locked, but I didn't ask too insistently – in the lavatories next to the monkey house.

There were occasional meals out with Bob and Mollie Bainbridge, teachers at St Mary's juniors, and once we were joined by Colin Barnett, a commissar in the National Union of Public Employees: Sancerre socialism, sycophancy and a shiny suit. Even in emancipated Oldham there were one or two organisations to look at and I went to say prayers every Wednesday for the Autumn Tea Club. (Manager: Mr Harry Hall from the Parish Hall).

Distraught Ida Webb, its oldest member – a lady with such powerful halitosis that they might have used it in the trenches as poison gas – came across and complained:

"I don't like this new name, Autumn Club. It were all reet when it were Over Sixties. But Autumn – there's ony one way ter go after autumn, int there?"

Every Thursday I used to say the 8am Communion Service in the Lady Chapel. One morning Virginia, a pretty woman of about twenty-five, hung back when the other half dozen worshippers had left. She wept continually and wouldn't, or couldn't, speak. I sat with her until ten o'clock and suggested more than once that we go for a cup of coffee and she could tell me what was the matter. At last, the string of her tongue was loosed and she blurted out:

"You can't do anything for me Father. No one can. I saw a vision of the Virgin Mary last night and she told me I'm damned."

"Now why should she do a thing like that? The Mother of Jesus is your mother too. She is infinitely tender and she loves you forever. You are not damned. Now come on, let's get that coffee."

If only the exorcism in Crossgates had worked as well...

Virginia lived down the road in Chadderton and I took her home. It was a second floor flat on a pleasing private development. She lived alone. She had been engaged to a violinist who was studying at the Royal Northern College of Music in Manchester. He had slit his throat.

That evening I went alone to the pictures. A Clockwork Orange. And the next day I thought I would go and visit my friend Geoff Allen who had been my tutor at theological college. When the college closed in 1969, the Staff were appointed to posts which were supposed to be of equivalent status to senior lecturer. The daft Principal, Arthur Widdess, a former missionary in China until chucked out by Chairman Mao in 1949, became Treasurer of York Minster and, following swiftly on his appointment, his Bursar was prosecuted for nicking some of the treasures. The Vice-Principal was made a canon of Durham. The New Testament specialist went to teach at a College of Education in Cheshire and Geoff was inducted Vicar of Ardwick, a post he was meant to combine with that of Diocesan Director of Education. His appointment was a colossal and typical piece of insensitivity by the numbskull church authorities.

Ardwick was an inner city shit heap for which the phrase urban dereliction might have been especially coined. Hardly anyone lived there. The vicarage, a large detached house in the Georgian style, was next to The Church Inn in the middle of a lorry park. Just the place to which to exile a highly intelligent, musically gifted, shy homosexual with a too much liking for the bottle.

I rang the bell. No answer. A lorry driver leaned out of his cab and shouted,

"He's in the church, mate!"

I set off across the road.

"Not in there! He's in the pub! He's always in the pub!"

I went into the pub and found Geoff on a bar stool swigging Carlsberg Special lager. Big round face, a bit shiny, wisps of ginger hair and a fag on the go. He spoke into the space between me and the landlord:

"What are you drinking, Peter? How did you know I'd be in here? I suppose you guessed you'd find the vicar in The Church!"

It was a quarter to one in the afternoon and his speech was slurred. Not slow and deliberate, maudlin and repetitious like any old soak, but sharp-witted, articulate , animated. Still slurred though.

"We'll have one more, Bill. Then I'll show Peter the parish."

His clothes were filthy and he niffed a bit of other rarefied pongs as well as the booze. He rolled down off the bar stool and frowned critically at a cigarette burn in his sleeve:

"Good job I know where I can get it invisibly mended."

"Invisibly mended! It belongs on the bloody Guy Fawkes, Geoff!"

He was not much taller than the bar stool. Rotund. Bad on his feet. Bored silly. We set off back to the vicarage. Someone shouted,

"See you tonight, vicar!"

"I've a Confirmation class. I'll not be in till about nine."

Then, as he hobbled across the road:

"I've only one candidate. No one lives here. She's a strange woman. From Rusholme. Says she used to live in Ardwick when she was a girl. That's why she wants to be confirmed here. Her father was Russian. She speaks Russian."

I remembered that Geoffrey spoke Russian. On national service MI6 must have noticed that he was better in the head than on his feet and they snapped him up, gave him the job of listening to Russian broadcasts to Europe on the short wave. Blue smoke from the rush hour traffic poisoned the afternoon. The noise was unceasing. Geoff's vicarage, isolated in this urban rot, was no place for a human being. And Geoff was one of the kindest, most talented human beings I had laid eyes on.

"What's up, Padre? Pissed already?"

"The lorry drivers are very affectionate. They're my parishioners, really."

The vicarage had large, high rooms with picture rails. There was a stone fireplace, and an arched doorway led into a wide kitchen. The sitting-room had a thick, dark green carpet worn only a little by the sustaining pedal on Geoff's Bechstein. By the wall opposite the piano was a new stereophonic system and about a hundred long-playing records – Beethoven mostly. The place stank of stale piss, damp dogs and un-emptied refuse bins.

"Let's have some lunch."

I sat on a chair by the cooker. As soon as he switched it on there was the sweet, sickly stench of decayed food, scorching. The table top was coated in grease in which dog hairs were embedded. My chair was the same – as I noticed when I stood up. There was a fruit bowl, empty except for cigarette ends. Another ashtray on one of the hot plates on the cooker. As if my imagination could do nothing but complete the picture, I asked,

"Where's the dog?"

"Out for a walk with Amanda."

"Amanda?"

"Yes, you remember Amanda – the college housekeeper?"

I did remember her. Amanda Utley had taken over the kitchen in my second year. The transformation was miraculous. We had been accustomed to the lukewarm sediments of institutional cooking but Amanda gave us haute cuisine – and all within the budget of the local education office's student maintenance grant. She also worked the trick of water into wine and so, occasionally in that dry evangelical prison, gentlemen took a glass or two of Burgundy or Hock at dinner.

Before Amanda's coming, Puritanism had fastened on the place like a pair of tight trousers. Widdess was so innocent of the world's ways as to be virtually ethereal. The rest of the senior Staff prevailed upon him one year for wine to be provided at the Christmas dinner. Afterwards gentlemen sang carols in the common room and, upon hearing this jolly wassail, the Principal, outraged, declared that there would be no more wine next year, if this was the sort of thing it led to. Widow Amanda and bachelor Geoff thrived as a double act. She was Roman Catholic, wiry, mischievous, refined. He was intellectually subversive like a too-intelligent schoolboy. Both smoked and drank vocationally. Neither had anyone else. She was the saving of him. They couldn't abide the lowbrow censure of wide-eyed Widdess or the polite malevolence of his fat gossipy wife. For Geoff and Amanda, vulgarity was the chiefest of sins. Geoff's parents were long dead, so he spent the vacations in college taking his evening meal with Amanda. Stretching out the hours with talk of food, drink and dogs.

"Yes," he said emptying a tin of mushroom soup into a saucepan containing a lump of margarine,

"Amanda is staying a couple of days on her way to Scotland. She gave me this recipe, actually. Pass me the sherry, will you?"

There was a sticky decanter on the shelf above my head. It doubled as bluebottles' HQ.

"He sells this in the pub for £1 a pint. You can't go wrong – for cooking!"

The combination of smells was vile enough to put you off eating forever.

There came a crash from the next room, so loud one of the heavy lorries might have burst through the window. Enough barking for a pack of hounds and then a smoky aristocratic contralto:

"Hello, Hello"

Amanda and her cigarette were dragged in by the two animals

"You remember Peter?"

"Yes, of course. Do stay for lunch."

We balanced the soup dishes on our knees and the dogs were glad to receive such morsels of bread soaked in sickly concoction as fell from their master's and mistress's table. There were in fact two courses of the foul medicine. Geoff and Amanda smoked and drank throughout. After lunch we retired to the sitting room and Geoff, squinting over the umpteenth fag dangling from his lips, dashed brilliantly through some Beethoven – the Opus 53. Then they drank alternately coffee and more of the lager from the gold coloured cans.

What would he do when she had left for Scotland?

The stories rolled forth like a royal procession:

"D'you remember that stately home in Cheshire where you played the piano after Evensong, Geoff? And you accompanied a woman in a couple of songs. I remember your saying to her, 'You're really not bad you know.' And she said, 'I am Isobel Bailey'!"

"And that other woman who'd had a frontal lobe leucotomy and she came up to you and said straight out. 'Good God, you're an ugly one aren't you'?"

Enough laughing and coughing to make the welkin ring

Back Home, I phoned Neil and told him I'd seen Geoff:

"Filthy beast!" he said. "I went in and mucked him out the other week, but I bet it's stinking again. He has all the lorry drivers in and then doesn't know what to do with them when he gets them there. He sleeps with that bloody dog, you know. There's a film on in Manchester called Dirty Harry. Bugger Clint Eastwood, they should have cast Geoff."

Two other college friends – Mike Redfearn and Gerald Garbutt - had parishes in Manchester and they too used to take turns at cleaning Geoff up. Gerald was tall, diffident, laconic, theatrical. Born in the next street to Alan Bennett in Leeds. He had something of Bennett's maudlin style. Once in the car on our way to some tedious diocesan function he said,

"Look at that sign, GET IN LANE. That's no way to talk to a gentleman!"

James and I went to the Consecration Service of Neil's new church. Bright red brick and fluorescent lights under which the pop art altar frontal and vestments dazzled like a gaudy transfiguration. The bishop presided sonorously. Neil was chirpy, urging his youth choir on through their bawling out of Heavenly Sunshine and Amazing Grace to the schmaltzy vibrato of the electric organ. The moment the service finished, a screen was rolled back and the building converted into a working men's club: bar, pies, peas and parish Bingo. The bishop wore the expression of a visitor from an alien religion.

A few weeks later and James arranged a parish trip to St Paul's, Salford to inspect the church which had been re-ordered in the style recommended by Mr Dykes-Bower. The impression was of a gents' washroom into which someone had shooed an art class with the solitary instruction that they were to try to alleviate the overpowering glare of whitewash with whatever mixture of colours they might fancy. The result was lots of gold edging with red and blue stars. Coronation Street baroque.

"It's beautiful!" squealed Mollie Bainbridge.

"But it's not like a proper church," said Harry Heap.

I sat with the old ladies on the way back to Oldham and asked what they thought of St Paul's:

"Very nice."

"Contemporary."

"We went to the abattoir with the Autumn Club, and that was very nice as well."

Within six months St Mary's Oldham had been fashioned in the image of James' vision.

X

We were exhausted. The long re-ordering project had been fought inch by inch and line by line by the old timers on the Parochial Church Council. Ancient animosities among such as Harry Heap, Reg Burton and Ellie Tasker had been set aside as they all united to wage war on the vicar's scheme. The fact that James managed to achieve his ambition was the eighth wonder of the world. And now we had to stir ourselves for the annual glitterfest, the Mayor's Parlour.

I called on James and found him shaving in his basement bedroom. The leader in his bunker. Without trousers. His socks attached to suspenders which fastened at the knee. Brown shoes. His cut throat razor wielded like a baton. The scene might have been the dressing room at the Oldham Rep for a performance of Sweeney Todd the Demon Barber.

"I suppose we have to go to this, James?"

"Think of it as earning time off Purgatory."

We walked up the hill and James paused to take a deep breath and admire the church stonework which had been cleaned and now shone in the lumiere – what Harry Heap referred to at the last PCC as,

"...them unnecessary and expensive lights. More bloody bulbs than Blackpool illuminations."

In the town hall the band was playing a quickstep. The gentlemen of the borough whirled arthritically in their monkey suits and their hefty ladies in their gold lurex looked like dangerous tropical fish. We went straight to the bar and James ordered whisky. Then another. The Mayor wore a chain so stupendous that, if he had been a racehorse, it would have been his handicap. The Mayoress was buried in something so voluminous you might have thought she was being suffocated. She was disdainful, above the herd. I thought she looked like Queen Victoria at Albert's funeral. More whisky. The whole topic was the church restoration and happily most expressed their pleasure at it. Most but not all. Not Reg Burton who I overheard whining to his anorexic sourpuss of a sister,

"I expect bills will be coming in for years and years."

More whisky. James was quiet. His eyes were like slits. But in an instant he brightened and made off towards the exit which led down the long corridor to the Mayor's office. Standing beside the piano was a lady aged about fifty and so impossibly voluptuous and flirty that she reminded me of what Mozart said about his lascivious pupil Elizabeth Auernhammer:

"One look at her and tartar is the only remedy."

"O come on James, let's get out of here!"

I was relieved when he came along without more fuss.

"We'll go to The White Swan. But I need a pee first."

He insisted on doing it in the churchyard lumiere.

"Look at that stonework, Peter! I told old Kirkman I'd put the place on the map."

I had a nasty feeling we were being followed and, yes, a weaselly little man with a rubbery face entered the pub just behind us. He carried notebook and pencil:

"Excuse me Mr Bentley..."

"Doctor Bentley if you please, my friend."

"I've been quite close to you all evening..."

"That's funny. I didn't notice a smell."

"And I heard what you said to the Chief Superintendent's wife."

James looked towards the bar and ordered two pints of beer. The weasel closed in.

"I heard what you said to the Chief Super's wife and I wonder if the church hierarchy might like to hear it too."

James turned savagely, lifted the reporter from The Oldham Chronicle on to the bar and said through clenched teeth:

"I am the fucking hierarchy!"

A great cheer went up and Mavis Rudge the landlady shouted, not frightfully annoyed,

"Boys – behave yourselves!"

The weasel slunk off. We finished our pints, then I chaperoned James through an unsteady three minutes stroll back to the vicarage. In the morning we spoke on the phone and I said,

"I hope that bloody man from the Chronic doesn't print anything."

"What man from the Chronic."

I left him to his alcoholic amnesia – what was the technical term? – Korsakov Syndrome. I drove out along the Shaw Road and up to the edge of the hills. Such heaviness. And not just last night's debauch, there was something else, something deep and raw. I felt fucked and thwarted. Three years since ordination and I couldn't work out what this job was supposed to be about. Perhaps there was no generic 'about' at all? Every priest I had met was different. You couldn't put Broadstairs in the same bag as Bentley – what, and then add such disparate characters as Neil and the senior curate, Frank Lindars and Geoff Allen?

I took the car up to a high ledge where you looked over the magical village of Delph, down there a long way and Yorkshire beyond. Delph with its redundant mill and its mill cottages inhabited now by commuters from Manchester: accountants, solicitors and their kids at private schools. Just like the commuters in Crossgates actually: away to the office before sunrise and then meet their mates in the City pubs for long, boozy lunches all on expenses, while back in Dingly Delph their coutured wives went up the wall with boredom and frantic with unrelieved lust. The cottages torn apart and reconstructed in whatever loathsome style of interior design was in vogue. Like the gormless Dykes-Bower St Mary's. The day was still – a rare event so far up on the Pennines – and white smoke drifted vertically from the chimneys. Only the old mill chimney gave out no smoke. Dereliction and ghosts. It came on to rain, slow, deliberate drops, heavy as curses. I looked back towards the town and...Oldham Edge:

Wet pavings in the rain,
The last of September afternoon,
A steep ascent to the driven moor
The sky a seamless grey.
You fear to turn and look down on
The chimneys, the vertical smoke,
The too white steam from the goods yard
And the black spire indicative
Of the last time you came this way
With your burden, under a silver
Intolerable sun, the haze and the
Traffic's distant lament

Or the time before, woolly, snowbound
Under the still excitement of silence.
And when the harsh spring flung
Watery shadows across the town.
This is not a seasonal landscape,
For the burden is always the same: as
Self-disgust looks skyward desiring grace,
Discovering only disturbances of weather.

I know – you must not wallow in your own subjectivity. Your feelings don't matter. Think about something else. What was it Kierkegaard said:

"Most people are subjective towards themselves and objective towards others. The task is to become objective towards yourself and subjective towards others."

That must be the priest's vocation. That and prayer – whatever prayer was, Mr Eliot, the occupation of the saint. That was the intersection of the timeless with time, marked by the rising smoke and the melancholy smokeless chimney. Restored cottages and the stonework tidied up too much. Little gardens and white fences. These things did not belong on that moorland with the hum of its industrial history recalled in the still air. Dead Delph. Dead souls.

My mind went back to Liverpool and to how I'd found the bus conductors so chirpy, so hopeful, after all the miserable buggers in Leeds. I shuddered as I recalled the psychology lectures. Psychology was institutionalised mental subnormality – if I may be allowed to introduce the word mental in the context of a discipline which had abandoned the concept of mind. They were all in the grip of strict behaviourism. We actually did tricks – experiments – with flashing lights, bells, mazes and wrote up the whole fucking crap in terms of negative and positive reinforcement, extinction, rewards and punishments, affect, conditioned reflex. Fucking crap.

We worked in the lab every Monday afternoon, with cages and Galton bars and electric shock machines and God knows what other crap. And we were supervised by a dumpy little dolly bird, rather like an outsized version of one of the straw haired, mini-skirted Barbie clones in the modern languages department. She went in for positive reinforcement. Lots of ticks in your exercise books and tantalising comments like the one she once wrote in my book:

"Good, very good. With a little more effort your work could be really excellent."

Not in a million years baby.

And I wondered what Sheila Kirby was doing these days. I came across her in the modern philosophy section of the university library in February 1970. She had a wide and open face that could turn ironical and mischievous on a whim. And she abjured the miniskirt in favour of little print dresses in pastel shades. She looked unhappy. And she caught me watching her. She said,

"Bertrand Russell died this morning. Ninety-seven. And I thought he was going to prove the exception to 'All men are mortal'."

Her intonation so canorous, like an afternoon stroll with Susanna from Le Nozze di Figaro.

"Peter, it's wonderful! A Midsummer Night's Dream. So drowsy with bees and honey."

When she spoke your name like that....and the evening and the morning were the first day of creation.

Sheila had bought a flat not far from the windmill on Bidston Hill out of some money an aunt had left her. We took to walking to the windmill and then returning through the woods to the flat. The Wirral view from her upstairs window was mesmerising. You could see as far as the estuary By West Kirkby and Hilbre Island. And, if you looked in the other direction, the stately buildings on the Liverpool Waterfront. But there was often a mist – thick as the Scouse accent. We drank white wine and played a lot of Mozart. We also played with her electric train. It was a beauty, all set out in the basement. The train was often stuck for a long time in the tunnel, hot, agitated.

Nostalgia slips easily into self-pity and I scolded myself for being so maudlin. It was not so easy to snap out of a bout of deep exhaustion. Well, what's so exhausting about being a parish priest – it's not exactly the coal face? My father used get up at six every day and go to work – usually inside a broken turbine – at Skelton Grange power station. What is saying Mass and sipping tea with parishioners compared with such hard labour?

Well, you pick up people's anxieties by osmosis. If you don't succeed in doing this, you're no good at the job. If you do succeed, to some extent anyway, you're buggered. In order to function as a priest, you have to enter imaginatively into the interior mental and spiritual states of your parishioners. As a vaccine works by giving you a taste of the disease against which it is the protection, so the priest's identification with a suffering parishioner is what allows him to be a help and comfort. When St Paul said, Rejoice with them that do rejoice and weep with them that weep, he wasn't recommending play-acting. He meant it. As he also said, Bear ye one another's burdens and so fulfil the law of Christ. The so-called law of Christ is to love your neighbour, and loving your neighbour means trying to understand his feelings, as it were, from the inside, to take upon yourself something of his suffering. Sympathy is from a Greek word and it doesn't mean feeling for, but feeling with. So every day the priest both endures and enjoys the whole panoply of sensations and moods: a little exhilaration here, a little dejection there. Here a shard of ecstasy. Now a little death.

To preserve his health and his sanity, the priest must rely on prayer. He must pray vigorously and regularly. And I'm not sure I'm any good at praying. In any case, prayer too is exhausting. As usual Mr Eliot has us bang to rights: We only live, only suspire, consumed by either fire or fire. Moreover – and let's be honest here – the priest is not only commanded to enter his parishioners' feelings, he is tempted to mess around with them. Not just to mediate God, but to play God. So he must every moment offer the closest intimacy while preserving the utmost detachment. Now do you see why I'm fucking knackered?

Something similar applies to the church services. If in his pastoral work the priest must identify himself with his people, in his liturgical work he must identify himself with Christ. As that pest St Paul says again, we must put on Christ. And, for Christ's sake, how does a man do that without hubris, without blaspheming? I think it was Anton Rubinstein who said,

"If I don't practise for a day, I know it. If I don't practise for a week, the orchestra knows it. And if I don't practise for two weeks, the audience knows it."

Something similar goes for saying Mass or reading the lesson. If you do it by rote, it cannot be right. Chesterton said that one of the worst things in worship is the priest who performs a casual solemnity. And the other extreme is to affect intense piety, to put on a holy voice. Don't do it. False piety and the parsonical voice are spiritual bromides. Again, you can't distance yourself. In church you have to be both yourself and not yourself. When reading the lesson – the parable of the Good Samaritan, say - the priest has to present the scene directly, indubitably, so that the congregation actually enters into its reality. So the priest in church has to be an actor. But his act has to be sincere!

"Now when he came nigh to the gate of the city, behold there was a dead man carried out, the only son of his mother and she was a widow..."

That's a killer. If the priest reads it properly, he might break down in tears. And if he breaks down in tears, this will be a distraction and spoil the telling. But if he does what I have done on occasions and, in heartbreaking readings, dislocates himself and sets his mind on something else – say, mentally reciting the names of the England cricket team – that won't work either.

Oh well, I might as well do the bloody job properly....

"...and stood at his feet behind him weeping, and began to wash his feet with tears, and did wipe them with the hair of her head, and kissed his feet and anointed them with the ointment... wherefore I say unto thee, Her sins which are many are forgiven; for she loved much."

Try that.

"This is my Body...this is my Blood."

How do you say that then?

The priest is like the tightrope-walker and he is not like the tightrope-walker. He has to do the high wire act but whereas the tightrope walker does it as an advertisement of his skill, the priest has to do it and yet not draw attention to himself at all.

Christmas Eve and the snow began in great meandering flakes, building and thickening until it drew a white curtain between my window and Oldham Edge. The Pennines blazed white, their lineaments picked out with startling clarity. Peace on earth – or at least on this small Lancashire portion of it. On the day itself the congregation in ones and twos drifting towards St Mary's. Seeing them from a height and distance, you understood L.S. Lowry's inspiration for his matchstick men. I recalled he had been born in Stretford. After Festival Mass I sat by the open fire in The George and bundles of words came tumbling in:

Picture a snowbound lake and a burning barn,
Or a house inhabited by the moon:
See how the beams of cunning silver light
Send out the radiance of the Eternal Girl.
See now a cowshed in the dead of winter,
And in the thickening darkness, fire
Like a galleon ablaze upon the sea.
The pinprick stars nod in their wisdom;
Three bare trees bend on the horizon
Under all that silveriness
To remind us that birth and death are
The start and end of the same reality.
His mother holds him now
As she will hold him again
In thirty years, under that sparse hill:
Mary, Maria, Mater Dolorosa, Ewig-Weibliche, Princess
In the crib of thine arms is our salvation born.
But today it is the angels' song
Brash, radiant; fire and the flicker of fire,
All incipient, telling us what we do not want to know:
That darkness will cover the earth
From the sixth hour to the ninth;
And that the spirits of the saints will
Walk abroad on a Friday afternoon.
Only, for this moment
Heaven and earth are in this barn:
She looks and he looks back at her:
There is a small movement –
The slight adjustment of his shawl;
Her hand moves in a half-light gesture, slow.
As kings and shepherds, stars and distant worlds
Behold the little boy from heaven:
Darling Jesus,
Emmanuel, thou art come,
Come, rejoice us,
And turn our hearts to thee

Part 2 : Purgatorio

XI

Having put Oldham on the map, James was talking more and more expansively of leaving. He was bored.

"Angst," he said "is an affliction like dry rot for which the only cure is work – and sex and drink and sleep and death."

He persuaded the BBC to come to St Mary's and broadcast the Sunday Service, live. The BBC's attitude to church services, like its attitude to nearly everything else, is to erect a mountain of clichés around it. Naturally, this kills off the religious sense altogether. Producers have, for example, this weird notion that churches should be filled with lighted candles at all times. We only had the two on the altar at St Mary's, so vulgar little night lights had to be brought in and placed on every ledge, shelf, side altar, the font, the lectern with the result of making the church, as James studiously remarked,

"...like a tart's boudoir."

Yes, but it would also be a tart's boudoir which echoed to the din of a certain kind of hymn tune. The BBC hates authentic tradition and prefers Kitsch, as we know from their self-trumpeting award-winning historical drama series in which, for instance, Jane Austen's characters' acid drop bitchery is reduced to the speech patterns of the soap opera on the grounds, as a senior drama producer told me,

"The literary language goes over people's heads today."

Why do BBC types imagine everyone in the country is thick? So along with the clichés comes an always effete and patronising smugness.

And so with the choice of hymns. Nothing authentic must be heard. Not Fight the Good Fight or O Thou Who Camest from Above – and certainly not I Vow to thee My Country – because that involves another of the Corporation's pet hates, patriotism and the love of our native land. The Beeb prefers internationalism, political abstractions and the bureaucratic straitjacket of the European Union. I Vow to thee My Country also glorifies war – according to the BBC producers who talk here in another set of clichés: those of the gung ho Hollywood war movie. Try telling the BBC types that there is the world of difference between glorifying war and giving thanks for those who died for our country. Trying telling them that soldiers of all people have the most reason to hate war, since they are the ones who have to fight it. Try telling them that, while war is certainly evil, there are worse evils – such as occupation by a dictatorial foreign power and the enslavement of the population. Try, above all, explaining to them that appeasement does not work. Appeasement causes wars. If you appease a man-eating crocodile, it doesn't reward you by not eating you: it simply eats you last.

The hymns have to be modern and have a beat. Try telling them that all music has a beat. That's what music is: melody in a particular rhythm. So what modern hymns do they choose to inflict upon the churches they favour with their generous offer to broadcast their services?

I danced on the Sabbath and I cured the lame

The holy people said it was a shame

But if those words are banal, what sort of language are we left with to describe the merits of:

Kumbaya My Lord, Kumbaya. Kumbaya My Lord, Kumbaya. Kumbaya My Lord, Kumbaya. O Lord, Kumbaya?

Or this favourite piece of tripe:

All that we need to do, be we low or high, is to see that we grow nearer the sky

And the lessons must on no account be read from The Authorised Version of the Bible. Again modernity is the shibboleth. Any Bad News Bible will do – so long as it's modern. And the sermon must be relevant, which means it should include as many references as possible to current TV soap operas and games shows. I remember the producer heartily congratulating some fucking aging trendy cleric when he revealed at the rehearsal for the service that he intended to begin with

"Hi there, guys. How're you doing?"

Anyone with any taste, please feel free to throw up now.

Part of the demand for relevance means also that the sermon should reflect the political views of the metropolitan elite – that is of the BBC types themselves. Much should be made of the fact that Jesus spent a lot of his time with the poor. But there will be no mention of the many lavish banquets he enjoyed with the rich. The sleight of hand here is that which identifies the colourful Galilean peasants with the wilfully shiftless layabouts on the sink estates.

Other rules of thumb: if you must quote culture, make sure you mention lefties such as the Champagne socialist windbag and rabble-rouser, Harold Pinter or the pedantic and anarchic sentimentalists Weill and Brecht. Prefer the developing world, What, by the way, is the definition of the developing world? It is those parts of the world which never develop. Hate America. Avoid classical music. Make relevant analogies featuring excruciating pop music. Generally, the preacher should demonstrate that he is a fully paid up participating member of the popular cultural establishment. The BBC religion producers, like the BBC politicos, regard themselves as cutting edge anti-establishment. Laughably, what they don't understand is that they themselves are the establishment now. Like the BBC comedy shows which promote themselves as full of the edgy wit of the outsider but actually are merely peddling the stale crusts of metropolitan-chic prejudices.

The preacher must have no truck with miracles. Explain the Feeding of the Five Thousand as an example of what we can achieve if we share. Similarly, the Bread and Wine of the Eucharist is not actually the Body and Blood of Christ but, when the Sacrament is taken together it is a sign of community. Christ's casting out of demons is to be understood as his powerful insight into psychiatric illness. The dumb demoniac who threw himself about all over the place and rolled uncontrollably on the ground might be said to have suffered from learning difficulties. Of course there was no physical Resurrection at Easter. Instead, after Christ's death, the disciples simply experienced a new sense of life. Naturally, it must be left unexplained how this happened if Christ remained dead.

He must emphasise Christ's commandment to turn the other cheek as proof that he was a pacifist. On no account mention some of his other sayings to the contrary such as, Think not that I come to bring peace but a sword. When Jesus asked Who is my mother? Who are my brothers? Claim that this is a clear rejection of the nuclear family and an affirmation of the commune. Well, we know that Christ said the only permissible alternatives in sexual relationships are marriage to one person for life or abstinence. That was then. This is now. And, in our progressive enlightenment, we now know that what were once regarded as mortal sins – homosexuality, adultery, fornication etc - are now only lifestyle choices and signs of openness and diversity.

To the solidified delight of Colin Barnet, the industrial chaplains of Manchester and just about every Christian Marxist in Lancashire, James brought across Professor Jurgen Moltmann from Germany and we all gathered in St Mary's to hear his mish-mash of Marx, Adorno, the death of God, liberation theology and the revolutionary meaning of hope. Sociological jargon in broken English. From this professor of theology, and the gang who turned up to listen, Marx, Habermas, Marcuse, industrial alienation – anything but Christianity.

James, it seemed, could keep himself alive and afloat only by a series of emotional shocks orchestrated to terrorise the bourgeoisie. At the same time he was the embodiment of a willed existentialism, conjuring the experience of life only by repeatedly hurling himself towards the very centre of the things that could destroy him. The theatre director and sweets to the sweet. Danny La Rue. The sensation in the Mayor's parlour – and a dozen like it – with the predictable fracas to follow: plonking the prying journo on the bar in The White Swan.

With James even this vertiginous existence became boring after a while when it was all played out in the same location. So he was on the move again. First to Sussex University for a year and The Maurice Reckitt Fellowship in Christian Social Thought. Light years away from Trafford Park, Colin Barnet and industrial alienation. Dialectic among the Brighton deckchairs – not to overlook the rarer delights provided in that town.

"Then," as he told me over the phone "I saw this advert in Times Ed Supp for the job of Conduct and Senior Chaplain at Eton. I thought, this is just me! So I applied. And guess what? I got the fucking job!"

It would have been his brilliant Oxford career that impressed the interviewing panel. Good God, I could imagine his performance in front of that lot: his voice even softer, even more mellifluous, his demeanour a study in refined humility, his directing the conversation into subtle, aristocratic milieu. And all done so quietly with a brow that showed just the right amount of furrowing. His burning contempt for the lot of them concealed completely. He told me he had found the interview exciting:

"There was this lady philosopher. She blushed when I smiled at her. I wonder if she knew, but a little, how I was contemplating her not quite geriatric cunt?"

From time to time he would phone and relate exploits:

"I love the job. I love teaching. I just can't stand the other masters. I can't stand being in a classroom. And I can't stand the boys."

"Apart from that, it's great, eh?"

"The other day, this little prick at the back whispering to his toffee-nosed neighbour. I shouted, 'Hey, you – what's your name?'"

"'Maximillian.'"

"Maximillian what?"

"Maximillian, Sir."

"Not that – you idiot! Your surname?"

"'Habsburg, Sir!'"

James did not stay very long at Eton. He left in circumstances which even for him were complicated and more mysterious than usual. Anyhow, triumph and disaster came alike to James. You might say Kipling's famous poem had been written with him in mind. He went off and did what he liked to do: visit exotic places, chat up the local women, drink the local drink – then sit up all night writing travel books. He went to live in glory in the Dordogne. There is more to tell about James, but it will have to wait for another day and another volume of these recollections.

After serving two curacies, a priest might reasonably ask the bishop to give him sole charge of a parish. I was reluctant to continue with what seemed to me like more of the same. My own parish one day – certainly. But I needed a break. Do something else for a few years. I applied to be Head of Religious Education at Whitecroft High School in Bolton. The High was misleading. Bolton had a policy of selection and the High Schools were bottom of the pile after the public schools and the grammars. Whitecroft was described in the jargon of the Education Department as non-selective. And, when I enquired of one of the educational advisers what this meant, he said,

"Whitecroft takes the kids who are left when all the others have been selected."

Bolton had a fine town hall, built by the same hand that made the corresponding hall in Leeds. It also had a precinct of course, but no cathedral. Instead there is the beautiful Victorian Gothic structure dedicated to St Peter and designated Bolton Parish Church.

While Oldham was always the first to close and the last to reopen during the cotton slumps, prosperous Bolton, further down the Pennines, never closed. The town is built in a valley and the southern suburbs merge indistinguishably with north Manchester. Wide roads run north and north west to the hill country around Rivington and Belmont, to the spectacular reservoirs with spectacular names such as Anglezaark. Rivington Pike was topped by a Victorian folly, a stone pillar and its softly curving slopes with that blob on the top which caused the locals to refer to it as the hill with the tit. Bolton is - well, I should say was, since I haven't been back for years – a cheerful, clean, airy town, extravert where Oldham was introvert. The people were healthier less pigmy-like. No rickety bandy legs. There was not the same sense of poverty's jaws always about to snap shut.

It was a twenty miles drive westwards down the M62 from my flat in St Stephen's House. This part of Lancashire is not so much dark satanic mills as green and pleasant land. Five minutes out of Oldham and I could see away to my right the TV transmitter on Belmont Moor and the other hills sweeping in a great curve beyond Rochdale and as far as Pendle with its legend of witches. Whitecroft School was on the north west side of Bolton, a mile from the town centre, up the Chorley Old Road. On either side were well-kept 19th century terraces, more opulent than anything in Oldham. The houses around the school had belonged to men who had spun cotton in the boom years. Now that the old mills had closed – and, yes, people really did gather in great crowds to watch the detumescent tumbling of the tall chimneys – the houses were occupied by bankers, sales-executives and other professionals – a few teachers among them.

Before my interview the deputy head teacher, Max Makin, gave me a tour of the school:

Corridors built on a square and a quadrangle hectic with girls in blue shorts and bouncing sweaters playing hockey. A couple paused to glance at the new teacher. The new teacher felt his cheeks beginning to burn. There had not been entertainment like this in Oldham. It surpassed even looking at the Girl Guides for well now Mr Broadstairs. There was a large assembly hall which doubled as a gym. A stage. A Steinway grand. An indoor swimming pool and eight acres of playing fields. There was even a library. The Headmaster's door was bordered by an impressive frieze which supported bell-pushes and different coloured lights to let you know whether Mr William Barnes – Billy Barnes to the kids – was in his office and, if so, whether he was desirous of seeing you.

He met me on the front step. Of average height, slim, balding, about fifty-five. His face wore that ironical, mildly shell-shocked smile which I learnt is the common result of surviving thirty-odd years in teaching. He threaded me through a crowd of unheeding second formers and into his office where he asked me for my DES number.

"What's that?"

I felt like the man in the gospels who tried to get into the feast without a wedding garment.

"Your Department of Education and Science reference number."

Max Makin, moustachioed with bushy ginger hair on either side of his polished dome said,

"Every teacher has to have one."

Any minute I would be cast into outer darkness and there would be weeping and gnashing of teeth.

Barnes had that serene look which I came to know well:

"No, Max. You don't have to have a DES number if you've got a good honours degree. So you see a proper education still counts for a little in our current Philistia. Not everyone goes to teacher training college. You know the difference between as university student and a training college student don't you, Mr Mullen? Tell him, Max."

Max looked as if he had suffered this persecution before. He said nothing and his head dropped, so revealing the totality of its vast shiny expanse.

"Well, I'll tell you," said Billy Barnes. "When the tutor enters the university lecture room and says 'Good morning', the students replay,

'Good morning.' When he says. 'Good morning' to the training college types, they write it down."

He threw back his head and chortled. A good impression of Mr Toad of Toad Hall. His laugh was so loud it hurt your ears.

"English Literature. Drama. Music. Cricket." I tried to give the words capital letters as I answered his question about any other interests, apart from,

"...religion."

He uttered the word as if it signified a necessary evil.

"As a Christian minister, how do you see yourself getting on with the Indians?"

I was struck with images of war paint and wagon trains forming a circle.

"...and the Pakistanis," said Max, relieving me.

I waffled something about mutual respect . I was still hating that word minister.

Barnes went back to his chair in the corner, like a spider retreating into its web. He folded his hands and lisped words which sounded like part of a prepared speech.

"You won't get much academic stimulation here, Mr Mullen. Most of our lot are nice enough but they're thick as ninety-five lavatory seats. All I want you to do is knock a bit of religion into them: honesty, manners, the good of the school..."

Another cup of tea and I'd got the job. There didn't seem to have been any other candidates. Billy and Max shook hands with me in turn as if welcoming me to death row. Billy gave me the Masonic handshake, that of a master mason, third degree, thumb pressed firmly into the correct finger joint. I didn't return it. Two years later when Barnes invited me to join the masons, he was shocked to discover that I knew most of the rituals of the craft.

"But how? They're secret!"

"Darkness Visible – a book about freemasonry by Fr Walter Hannah who infiltrated the Lodge and wrote a spoiler."

Barnes was distraught – as if he'd found me cheating at Bridge.

All I had to do before I was formally welcomed into the glorious company of the non-selected was to pass a medical and obtain that DES number – not as a qualification but so I could be put on the payroll. The doctor said I was a little underweight at nine stones six pounds – or whatever the equivalent in foreign money. The magic DES number arrived in the post. First the weigh in, then the ball and chain.

Staff rooms were smoke-filled in those days. Most schoolteachers are of the anything-for-a quiet-life temperament, adept at finding tricks and dodges to avoid confrontation alike with kids and colleagues. Every staff room has its resident politico and at Whitecroft this was the ideological Marxist Tom Handley – the Althusserian, post-structuralist, composite motion sort. The full rule book. Decidely not the romantic ragged trousered philanthropist type of whom it is said that they couldn't blow their noses without lamenting the conditions of employment in the handkerchief factories.

On my last Sunday in Oldham, Reg Burton, in a tone that suggested I was deserting the front line, said,

"So you're leaving the church, Peter?"

"No – I'm still a priest, Reg, but not with a parish."

"What's a priest without a parish?" And he shuffled off, disgusted.

The Church of England changed more drastically in the years between 1970 and 1985 than it had done in the previous five hundred. New, illiterate translations of the Bible were produced along with dumbed down modern liturgies and more of those doggerel hymns with tunes like advertising jingles. The historic consanguinity between sacred scripture and secular literature was destroyed. The cultural links that had for centuries bound together the way we spoke in church with the way we talked in the street were being severed beyond repair. The great English novel is full of biblical quotations and allusions. But when the Authorised Version of the Bible was cast aside, it necessarily took with it into the darkness much of the sense, idiom and nuance hitherto discovered in our great literature. The modernisers in the senior clergy and the synod were philistines and they couldn't care less. It was worse than that: they actually despised our national history and culture. It was all so much elitism to them. The shepherds who were meant to guard the sheep were become wolves who devoured the sheep. The utter debacle, the destruction of the English Church, could not be seen in its entirety back in 1973, but the signs of what was to come could be read. Was I leaving the church? Not exactly – but it was a good time to be going.

I began at the chalk face on Monday 7th January 1974. It rained. It rained all that month, saturating Pennine rain that turned the landscape into a mist and the motorway into walls of standing water not seen since the crossing of the Red Sea. The daily drive, though at no more than 50mph under Mr Heath's restrictions owing to the coal strike and the oil price hike, was slowed down even further when the car began to take in water. The staffroom was all brollies, plastic macks and stoicism. World weariness kept at bay by teachers' semi-hysterical banter. Purgatorio.

XII

It is easy when writing up memories like these to retreat into an easy fluency which merely records the things which took place – to settle for the quotidian and the anecdotal. What's really required is to smash together the whole riotous, bilious, phantasmagorical, tedious continuum that school is, was and ever shall be: the morning assembly with all its farts and dog-eared formality, the stentorian tones and the sports results, livened now and again by the crash of someone fainting. What is it about schoolteachers – as a breed, I mean, or as a species in permanent personal decline? The sex-starved displacement activity of the thirty-odd years English and modern languages teachers whose husbands had, unaccountably, given the perfumed, empty-headed gorgeousness of these house-trained Barbies, long eschewed the delight of pleasing them. Why? What is the atrophy which assails middle class marriages after a few years and substitutes for ecstatic strife below the hip bone, conversations about mortgages and damp courses?

Still it rained. Children go beserk when it rains. The only sorts of weathers which drive them crazier are snow and fog. Rain is just the chaos of snow and fog without the romance of pretending to be lost in the eerie silence. You cannot keep the kids dry, short of nailing their feet to the floor – a practice of which the Local Education Authority – though not most headteachers – tends to disapprove. They hurtle around the muddy corridors. They slip on the wet floor and have to be taken to Casualty, or at least as far as the deputy head's office for a bandage. They drape sodden clothes over the radiators. Everywhere there is the sickliness of sweat and farts and drying rubber boots.

Billy Barnes was magnificently incompetent. Already the first week in January and he hadn't completed the timetable. So each teacher sat with his own form all morning searching desperately for something to assuage the boredom, listening to tales of Christmas exploits of who ate and drank the most and who was most sick. My form of fourteen year old boys and girls was 4Y. The brainiest was the X stream – or as Max Makin said, the least unselected. The thickest was the G stream – G for General or Gormless, according to one's affective disposition. The system was called Mixed Ability Teaching – which was supposed to apply to the pupils and not to the Staff.

But, for instance...Harry Booth, the chunky, whiskery maths master, popped in from next door to borrow my calculator so he could work out his form's dinner money:

"I haven't got a calculator, Harry."

"However do you manage?"

He had barely been gone a minute when Louise Burkitt said,

"I've got a calculator, Sir. He can borrow it if he likes."

"That's very nice of you Louise. Take it round to him, will you?"

This for the maths master who couldn't add up.

Just then there was a commotion from Harry's room like the opening of an artillery barrage. Louise came back and I said,

"What's going on in there?"

"It's Mr Booth, Sir. He's standing on his desk trying to get 4G to be quiet, but he can't control them. They're all banging their desks and that."

And that.

My girls sat in lumps and talked about clothes and disastrous dates. Some of the lads tried to make me welcome:

"It's lousy here, Sir. But it's not as lousy in summer."

So – it was not only the Crossgates bourgeoisie who went in for minimalist syntax. Everybody was bored beyond limbo.

School uniform was a queasy green. Green trousers for the boys and, by concession to their perceived womanhood, fifth form girls. Otherwise green skirts and cardigans for them – with white blouses underneath. A fifth form girl came in just after ten o'clock. All in green. The trousers sort of gathered at the waist and then wide and loose around the thighs. Bottoms were wide, though flares were not allowed. She had a face white as chalk and a voice like acid indigestion:

"Wet playtime," she said and departed. There was a groan from 4Y

"Can we play cards, Sir?" This from one of the lads already flicking through his deck.

"No, I don't think so."

Another groan.

"Look all of you..." I made a gesture of clapping my hands, walked about a bit. "...why don't you tell me all about yourselves."

A louder, more heartfelt groan.

"It would be a help to me – getting to know you, I mean, if we all sat in our proper places."

The lump of girls flaked off at the edges and, because even to have to do what they were told was some small relief of the boredom, they all went to sit at their own desks. They talked. They told me where in Bolton they lived: Halliwell, Moss Bank, Farnworth, Astley Bridge...

They were friendly, affectionate even. But not with one another. There was a desperate cruelty. School kids live on Schadenfreude and the comforts of ordinary friendship are not counted worthy to be compared with the glee felt at a classmate's tribulations. Except this is not quite true: for the expressed glee is a corporate glee, and camaraderie consists in sharing a voyeuristic and mildly sadistic fascination for the misdoings of one's neighbour.

All was partisan. When one told me which part of town he lived in, the others would cheer if they lived there too and boo loudly if they lived somewhere else. Egalitarian theories in education will never work in practice because the kids are competitive to the point of cannibalism. This competitive class mentality covers truly elevated concerns, such as whether Bolton Wanderers are the best football team in the world – no, in the whole universe – to matters giving rise to mere contempt and ridicule, as in,

"We're not talking to Christine any more?"

"Why ever not?"

"Her pumps are not lace-up."

I have seen children die of shame at much milder accusations.

While we played this game of introductions, there was a further outbreak of comradely viciousness. A girl with wet, stringy hair on the back row, having received no obvious provocation, shouted:

"Brian McGready's stupid, Sir. He once swallowed three live tadpoles!"

Every eye switched on to poor, purple-faced McGready. Flustered by this surreal disclosure, all I could do was ask limply,

"Where?"

The girl with the wet, stringy hair came back at me with chapter and verse:

"Outside the boys' lavs, Sir. Last year."

You could have expected lavs to raise a giggle – but last year! I quickly learnt that not one jot or tittle gets erased from the pupils' corporate memory – not even after they have long left school. It wouldn't matter if Brian McGready had gone on to score a century against Whitecroft's deadly enemies, English Martyrs RC Secondary, or if he had become the first kid to earn a grade one CSE pass in Maths, he was forever marked as the oaf who once swallowed three live tadpoles outside the boys' lavs.

Late morning, a completely green fifth form girl came in and asked, "Is Pauline Dunn here?"

Pauline blushed and the class fell unusually silent. The green girl said, "Pauline, yaffat go see Mrs Westcott at dinner time."

The green messenger went away and the Greek chorus let out a lascivious

"Ooh!"

"She's been..."

But I didn't hear the rest for the waves of uncontrolled laughter. The others had heard well enough and, whatever it was that Pauline had been up to, it excited them more than all the rain, snow and fog of that January. I should explain yaffat. So far as I know, it is an expression confined to Bolton. They did not say it in Oldham. It means, You are under an obligation to...; You must. The fifth form tutor John Humphrey told me it is an abbreviation of, You have for to... followed by the verb – and that it probably comes from the French. God knows how the Gallic intonation made inroads as far as Bolton.

The bell went at 12.15 for wet dinnertime. A few of the boys got up to leave. I said,

"Wait a minute – where do you go for wet dinnertime?"

"We affat go see Mr Platt about Jim, Sir."

"Jim?"

"Gym, Sir."

Pushpa Mistry – lovely name, suggests doing press ups with a sexy archangel - sang out the missing information:

"They're going for a smoke, Sir!"

"No, we're not, Sir, honest."

The evil eye having been cast on Pushpa.

"We're just off to see Mr Platt, go to lav, and that."

And that.

Meanwhile, the girls showed no inclination to leave the classroom. They congealed again around and upon one desk.

"Can we stay here, Sir? We'll be good – honest."

I had noticed the outbreak of honesty.

School dinners were consumed in the dinner hutch, a white-painted brick building by the side of the new ROSLA – Raising of the School leaving Age – classroom known as Colditz. This housed the most disgruntled pupils in the whole school – those who adffa (had been compelled by the new statute to) stay on for an extra year. They hated it. As Derek Spivey put it to me:

"It's not fair that we have to piss around here for another year when we could be out earning some dosh."

It was hard not to sympathise.

I saw Harry Booth again in the staffroom. He wore the look of a man who had just been let out of jail. There was Cheryl Gyte, the adenoidal gym mistress whose name one day was to give rise to the utterance of an awful Spoonerism. And there was spindly Kate Murphy, Labour Party activist who taught bits of all sorts.

Philip Oliver, the lanky, laconic, sardonic physics master was on dinner duty in the hutch, so there was no trouble from the kids. Phil had taught at Whitecroft for so long that he had refined teacherly techniques to a perfection which was nearly supernatural. He exercised discipline unconsciously. A slightly louder than conversational utterance, "Er..." and silence would immediately fall on the room like sleep. He was also a master of the pedagogic ironical style which is the only language the kids respect – since it contains, beneath its urbanity, something of the nastiness of their own ways of talking to one another. So, for example, given a case of bad table manners:

"Er... Jason Stevenson, your mother would not be exactly pleased to see you putting your knife in your mouth like that. Your father might, though – hoping you'd cut your throat."

All from his great height and in the resonant sardonic tone. Phil's utter – though perhaps it was only a device? – contempt for all things juvenile had the double effect of flattening the offender and, his apparent cruelty capturing the attention of the others, of quietening the whole room.

Back in the staff room, teachers were hugging the radiators and saying it had not seemed two minutes since the end of last term. There is always a PE teacher coming in or going out, bouncing a football. There is always a posse of kids at the door. They are always looking for the PE teacher. At 1.45 4Y sauntered into the form room looking even more bored than they had been at the start of the day. And now, after double helpings in dinners, they were drowsy as well. I called the register:

"Anyone know where David Midgeley and Sandra Grant might have got to."

"I do, Mr Mullen!"

It was Phil Oliver, suddenly appearing at the door, holding the two absentees by the nape of their necks like kittens for the drowning:

"I discovered them engaged in a loving act, in the romantic location of the boys' lavatories!"

Uproar.

"Er..."

Silence.

Whitecroft was proud of its range of extracurricular activities. There was chess and there was fencing, football of course, netball and swimming. Then there was the drama mistress, pixie face Jill, tall, musical, with the infinite legs which moved like silky serpents in a synchronised swim. The movement conjured obscure recollections – such as that parallel lines never meet. They did meet, though.

There was Dorothy Bedford, head of English. She was like everyone's mother. All anyone ever heard her say to a pupil was, "Now look!" – with the Lancashire intonation, "Newe luke!"

And the autodidact John Davies, standing under the clock in the staff room and doing his impression of the headmaster taking assembly. There is one of John in every staff room – the theatrical cynic, all disillusion and bile when holding forth, but suffering the little children like gentle Jesus himself. John seemed to hate himself for loving his job. Never tired of complaining how he was colossally victimised by the philistine headmaster, but putting in all the hours that God sent with the most unfortunate and least capable of the kids.

John was well into his Billy Barnes impersonation:

"Now then, Mr Davies, at the beginning of this new term, and refreshed as I am by many nights drinking at the Lodge... and, as a token of gratitude for all you have done for our great school these last eighteen years, I am for the tenth year running putting you in charge of F4..."

F4 were the lowest class of the first year. According to the Education Department's official tests, their brains glowed with even less candle power than a Toc-H lamp. Many of them were the children of Ugandan Asians, recently thrown out by the dictator Idi Amin. Some of their older brothers and sisters were intelligent and good humoured but these, the smallest and most speechless, were cold and afraid. All scuttering about the place like mice. All with big brown helpless eyes. But John gave up his dinnertimes to love them. Then his classroom was a magic theatre. He read fairytales aloud, doing all the voices. If you passed his room at these times, you might hear a snatch of a Beethoven symphony. You would certainly hear children's laughter.

John tricked me into agreeing to go with him and some of the F4 and F3 pupils on an educational trip to the Manchester ship canal – understanding our local industrial heritage and all that. It was a grimy February morning when we set off in the coach on a hopeless crawl through the perpetual north Manchester traffic foul-up. A heavy drizzle descended as we disembarked and walked the cold quayside into the bleakest stretch of concrete and cast iron in the whole dilapidated industrial wasteland. Small ships' horns, melancholy. Men in the distance hammering on the cast iron with steel hammers. Like being in an echo chamber from hell.

Laschish Patel was walking beside me. He said,

"Great, isn't it, Sir!"

His face like the beatific vision. I had never seen anyone look so happy. The rain came on more heavily and John found it hard to make himself heard over the penetrating wind. He was telling the kids they could have an hour's free time to explore but...

"No leaving the safe area, is that clear? Is that quite clear? Do I make myself clear?" teacher-speak repetition for:

"I really mean this, and if anyone disobeys, they're done for."

There was a structure which looked like the punishment room in a concentration camp. This was the museum of shipping, full of whirring pulleys and levers and phantasmagoric gadgets that went CHUNG! The true attraction for the kids was the snack bar at the far end. John, the geography mistress, a student on teaching prac at Whitecroft for that term, and I went in search of a quiet spot there to consume our sandwiches and gather our strength for the long afternoon's tour of the high gangways and the cavernous locks, now no longer in use. This tour lasted from 1.30 until 3.45. It was like doing hard labour.

The highlight of the trip was a boat ride in the old ferry down the canal, dispiritingly lined by the collapsing warehouse buildings. John instructed us enthusiastically,

"These would have been bustling with trade a hundred years ago."

The effect on our gang was as if he'd said,

"I was alive once – but I'm dead now."

As we approached the dock, I saw the boy Geoff Collins leaning over the side. He was throwing up with a vigour I didn't think he possessed. I kept an eye on him for a while and became worried when the was no end to the vomiting. He could have won prizes for it. I went across and put my arm around his shoulder. In a rare pause between emissions, he said cheerfully,

"I'll be all right, Sir. It's just 'cos I ate thirty-three Curly Wurlys this morning!"

The whole day was like a Purgatory Acclimatisation Course. I arrived home at 7.30 and went straight to bed.

Every morning the whole school piled into the hall for assembly. The teachers stood along the walls surrounding the five hundred inmates like warders at Wormwood Scrubs. This morning Larry Johnson, music master – universally mocked as Sticky Fingers – was embroidering a two part invention by Bach. The reassuring rhetoric of Philip Oliver wafted across the hall like a zephyr:

"Now then, Lester Briggs, we're not going to be able to sing like a song thrush if our mouth is stuffed with chewing gum, are we."

Lester shyly removed the gum and slipped it into a handkerchief the colour of an oily rag.

The men wore sports jackets – with leather patches on the elbows - and flannel trousers. The women were in two piece suits. There were exceptions: no one would expect to see Roy Platt in anything other than a track suit. (I didn't recognise him for almost half an hour one Christmas at an end of term drinks party when he turned up in a shirt and tie). Or Mrs Gyte without, as it were, her netball skirt and, hanging from her waist, her whistle. Now here comes the exception: Mr Barnes, ascends the rostrum not only in suit and club tie, but wearing his academic gown. An academic gown at Whitecroft was like a bottle of gin at the Methodist Conference. There was not just the outward and visible sign of solemnity, but its inner reality. In the sweaty silence, he intoned the versicle from The Book of Common Prayer (1662).

"O Lord, open thou our lips."

It seemed he was making a heroic attempt to sound like what parsons are instructed never to sound like. A booming vibrato. Clearly, he was trying to put meaning into his words and astonishingly the kids replied in like manner:

"And our mouths shall show forth thy praise."

We had The Lord's Prayer and then Larry Johnson tickled the Steinway through Morning has broken. Billy Barnes read the Bible with all the cheerfulness of Mr Sowerberry the undertaker in Oliver Twist. It was the opening of the Sermon on the Mount

"He always reads that!"

4Y's Christine Brockbank told me later.

After this glimpse of heavenly things, we were obliged to turn our attention lower – much lower. Barnes, still with the hint of Canon Adenoid, in his voice said,

"I must make a report..."

Someone farted authoritatively.

Thunderous laughter and applause. Many of the teachers smiled too. Not Mrs Gyte, thankfully. Manfully, she strode into the thickest clump of hilarity, seized the proud culprit by his red left ear and, to trumpeted cheers, marched him out.

I'm not sure that I accurately recall the order of events after this. Certainly, I remember Mr Humphrey shouting something vaguely apocalyptic over the tumult. Then, when the giggling and rustling had finally stopped, we were all left gazing towards the headmaster. He did not utter a single word, but his regained control over the hordes was complete. What he had not been able to do by his voice, he now accomplished by silent gesture. First, he folded his arms across the lectern, narrowed his eyes and stared straight ahead with an absolutely calm viciousness. Then he turned his head swiftly to the right, affecting to notice an insubordinate blink or sniff. Next, he turned again, giving them the benefit of his other profile, towards the high windows so that his face was illuminated like that of the victim in The Martyrdom of St Sebastian. Finally, he stared out over all their stricken faces and shook his head slowly in a motion of infinite sadness. One tug at his gown, he turned and left the rostrum completely victorious. At times like this, Larry Johnson knew not to play a recessional. Once the headmaster had disappeared at the end of the corridor, there was the beginning of slovenly movement from the vanquished. This was put a stop to. Philip Oliver's laconic command:

"All right – nobody moves!"

Then Max Makin appeared on the rostrum with papers in his hands:

"Mr Barnes would like to see the whole school in here at 4pm."

He spoke in such a whisper, you could have thought a child had died. In fact, they had all been quietly and professionally murdered.

XIII

"Yaffat go see Mr Barnes in your free period, Sir."

That was the 4Y register monitor bringing a message from the Presence.

So I went.

What a change. The old sod was genial as Father Christmas:

"I've asked Caroline to bring us a pot of tea."

He strolled out from behind his huge desk, imperiously as Nelson might have strolled the deck of his flagship. The wide windows looked out over the car park and towards a row of detached houses, upon one of which there was a red and white banner: VOTE LABOUR. The uninterrupted sight of it must have been a torment to this dedicated freemason and lifelong member of the Bolton Conservative Club. The wall behind the desk featured portraits of headmasters past, and opposite there was a picture of The Fighting Temeraire.

"You were in assembly this morning, I think, Mr Mullen?"

"Yes. I was beside the piano."

"I thought I saw you. You were almost obscured by Clark Dunderdale. D'you know Dunderdale? He's a big lad. Nice chap. Nice chap. Not very bright though."

Not very bright, Dunderdale – and there was I almost obscured by him. Barnes was still and silent for a long time and then suddenly his face cracked like crazy paving and he smiled with the most illuminated benignity.

"I wonder, Mr Mullen, if you would like to lead the occasional assembly yourself? I mean…as a professional…with your experience… No use having a dog and barking yourself eh? Or should that be a dog-collar. Ha! Ha!"

Even a dog – and its collar - partially obscured by the not very bright Clark Dunderdale.

In came the tea lady, secretary's assistant, thin as a mop handle. She stared at me and then at the carpet, as though wondering whether I was quite housetrained.

"Thank you Miss Sope."

He dismissed her with a gesture that was such an extravagant benediction that I felt ecclesiastically outclassed.

"Well, yes, Mr Barnes, I'd like very much to take the occasional assembly."

"Tomorrow morning then. Now I suppose you'll be wanting to get back to your classes."

No whacking could have come as more of a shock than what I had just experienced in the headmaster's study. On my way back to my room, I called in room 25 where Max and that other incarnation of deputy headness, Thelma Westcott, - great niece of Bishop Westcott of Durham, no less – devised endless lists and invented fresh reprimands. Max was in full expostulation even as I entered:

"But Gary, not with a milk bottle and an umbrella, surely?"

"Why not?" said Thelma, with that look on her face.

Corridors are to the school what aisles are to churches: they are where all the action takes place. Corridors are the places where, though told a million times not to, children habitually run. Shouting takes place in corridors. Furtive thumpings and other minor acts of malevolence occur there. Recalcitrants ordered by teachers to stand outside lurk there sulking, only to be asked by every passing teacher the nature of their offence. Corridors are where litter is discarded and where schoolbags are kicked about, where windows are broken and fire-extinguishers wrenched from the wall, where teachers laden with great stacks of exercise books are ignored by the manic hordes jostling their way from the last misdemeanour to the next act of irresponsibility. The atmosphere of the bullfight is now and again pierced by the unavailing cry, Don't run! or, as it might be, Keep to the left, I tell you! The way is often blocked by the entertaining spectacle of a red-faced teacher chastising a runner, a smoker or a hurler of satchels. Corridors are also places where teachers accidentally catch up with pupils for whom they have been on the lookout. A theatrical act of this sort was taking place even as I passed by. Mr Todd was enquiring of an all-in-green fifth former:

"Just what had your – naturally unfinished - metalwork project to do with Samantha Cochrane's jumper?"

"Dunno, Sir!"

When I reached my room, I found half a dozen boys sitting on desk tops playing some form of gambling game with cards. A few girls were chattering nearby and practising their nonchalance. They were all in 5R, the ROSLA set, surly and aggrieved because they were being made to stay on that extra year when they might have got that job in the segs factory and earned money for beer or, dressed in a different uniform, been discovered waiting at tables in one of the fashionable cafes near The Octagon Theatre.

There were a few girls from 5X – la crème de la crème – sitting in the far corner doing their nails. Everyone ignored me.

"Good morning!"

The only reply, the slap of playing cards on the desk top. I walked across to the card players;

"Now then, and what are your names?"

Nothing. Some light giggling from the 5R girls.

"Go on Trev, it's your go! said a swarthy card player to the lad on his left. Just then a green runner arrived in the doorway. She too was from 5X – the examination form. She looked cleaner, softer than the ROSLA lot:

"Excuse me, Sir..." with something like the ghost of a courtsey, "... Mrs Westcott says 5 ROSLA affat go see Careers Officer."

A grating of chairs over the bare boards and the ROSLA girls were up and on their way to room 25. One girl did not move:

"Come on, Sandra. Yaffat see Mrs Westcott," said the green runner.

"Tell her to fuck off!" was the proposed greeting from somewhere in the card school.

I had expected to be angry but I found instead I was degenerating, turning sentimental. A right old softy. I could have wept for the predicament these kids found themselves in.

"Sir," said the 5X messenger with a look of wan apology, "Yaffat have some 5G and 5P lads in with you."

Another little curtsey and she went off, this time accompanied by Sandra.

The 5G and 5P lads rumbled in. Gum-chewing, mumbling in the lower reaches of the bass clef, they clattered about and threw themselves on the furniture. Some tried to join the card school. I stood in the middle of the room, at the front. I took the wooden blackboard duster and banged it on my desk. And again:

"Bring me those playing cards, please."

"What for?"

"Because I asked you – that's what for!"

They were such a sorry mix. Some so creased with apathy you wondered if they could last another day. Bored with everything, even rebellion. Others looked catastrophically sorrowful, it was all I could do to stop myself bursting into tears. Only a few looked as if they were using the ROSLA block as a transit camp on their way to Borstal. One of them savagely overturned his desk.

"Pick it up, please!"

He didn't, but one of his pals did.

I took the playing cards from the boy who had brought them to me.

"And I want 'em back! They're me mam's!"

I put them in the top drawer of my desk and sat down.

"Now, where are your books?"

No reply

I asked again. One of the apathetic ones at the back said; "At home."

I wasn't going to continue this teacherly litany. So I did not say:

"Well, they jolly well shouldn't be at home: they should be here!"

I felt things had got too miserable to play this game. I knew I would write this down one day: a small tragedy was being played out in my classroom and, it seemed, there was bugger all I could do about it.

"Dog's eaten mine, Sir!"

Laughter, The usual sounds and unpleasant smells. More laughter – but hollow as a reed.

"All right, since you've no books, I'll read to you!"

"What out of, Sir?"

"A book. It's a story."

"What is it, bleedin' Jackanory, Sir!"

I put the book down. I began to stroll up and down between the desks:

"So, you don't want me to read to you?"

"Aw, Sir!"

This was a surprise: one of them looked disappointed!

"Well, I'm a teacher and you're here to learn. What would you like to learn about?"

"Tell us how f't get VD, Sir!"

If one event stuck in the minds – if they had minds – of this poor lot, it was the annual visit of Dr Silver from the VD clinic:

"He showed us a great film, Sir..."

"I know. I was there."

"...there were, like, all these blokes with scabs and lumps. And your nose might fall off."

"I hope your nose doesn't fall off, Tom!"

"...and one of the Indian kids had never seen a picture of anyone's dick before, and he fainted!"

This was the stuff. They all joined in the joyous reminiscence of lurid pathology.

"And is it true you can get it off lavatory seats, Sir?"

I recalled David Midgeley and Sandra Grant: "Only if that's where you have sex!"

"Kung Fu, Sir"

"What about Kung Fu."

"Tell us about Kung Fu, Sir!"

He rolled up his sleeves and cracked his biceps.

"Don't bother, young man: the girls went ages ago!"

I sensed an outside possibility of a meagre redemption.

"Very well, Kung Fu it is!"

A few of them were out of their places and trying to cause mild havoc. I removed my jacket:

"Sit!"

For the first time, I shouted.

Amazingly, they sat and an unaccustomed calm spread throughout the whole fetid classroom.

"You – " I clicked my fingers, "a window open, please."

He obliged with rapid, eager movements, as if he was wondering what I might do next.

Slowly, I began to roll up my shirtsleeves:

"Kung Fu," I intoned with lapidary forcefulness, "is a martial art which dates from the time of Confucius. It uses not weapons but..."

My voice trailed off to a whisper, "...with it an expert can kill a man."

Then, very loud: "You, come here!"

I pointed to the one who looked toughest of the lot. And I kept pointing steadily towards him as he left his place and came forward in complete silence.

"Nearer!"

When he was so near,we could have rubbed noses, I said,

"Now, do you know just where the pressure point is in your neck – the one which needs only a finger and thumb and you're a dead man?"

"No, Sir."

He was red in the face.

"All right, does anyone know?"

They were already feeling their own necks as if testing for mumps. Not a word – not even from me as I shooed the tough back to his place:

"So you don't know? Not one of you understands the basic principles of Kung Fu? Then I shall have to teach you."

I sat on top of my desk and faced them:

"Kung Fu is a physical and spiritual technique – a noble art – which gives you complete mastery over your enemies, over anyone in fact. It calls for superhuman strength and power, power to dominate others. Power to get your own way. To control people. Would you like me to teach you that power?"

Unanimity broke out and, even more extraordinary, something like enthusiasm.

"But before you can dominate anyone else, you must learn how to dominate yourself. You must first prove to yourself that you are strong – really strong. You must achieve total self-mastery. Do you understand?"

"Sir!" In a muffled chorus.

"There must be no weakness, no giving-in, no let up in this self-domination. We shall start now. Lesson one. Sit. Upright. Backs against the chair. That's it! Arms folded in utter stillness..."

A glance out of my eye corner:

"...I said utter stillness. Head up. Chin in. Knees, ankles, feet together. You count under your breath and you blink only once every ten seconds. Do you understand that? Shush! Keep still. Good. Now your aim is to train yourself to maintain that position for as much as five hours at a time..."

There was not even a whiff of scepticism.

I sat down, took a sheet of paper from my desk and began to scribble a shopping list. They all sat like statues in a graveyard:

"...But today we shall practise for just a quarter of an hour."

There was a movement outside the window. It was the headmaster. He peered in through the glass. No one was distracted. Not a movement. There was not the ghost of a giggle or the hint of a smirk. Mr Barnes looked uncomfortable, as if he were being scrutinised, as if his suit did not quite fit. He tapped on the door and came in. I purposely did not notice him. He stood by my desk and looked out over the motionless beings. Talking at them, as it were, he asked,

"And what is this you're doing with the ROSLA group, Mr Mullen?"

"RE Sir. It's meditation practice."

He stepped reverently towards the front row:

"And tell me, Gary, what are you doing?"

"Practising complete self-control, Sir."

The lad spoke with such monumental disdain, as one in whom some deep purpose, recently awakened, had been interrupted by a trifle. Mr Barnes paused, nodded and uttered the one word,

"Commendable!"

Then he turned to me, his face out of their line of vision, and he grinned as he perused my shopping list:

"Excellent, Mr Mullen! Truly excellent! Excellent 5R! Really well done!"

And he tiptoed out.

"Now," I said "we shall maintain our position until the bell."

And they did.

Jill Legs the drama teacher was sitting in the staff room one day looking like a form mistress from a Carry On film. I was insipid in an armchair trying to recover from an assembly I had just delivered for St Valentine's Day. Impossible. The kids so grubbily romantic, hysterical over love tokens and, in extreme cases, fondling one another even as they stood in their lines. I was doodling a little verse of my own:

White upon white and frozen sense,
Mid-February's relief is Lupercal,
Licked by tongues of fire corporeal:
I have no need for shriving.
Intention in the fingertips and palms.
(There will be palms again
And tongues surprising with their ecstasy)
Lips to find your warm and central sense.
St Valentine martyred on the Flaminian Way:
That is another story of man's love
Living still as Christians put on ashes,
While the people of the woods attend their fires.

"What are you doing?" said Legs

"Nothing. I'm thinking of taking up smoking for the stress. They say it protects against brain damage."

"Are you going to come round for a drink?"

"What now?"

"Of course not now. Peter, they're showing Romeo and Juliet at The Odeon. Shall we take your lot and my lot?"

"My lot?"

"You do rule with fastidious majesty over 4Y, do you not?"

"So it has been said, darling."

"Are you feeling the least bit romantic? I mean, could you work yourself up to asking Billy Barnes if we could take the kids to see some wild Bill Shakespeare?"

"Why?"

When she stood up as was as if the sphinx had not merely moved, but had loped into action with feline graces more at home in the jungle than the desert. There was nothing dry about Jill. Oh stop it, Peter! You can't start on that tack – not on a sodden February day in the Whitecroft penitentiary.

"Education," she said. "No I'm serious."

"You're fabulous!"

"I'll hold you to that."

"I'll hang on and try not to shout too loud."

"Too loudly."

"Yes, mistress."

There was no denying it. What was the point in denying anything? It took me back to Leeds where the Leitmotif was all denial – all that it were all right...it weren't bad. Let's try affirming things for a change! With such pathetic, dying enthusiasm I tried to ginger myself up.

So there we were on the bus on a sullen day at the back end of February 1974. That bubble cut Christine Brockbank from 4X asked me straight out on top of the bus – God, where do these kids get it from! –

"D'you fancy her, Sir?"

The Sir somehow made all the difference. If she'd merely said, "D'you fancy her?" it would have been insolence. The Sir made it sound like pastoral care.

Brockbank herself was more than a handful. Bright as a sparkler.

Looking straight past her – displacement activity - I said:

"Put that cigarette out Claire – that's a good girl. We don't want the good burghers of Bolton to think we're not ladies, do we?"

I heard myself picking up the tones of the great Phil Oliver.

"Aw, Sir, Miss Crawford always lets us smoke on trip if we want!"

"If you want? And if you don't want, does Miss Crawford smoke on your behalf? And in any case, I'm not Miss Crawford."

"We had noticed, Sir!" said the ludicrously pulchritudinous Katherine Kolomijzeck, 4X

They all yawned through the travelogue and I wondered what they would make of the film. The girls liked Juliet's dress but wanted to know why the cast were talking funny. And in Zeffirelli's love scene – nightingale, lark and all – Romeo was loudly admonished by one of our lads:

"Get it up her!"

In the darkness crisp packets crackled like static. The girl immediately behind me whispered to her friend:

"There – that's where Paul and me sit when he..."

I didn't hear the friend's response above the prolonged giggle. They had all yawned through the travelogue and shouted the 10...9...8 countdown before the main feature.

But the tragedy reached some of them:

"It's not fair, is it Sir, when they died like that. It made me cry. I like happy endings best."

And inevitably:

"Will we affat write about it tomorrow, Miss?"

Miss Legs told them they would start a Shakespeare project.

It was now almost Easter and Mr Barnes had not called on the Lord to open thou our lips in Assembly since January. The fact that our lips had remained open was owing to my having mounted the rostrum every morning for the last eight weeks. Barnes had his dog and was delighted not to have to do the barking himself. Effectually, he had retired. He didn't even come into Assembly – not for the prayers and the hymn anyhow, but only when he had roused himself to deliver some reprimand or announce sports results. The darkness of these maladroit appearances was lightened on the last day of term. Barnes reminded the whole school that it was only two years since James Stevenson had drowned in one of the deep mill ponds known locally as lodges.

"So, all of you, keep away from the lodges."

"Same to you, Sir!"

- like a jumping cracker from one of the ROSLA lads who was demob happy and didn't give a damn for the old freemason's reaction. Everyone chortled and astonishingly, so did Billy Barnes. The scene like Scrooge's parlour on Christmas morning.

For eight weeks I had discovered a fresh topic every morning, usually concocting the mixture while driving down the M62 from Oldham. I knew I had to get their attention within the first twenty seconds or else they would only shuffle and whisper and fart indifference throughout. So I turned my evenings into purgatory by attending to the tripe they watched on the telly. Making righteousness relevant, as they would have said in the Teacher Training College. But there was, after all, a limit to the ethical mileage – to say nothing of the spiritual elevation – to be derived from The Six Billion Dollar Man or The Bay City Rollers.

I was agreeably startled in that last week of term, the week before Holy Week, to discover that what the little buggers wanted was the real thing – provided you were reckless enough to give them it straight. I simply read the account of the trial and death of Christ from The Authorised Version:

And when the sixth hour was come, there was darkness over the whole land until the ninth hour. And at the ninth hour Jesus cried with a loud voice, saying, Eloi, Eloi, lama sabbachthani? Which is, being interpreted, My God, My God, why hast thou forsaken me?

The silence was so thick it was like being enclosed in velvet. I asked them to imagine what it must have been like to be there, to be Peter, Mary, Judas, Pilate... Jesus himself. There were daffodils around the playing fields and the spring sunshine slanted into the hall through the high windows. 4X performed a Passion Play and the school sat still. Not one raucous comment and fewer farts than were customary. They sang Passiontide hymns in the yaffat dialect. The young boys were clear-eyed, taking an interest, on the note. The girls all fresh in the April morning, but strangely sorrowful, older somehow when they sang. They were already starting to look like their mothers.

Did e'er such love and sorrow meet

Or thorns compose so rich a crown?

So much for those philistine bastards, the modernising bishops and members of the Liturgical Commission who, on the lying pretext that the real Bible is beyond ordinary people, had set about depriving them of their glorious, tumultuous, numinous spiritual heritage in English. The sheer awfulness of the filth they were putting in place of the language of Shakespeare and Cranmer:

Pilate could see that nothing was being gained, and a riot was starting...

Who, but a bishop or a member of the Liturgical Commission could imagine such crap could ever pass as a replacement for:

When Pilate saw that he could prevail nothing, but that rather a tumult...

Or: After fastening him to the cross...

for the spare, heartbreaking, And they crucified him

These illiterate iconoclasts revised St Matthew to read,

King of Israel indeed!

What is this bourgeois, housetrained, euphemism indeed doing on Calvary?

What idiocy! What blasphemy!

One of the criminals who hung there with him taunted him, 'Are not you the Messiah?'

For God's sake, do they really think such an effete phrase represents the syntax of a man being tortured to death?

They were bringing out emasculated forms of the Holy Communion service too. These left out the words Body and Blood from the revised Prayer of Humble Access. The new Confession omitted the words

We acknowledge and bewail our manifold sins and wickedness – presumably because modern man, come of age, had divested himself of all his previous faults. No sin? So what's the bloody point of proclaiming the forgiveness of sins then? Just when you think they can't get more crass, you see that they have replaced It is very meet, right and our bounden duty with It is indeed right. Yes, that precious indeed again! Soft-soapy talk. The lingo of the sherry party or a lunch for chartered accountants: It is indeed Mr Limbo and Mr Vacuity – financial advisers to the General Synod.

All the children blew away cheerfully for the holiday and I could have cried. I'd wrestled with them hammer and tongs for a whole term and prayed for respite. Now I was missing them. Was this love, or what? Was I finding out at last what it is to be a priest? Don't ask me. I sat in the staffroom and watched the blossom falling like snow across the cricket field. Dorothy Bedford came in and asked if I would help produce Toad of Toad Hall at Christmas. It was eight months away, so I said Yes. Meanwhile, I had managed to raise the deposit for a house in Bolton. Actually, for the first time in my life I was beginning to feel well off. £600 a curate's stipend. My starting salary at Whitecroft was £2029 and this had increased to over £3000 within a single term owing to Edward Heath's insane policy of trying to defeat rampant inflation by index-linked increases – a policy continued by the socialists who were returned under the spiv Harold Wilson that February.

My house was in Bromley Cross, ten minutes drive around the ringroad to school. You could see the moors over Belmont from the window. And Bolton itself was green enough. From my front door, Eagley Way ran a quarter of a mile down to a stream curling through wooded fields. And behind the house, on the far side of the hill, was Entwhistle reservoir – a three miles circular walk. Tall trees. Birdsong.

XIV

First day back after the holidays and I was involved in a fight. It was my dinner duty and I arrived at the hutch to find Clark – not-very-bright - Dunderdale with Steve Parker's knife at his throat. Knives were forbidden in school. I knew because, recalling the time of man's innocency when I was a boy, everyone had a penknife. So, in my early days at Whitecroft, it seemed to me there was no harm asking class 4Y if anyone could lend me one to sharpen my pencil. And a hush had fallen over that chattering assembly like the silence after the Last Battle. I can't remember what I did in the hutch that day, except I seem to recall trembling a lot and trying to fluff myself up to look as big as possible. Next thing I remember was having both lads by the wrist and carting them off to the deputy head.

Max Makin was at his desk swigging from a bottle of milk. He removed the boys to the headmaster's study, returned and offered me a cigarette:

"Oh, I forgot – you don't do you? I can understand that Parker getting up to no good, but not Dunders. A nice lad Dunders."

"And, as it happens, still alive."

"You should call for assistance in a case like that, Peter."

"I didn't know what the hell I was doing."

There was a staff meeting at the end of the afternoon and Barnes was at his shiftiest and most obsequious. He regretted the stabbing, "... of course" but hoped no news of it would leak out for this would be "most unfortunate" for the sake of "the good name of the school" – especially if any whiff of the incident should reach The Bolton Evening News. The commendation which I received for my "prompt action" was tinctured with his half-spoken hint that, if I had not discovered the brawl, it would all have blown over harmlessly. I said,

"I suppose you'd define a burglary gone wrong as what happens when the copper interrupts it?"

Suppressed merriment all round. Barnes glared around the room, no doubt noting those who had laughed most fervently and marking them down for extra playtime duties.

There were muffled squawks when the geography teacher – the mistress of the sardonic mode – whispered:

"Of course, we could always have left them to kill each other. That would have gone down a treat with the Bolton Evening News!"

Knife fights were becoming a contagion. Next day John Davies was stabbed in the corridor outside his classroom. Barnes visited him in The Bolton Royal Hospital and pleaded with him not to sue,

"...for the reputation of the school."

"What reputation?" said John.

The summer term was one long session of educational lunacy. Naturally, it was the season for cricket and school sports, the fundraising Whitecroft Gala and all the history and geography field trips. It was also interrupted by two weeks extra holiday to mark what used to be known as Bolton Wakes. This municipal vacation dated from the time when the local mills all shut for the same fortnight – a different fortnight, of course, from that of Rochdale Wakes, Blackburn Wakes or Oldham Wakes – and the workers buggered off with their families to Blackpool or Morecambe, leaving Bolton like a wild west ghost town. Not so much wakes as sleeps.

With all the mills now closed and present day Boltonians working in a hundred different sorts of jobs in offices and factories, wakes were an absurdity. But they were a traditional absurdity. And so the kids came back to school for four weeks after Easter and then the school closed again for the following fortnight. This perpetuated the double nonsense of disrupting the flow of the busiest term of the year and of forcing the kids on to the streets because their parents were at work.

John Humphrey told me, as we were on our way to turf some big girls out of the sandpit:

"I've asked the Head umpteen times to hold the exams in the spring term – get them all over with before Easter. All he ever says is, 'But wakes are always in June, John!' For monkeys' sakes, bugger the wakes! As if the exams were Oxbridge Finals. As if Lady-Wash-Hand-Stand couldn't come and dish out the prizes in March. I wonder sometimes why I stay in this madhouse."

He had been an inmate for twenty-eight years.

A highlight of the disjointed summer term was the visit of that wonderful Dr Silver from the VD clinic, with his recollections of Paul Ehrlich's magic bullet. The name Silver had just the right amount of decadence about it to suit the job: a blend of silver bullet, Long John Silver and werewolves. What grotesque ills might follow lascivious delights? Dr Silver will describe them graphically and with glee.

On he came with his silver hair and his metre ruler. The lights went down and the spectacular photographs of sores, gummata and terminal lesions appeared on the screen in glorious colour. The names of tertiary syphilitic complications were uttered softly, mystically, as if they had been the names of rare butterflies: aortal collapse, locomotor ataxia and, pronounced in a paroxysm of relish, general paralysis of the insane. Dr Silver told you how fatget the lot.

The kids loved the mucky pictures. As each technicoloured diseased organ appeared, Dr Silver would tap it vigorously with his stick and eyes began to water. The whole performance received in transfixed silence. I thought of the damned souls in the masterpiece The Last Judgement on their way to hell, but covering only one eye against the sights of demons and serpents as fascinating as they were horrible. If you looked out over the sea of cowering children, you could see right into their petrified brains, to terrifying recollections of a stolen kiss that might return to visit suppurating vengeance twenty years hence. You could see resolutions being formed there and then – kids taking silent vows never to play with their bits and pieces ever again. We also saw congenital syphilis, cheerfully described by Dr Silver as:

"The sins of the fathers visited upon the children unto the third and fourth generations."

And then almost with regret,

"Of course, there's a lot we can do with antibiotics these days."

Later, I challenged Barnes over the necessity for such cruelty:

"It's child abuse."

But his view was that of the old Army Medical Board who delighted in dishing out moral shocks:

"If even one child is deterred from experimentation which could ruin his life..."

"Experimentation – you make it sound like the bloody chemmy lab! Working class kids already have a bad attitude towards sex. You've only got to hear them talk. They're brought up to regard it as dirty, filthy – even sinful for God's sake!"

"I thought you, of all people, would understand only too well the sinful component of sex."

This threw me off balance, as I wondered for a minute whether he was referring to theological understanding or to something more, shall we say, personal. Gossip is a mandated part of the curriculum in all schools. Strange how it works, too: if you want to know which teacher is knocking off which other teacher(s), you should ask the stupidest kid. Slightly recovered, I said:

"I do understand it. But I want our children to know that we're meant to love one another – and sex is a big part of it. Gods knows, most of these poor sods have little enough love in their lives."

But he only smiled pityingly and turned away.

Little enough love in their lives? Yes, many came from broken or dysfunctional families and I learnt a lot about this in my second year at Whitecroft when I was put in charge of the first form, F2. Monday mornings were the worst. Half the kids would come in with the look of frightened animals. All weekend their homes filled with booze, shouting and fighting. Never given proper meals. The sheer hell of being eleven years old and forced to observe at close hand your mother regularly smacked or thumped by your father – or by whoever happened to be your father this week. Your mother cowering, crying, bruised. The desperate noise of violent sex. Kids' eyes stinging with all that cigarette smoke. No, Mr Billy Barnes, love is the last thing our kids will connect with sex. And then what? You're all for telling them they can get VD as well. It's sadistic.

And on those Monday mornings the children came in with white faces and sore eyes, their lips quivering. On the edge of breaking down utterly – and the only thing preventing it, the sure and certain knowledge that their classmates would laugh at them.

The first two periods Monday morning I had F2 to myself. They were subdued, resigned, apathetic. Some looked so sad my heart broke every week. Under the pretence of examining their homework books – what homework? – I would invite them one by one to come and show me what they had written. Nothing usually. Or perhaps an unfinished drawing. Each child searched my face, as if inwardly imploring me to do something. You spoke as softly as you could to them all: boys as well as girls – it made no difference

All they need is love.

God knows what comfort they get these days when anyone placing himself nearer than three feet from a child is suspected of being a child-molester. And they can't even give these fiends their proper description – child-molester – but have to bring in some poncy Greek euphemism: paedophile.

Once Dr Silver, having delivered himself of his little apocalypse, had departed, a sullen righteousness descended on the school like that which falls on a congregation very temporally convicted of sin by some lurid evangelist. But just as suddenly, after two or three days or some miraculous occurrence, such as Bolton Wanderers winning promotion to the second division, the Methodistical atmosphere would lift and the school sailed easily again into the habits of cheerful misdemeanour. But not before Barnes had seized the opportunity provided by that puritanical interlude, to beckon the children to more vigilant self-control. What does it say of human nature that all the children regarded Dr Silver as a marvellous bloke?

It was not only the pupils who were egged on to ever greater achievements. Teachers were subjected to a barrage of admonishments involving the latest educational fads: mixed ability teaching, modular learning, open plan classrooms, continuous assessment and a whole mouthful of a thing called a charter for excellence in the core curriculum.

The man or woman in the street knows nothing about how the educations system works. How can they when all they have to go on is the fading recollection of their own schooldays? Those were the days of talk and chalk before the coming of pupil centred education. Those were the days when teachers were actually expected to impart some real knowledge. Of course, in order to be able to do this, you had actually to know something first. By the 1970s all such aspirations were despised and rejected. No longer were teachers expected to do anything so substantial as actually impart knowledge – or even pass on a little information – but instead to teach the child how to learn. Nebulous. Meaningless. In fact that old rigmarole of reading, marking, learning and inwardly digesting became at best only ancillary to the truly important part of the education world: the Committee and The Advisory Service.

There was much political talk from Jim Callaghan's government of standards and teaching the basics. Unfortunately no one noticed that this was impossible, because the teachers themselves had never been taught. The 1970s were the second generation of that institutional ignorance provided by state education. Most teachers knew no grammar – between you and I – had no vocabulary – mitigate against – and couldn't spell – restaraunt. But that wasn't the worst of it. You knew there was no hope left when they answered criticisms of their ignorance by taking a pride in it: It doesn't matter.

Those who saunter through the green and cream corridors of the Local Education Authority's building – usually called by some implausible name such as Ventura House – are not only more highly regarded than the teachers, they are paid far more generously. If you would seek advancement in the modern teaching profession, you must understand that the examination results of your pupils matter far less than the number of attendances you can chalk up at the moronic courses devised by the LEA. So, when I was asked to become a member of ALSEB – The Associated Lancashire Schools' Education Board – and to attend its inaugural Curriculum Development Meeting – the most important get together in Europe since Yalta – I surmised that I was being dreamt of as possible future office material. This did not come upon me all in a rush and I should therefore describe the remarkable series of events which led up to it.

One day in June, I was sitting at the far side of the sports field, marking examination papers while the languorous girls of 3G lay all about me reading The Hobbit and making daisy chains. I saw, among the distant sharp shadows, Mr Barnes gliding towards me inevitably, like the ghost in Whistle and I'll Come to You. His trust in professional confidentiality would have been diminished if he had heard lovely flowery, brown Shilpa Patel say:

"Look out, Sir – here comes the spoilsport!"

Even in that heat, he wore his military tie and charcoal suit. He loomed, hands behind him, face wrinkled into an expression of genial disapproval:

"Ah, Mr Mullen, you seem to have taken root!"

Which, being interpreted meant,

"Why are you out here with your class rather than indoors behind the double glazing?"

It would have been ridiculous to apologise, snatch up assorted thumbed copies of the Great Bore Tolkein and chase my sunlit girls back into the classroom. So I said simply,

"Yes."

"Yes...er, Yes?" he took out a less than white handkerchief and polished his sodden brow.

"Yes, I said. Yes, I have taken root. With my class too. Far too hot to be inside, isn't it?"

Bumble bees dithered among the buttercups. Affectionate little girls lay propped on their arms, kicking their legs behind them. The old tyrant's face changed, softened, as if, for the first time in his life, and by some supreme intervention of the Almighty, he had actually been moved by something. He looked into the far distance, as if remembering a very distant summer's day. I would even say it was a tender look. Poor, shrivelled, disappointed Billy Barnes. What branches grew out of that stony rubbish?

Then he shook himself back into...God, into whatever cold personification he customarily inhabited and said,

"Well, you may be outside the classroom, but the girls seem well-behaved enough. Carry on, Mr Mullen."

It was the Mr Mullen that got me. Why didn't he call me Peter? I had saved his life by taking assembly every morning since the dawn of time. I played to the full my daft part in the running of his daft school. Couldn't he be a bit more affectionate, a bit more relaxed, than Mr Mullen? He would die like that. Twisted. Disconnected. I thought, the poor shit! Then I remembered what a shit he could be – had been – to such as John Davies and generations of kids who would have loved to have loved him as a father.

"Did you get a bollocking from Sir?" asked Max at four o'clock. Then,

"What a mean bastard! Anyone, half human, in his position would have gone round your 3G girls and asked them what they were reading."

Almost against my will, I said,

"Oh, I think he does have a trace of humanity in him."

"Well I've never seen hide not hair of it in ten years."

On my way home, I slipped a note under the head's door inviting him and Mrs Molly Barnes to supper. He came in the charcoal suit. But Molly was splendid, voluminous, hearty and wearing such a colourful dress that she looked like a flower arrangement. She ate well, while he nibbled his cheese and looked about the room in search of photographs to praise. She kept saying things like...

"Willie was at the Lodge, weren't you, Willie? ...Mind you, the Lodge isn't what it was, is it Willie?"

Then to me directly, plaintively,

"Well, he says it isn't."

And she had that dead look in her eye which had given up hope, except the hope of...well, one last shot at something approaching the life she had hoped for.

"I don't know that he takes the interest in the Lodge that he once did. And I always say that if you want to get something out, you must put something in."

I shall not describe the picture that rolled before my eyes featuring the gloomy headmaster and his voluminous consort. I went to the piano and played Mozart's Masonic Funeral Music. Then Molly got up with a great swish and played some Scott Joplin. Billy smoked a cigar and wore an expression as impenetrable as God's on the day before the first day of creation. It was after midnight when they left and the sky was still bright over Belmont moor. Molly kissed me – that no fuss, ordinary lass kiss – and said,

"He's really enjoyed himself tonight – better than I can remember. Well, we both have."

"Goodnight"

All under the high summer moon.

About a week later I was substituting for Mrs Gyte who was off school with a cracked something-or-other. 4X girls PE in the hall. They loved to tease with their gymnastic cabaret:

"D'you like taking 4X girls, Sir?" From the mouth of Pauline Squires, upside down on the wall bars.

"You ought to be X-rated by the BBC."

"The BBC, Sir?"

"Barnes Board of Censorship."

And behold, he appeared at that very instant carrying a long brown envelope.

"I hope the girls are no trouble to you, Mr Mullen?"

"Not in any way, Sir."

His face was folded again into that crinkly grin which, if you had not known him better, you might have construed as some small token of humour, of humanity even. He handed me the envelope and left.

"Have you got the sack, Sir?"

Jeanette Stewart doing sit-ups

The envelope contained a photocopied invitation to join the Bolton Lodge of Freemasons. Like an Unbirthday Present , it was an Uninvitation, for it began by saying that no one is ever invited to join the Freemasons. Then it proceeded to invite me by way of convoluted etiquette. I could almost hear the Mozart, see the bared kneecaps. Amanda Bagley nearly fell on me as she said,

"Look, Sir, I can do the flying angel!"

Next day I took the brown envelope back to him and said,

"I've always found the Masonic rituals very moving, but I think my connection with the brotherhood will never amount to anything more – you know aesthetic and – remembering the Mozart – musical."

He said, "I should very much like to borrow your gramophone records of the Masonic cantatas."

Then, as if all that had gone before had been some sort of set-piece, a formality to be done with, he said,

"Here's something I'd like you to do for the school, and it won't do your career any harm either."

It was as if he could not quite put out of his mind the masonic references. And the consolation prize came in a bigger envelope than that which had enclosed the bounty of the Uninvitation. It was the prospectus for a Bolton Education Authority course entitled

Education in a Multicultural Society to be held second week in July in the Teachers' Centre. He said,

"It'll mean the whole week out of school – and of course you'll receive your full expenses."

I couldn't estimate what proportions of gratitude and regret should sound in my voice.

"Twenty years in this purgatory and I've never been asked to go on a course, Peter – no, not even for half a day. The Powers-that-Be must be grooming you for higher things...."

This was John Davies for all the staffroom to hear.

"... and the geography teacher has been selected too."

True. The community orientated social geography geography teacher had petitioned Barnes to start a Community Service scheme in school. Miraculously, he had agreed. As she told me, he had called her in and said,

"Since half the potential burglars you'll be taking out with you to do old ladies' shopping will be black or brown, you'd better have a look at this."

This was an envelope just like the one he had given me.

The course was all bureaucratic tomfoolery and a bit of showbiz to promote Education Department policies – which, you soon discovered, were brought into being to promote Departmental Functionaries, their careers and their egos. Promoted to what? To their removal into an Educational Authority housed in a yet more salubrious and coveted area within the Nationwide Advisory Service and to the reward of the extra point on the Burnham Teachers' Scale: that ladder of perfection. And that was how the geography teacher and I came to be sitting in that carpeted oven at the Teachers' Centre, listening to the Chief Adviser reading from the Race Relations Act.

These educational professionals were even more infantilised than the bishops and the Synod, and just as politically entrenched. The second morning, we all had to colour our faces as if we were Indians or blacks and wander around Bolton in search of racial abuse. It was culture shock of a sort to see the aged needlework mistress from Upper Crompton Secondary School coming out of Yates' Wine Lodge with a fag in her mouth and wearing a sari.

In the afternoon we were talked to in Russian so that we might learn alienation and what it was like to be strangers in a strange land. Russian was easier to understand than the jargon-infested paper read to us on the subject of Racial and Cultural Stereotyping in the Multiethnic Society. It was all stereotypes and so metropolitically left wing it set your teeth on edge. To defer sleep in the late afternoon, I kept trying to set whole tracts of the speeches to tunes from songs from the shows:

Some young coloured immigrants

Feel an ali-en-a-tion

That sort of thing.

On the last day we went into a workshop in which we were all made to stand around the walls. Then each person had to run full pelt at the person directly opposite who was instructed first to gently arrest the other individual's progress and then demonstrate by the use of non-linguistic signs your welcome for that individual. Buy me and stop one. Somehow this circus was meant to be an exercise in fostering mutual trust. What we got were a few bruises. Apart from that, it would not do to describe the nature of some of the collisions which took place in too much detail. Anyhow, a lot of drink was drunk over lunch and we sat all afternoon hunched and dozing over our ballpoints as we were obliged, just like kids returned from the school trip, to write up what we had learnt from the role play. These reports were not to be works of individual genius but the correlated responses of the group as a whole. A whole week's bollocks courtesy of the Bolton ratepayers.

At the end of the afternoon, each group had to elect a reporter who would then speak for them all. I spoke for our group. I drove the thing so far into the realms of surreality and hyperbole that I ended up getting myself taken seriously, to the extent that, after the final session, the Senior Educational Adviser came across and said:

"Peter – you don't mind my calling you by your Christian name?"

(He could call me by my Amerindian or Polynesian name if he wished)

"...er Peter, 'er, I wonder... I mean, I think you would be very useful on one of our ALSEB sub-committees."

ALSEB? Associated Lancashire Schools Education Board –

except they were spelling board wrongly. Actually to be asked by a Senior Educational Adviser – an apparatchik from the office – to join a committee – sorry, a sub-committee – was a privilege for which most of my colleagues would have given the last sheet of paper from their clipboard.

In the long holiday I stayed in my father's caravan on Baildon Moor. I got pecked by a hen. I went to watch Yorkshire play Surrey at Headingley and in the evenings read The Brothers Karamazov. Night after night the sunset turned the sky over the valley a blaze of red and orange, with uncanny blue and green flashes and I wondered if these could be the northern lights. From the high moorland the view was down to the Victorian mill town built by Titus Salt on the banks of the river Aire, and so rationally named Saltaire. Decent houses for the workers, public baths, evening classes and a Nonconformist church – all paid for privately by Salt.

Pathetically, I was morose and sorry for myself. Thirty-two years old and sick to death of going through the motions. In this spoilt brat mentality, it seemed to me that, though there was usefulness and even enjoyment in being a parson and a teacher, there was also too much sheer tedium. And waste of time: the investing of trivia with phoney importance. Looking at the Girl Guides. staff meetings. It was all summed up really in that dispiriting acronym ALSEB: A Lengthy Session of Exasperating Bollocks.

That waste of time rose up before me like the bilious sky in a storm over Baildon Moor and I was sick. Twice I was sick among the trees beyond the camp site. All that phoney importance rolled over me like the damp mist that stretched down from the scudding clouds.

"All over Yorkshire," I said aloud like a mad man "all over Yorkshire fast clouds dropping dampness, going nowhere."

I was going nowhere, dropping dampness.

And yet night after night the air cleared and the sky burnt orange like an open oven. Clouds and fire. I read Hamlet and concluded that it's not that talking to yourself is a sign of madness, but too much talking to yourself is what makes you go mad. I was talking to myself too much. I was half mad. Hawks and handsaws. Clouds and fire. I said:

"Sir Titus Salt built Saltaire for his workers. Benevolent capitalism. An enlightened man."

And the rain came on again.

I stood under a tree and listened to the rain like applause and the thunder moderating far away over Leeds. Titus Salt and his men together made up a sort of unity, a sort of sense, as no doubt Titus Oates had thought he was doing with his gang.

"Timothy, Timothy, Titus, Philemon, Peter, Peter, John, John, John, Jude, Revelation."

Unhinged. The mind ran on, ever more desultory. Broadstairs and his vision of the Kingdom of Heaven as a vainglorious amalgamation of all the holy clubs in Crossgates. The Senior Adviser and ALSEB. They actually took these things seriously! Part of the time, I craved to be like them. I wanted to lose myself. To belong. But I didn't belong. I was only looking in on them like a stranger peering out of the darkness into the lights of a family Christmas. I was sick of merely moving among normal people, observing myself observing their absurdity. And of course I was overwhelmed with guilt for thinking these good and useful people, and their dutiful activities, absurd. At least they were doing something useful. They had a life, continuity...

Well now, I'll just total 4Y's dinner money and get ready for my ALSEB meeting....Janet Parker got 79% in the French oral... Broadstairs went on holiday in August...a Sacrament is an outward and visible sign of an inward and spiritual grace...the geography mistress is having a damp course put in. So what!

Mullen, you should be ashamed of yourself for such arrogant solipsism! Remember George Herbert: Who sweeps a room as for thy laws makes that and the action fine. Just who the hell d'you think you are Mullen!

The tops of the distant trees were gone now into the twilight. Street lights like a printed circuit stretched three miles away over Saltaire and the environs of Bradford. Saltaire and the environs of Bradford! Cappadocia and the country about Cyrene. Parthians, Medes, Mesopotamians, Elamites... And all the rest.

"And you think that's so clever?"

It's not always possible to tell who's talking.

Bradford had trolley buses once. Trolley buses. Trolley buses. And streets with Bradfordish names, different from Leeds. Woollen. Houses in stone, not redbrick. Liverpool had been only an oily mist.

All this among the dripping trees and past the pecking hens which had now gone to sleep. Purposeful activity of Dad's, that – to buy a caravan. Blue and cream wedged in by stones.

"That's its base, you see. A caravan has to have a proper base. And it has to be inlaid."

If you stared, the distant street lights came closer. They changed from red at twilight to the sulphurous yellow they burned all night.

"Or so they reckon...well, when I say all night...they reckon they're switched off an hour before sunrise. That's if we get any sun. Ha! Ha! Ha!"

No need to be so selfish. The caravan smells like plastic in the night. You can lie there, flat. The lights are still there, a string of magic beads over the fairyland of Sir Titus Salt. The salt of the earth. The lights are still there even when you're not looking. I had found something like a stone in my belly. I had no idea what it was but it never went away. I began to call it the central disturbance.

"Why?"

In the deep, dark silence of Baildon Moor:

"Why not write?"

"Write what?"

"Why?"

"Why not?"

"Why not write a book about Philosophy for the kids?"

"A simple book."

"There is one already. It's called Philosophy Made Simple by Richard Henry Popkin and Avrum Stroll."

"Sounds bloody American!"

"It is."

"There's no need to sound so disparaging. Why are you always so sour?"

"How To Do Philosophy."

"How To Undo Philosophy."

"Too gimmicky. The publishers won't wear that, you'll see."

"Too gimmicky."

"Won't wear it."

The pub stays open until past one o'clock and the caravaners come back pissed and singing. They have had a good time. It's not far from Wuthering Heights up here.

XV

Eternity in Less Than an Hour: The Fifty Pence Philosophy Course
Plato held the idea
That the idea held Plato
Jean Paul Sartre
The French fartre
(Following Descartes)
Declared one philosophical banker:
"Hell is other people."
Did he believe he was heaven?
What a wanker!
Kant said we ought
To pre-think thought;
Set down the conditions
In three admonitions:
"For all the human race,
There are cause, time and space."
Now he basks in God's glory
For inventing synthetic a priori
Hegel had a thesis,
He also had a cat;
The thesis spawned antithesis,
The cat, she ate a rat.
Indigestible synthesis
Sicked up in every place
While Hegel said, "We must press on
Through this Absolute disgrace."
Kierkegaard is hard.
He thinks less than nought
Of thought.
He has thought this for ages
In thousands of pages.
His finest one-liner is

"Vivat Regina!"
Hume had no room
For laws or cause.
He said to his mother,
"It's just one damn thing after another!"
Believing only in constant conjunction,
He deprecated Extreme Unction
Russell's perverse irregularity
Preferred the appearance above the reality.
He loudly addressed the Bloomsbury waiter,
"Your table is only a pile of sense-data –
Besides, there's a fly in my soup!"
The waiter replied, "That speck is no fly,
But only a perceptual trick of the eye."
Russell made answer, "That's all very well;
Now pick up the phone, get me Lady Morrell.
I sense an empirical change in my luck:
She's promised a logical-positive fuck.
Wittgenstein asked, "Had the phone rung?"
Frege said, "Is that Sinn or Bedeutung?"
He answered, "Sir, with the utmost deference,
That telephone requires no reference,
Nor ontology abstruse,
For its meaning is its use."
Philosophy today is all the same:
One interminable language-game,
Thanks to those two pals of mine:
Gottlob Frege and Wittgenstein.
"God is dead; beat the wife;
Fill your head with war and strife;
Disdain your fellow men as swine;
Carry a whip and don't drink wine."
Nietzsche then went mad and laughed;
(he called this frohliche Wissenschaft)
If you can copy him and think it fun,
You'll be an Ubermensch my son.
Arthur's philosophy comes in layers,

(He threw a woman down the stairs).
He said, "This sound advice I give –
Lie down, reduce the will to live;
Fear not to die, give up the ghost,
For life, not death, holds terrors most;
And when you're dead, you have no yen
To be wakened up again."
The woman lies now where Schopenhauer's bell hung
Clutching a copy of Die Welt als Wille und Vorstellung

I began the philosophy book in September, writing in agitated spare moments at school, in the small back bedroom and, now and then, in the local on Darwen Road – which was only thirty-nine paces from my front door – the most miserable pub in the world.

Casting for Toad of Toad Hall took less than five minutes during morning break. Dorothy showed me the music set for it. I said,

"It's fey. Not what you'd call music for listening to. May I try and write a few songs myself?"

That was how I got to play the Steinway. Pixie-face Jill directed rehearsals. Her short skirt looked even shorter, and her legs even more infinite, when she was up on the stage and you were at floor level. We were assisted by a good-natured, half-reformed hippie whose name I forget. He had been awarded a degree in philosophy by a circuitous route: The University of London via Bolton Institute of Technology which was widely known among its members – by self-conscious parody of the Massachusetts Institute of Technology – as BIT.

The term passed in chronic amateur theatrical panic. God it was wearing. The kids either couldn't learn their lines or, in the case of the ebullient thirteen-year-old spiv Russell Campbell, they ad libbed until you ended up doing a different play. I took one night off and drove Jill to Leeds Town Hall to hear Schubert's Third Symphony and Clifford Curzon playing the K. 488. Toad was a surprising hit. At the Leavers' Lunch on the penultimate day, Billy Barnes beamed and then asked,

"What operatic delight will you and Mrs Bedford give us next year?"

In my mixed madness of end-of-run anticlimax and end of term euphoria, I said, The Magic Flute.

Barnes didn't seem to hear me. He was out of place at parties. To see him pulling a Christmas cracker was like watching someone perform an obscene act, with reluctance. It was a beguiling lunch nonetheless, held at the Smithills Coaching House – a place off Moss Bank Way, with cartwheels in the cobbled yard in front of the old stables, and chicken-in-a basket in the so-called cocktail bar. Acting entirely out of character, Barnes himself had instituted this event in an earlier age of innocency signifying and representing the coming almost of age of the pupils who were leaving. It was the one time in the year when Billy Barnes demonstrated a latitudinarianism that was utterly obsessive. The pupils would not only be allowed to drink responsibly: they would be compelled to do so. Having treated them for the previous five years as if they had been recruits to the kindergarten, he now proposed to regard them as fully-fledged citizens with all the rights and privileges thereunto attached: including the celebrated right to get pissed and throw up.

The headmaster promenaded post-prandially among the tables, engaging in sophisticated conversation with pupils who, only a matter of weeks before – days, in one case – had stood awaiting his chastisement for going out of bounds at lunchtime. Form teachers had for weeks cautioned the Fifth Year concerning etiquette on this auspicious day. There was Mr Thompson's gently-expressed hope that he wanted

"...to see you all behaving like young ladies and young gentlemen"

Nicely contrasting with Philip Oliver's laconic threat,

"Woe betide anyone who comes back pissed or pregnant!"

Back in school, Philip was for once upstaged – and by the deputy head, no less. For weeks Max had been fulminating against Sharon Wilks, a pert and self-assured girl in 4X, for wearing earrings. Just before the bell for the last lesson, Max walked past Sharon in the corridor and saw, as he put it,

"...those great hideous green globes dangling."

He shouted loud enough to have been heard in Bolton town centre,

"Sharon, get them off!"

Well, you can imagine...

I finished the philosophy book in the Christmas holidays, mainly, over pints of Holt's bitter in The Black Dog under Belmont Moor, half my time staring out at the high television mast poking through the clinging mist. There was something else philosophical, aside from my book. One Friday afternoon I had the misfortune to have to sit in on the school's latest and ugliest cast of miscreants, 5P (boys). Their famed apathy was Zen-like. But occasionally one would goad another just too far and thuggishness would break out. Today it was Michael Hargrave's turn to compete for the Yob of the Month Award. Swearing, shouting, spitting. The others looking on in a sort of truculent daze. I grabbed him and said,

"Look here, Hargraves, I'm fed up with you. You're so stupid you don't even know you exist!"

Such serendipity! The Lord had delivered them into my hands. One lad half arisen from his dogmatic slumbers said,

"How can you prove you exist, Sir?"

And that was it. Beginning philosophy. I chucked a few chestnuts at them including,

"Is a red rose still red in the dark?" and "Is this a proper question?"

Suddenly they were all mine. They petitioned to be allowed to come back after school for more of the same. They called these sessions "Boggling lessons." Almost as if "Tell us how f't get VD, Sir" were transformed into "Tell us how f't understand the Ontological Argument, Sir."

So, with the aim of attracting a publisher for my book, I submitted an article to The Times Educational Supplement on my experience of introducing philosophy to schoolchildren. A fortnight later I got my very first rejection slip. So I sent the piece to the Tuesday Guardian Education. They published it and within a week I had received sixty-seven letters in reply, including an offer to publish my book from Mr Nicolas McDowall of Edward Arnold (Publishers) Ltd of 25 Hill Street in Mayfair. My manuscript was reviewed by two readers and within the month I had signed my contract. There were stuttering letters between McDowall and me in which we bickered good-naturedly over the title. My Baildon Moor prophecy had come true:

"But you can't call it How to Undo Philosophy – far too gimmicky."

I managed to protest his kiss-of-death alternative, An Introduction to Philosophical Analysis and we settled on Beginning Philosophy.

All that year my ALSEB committee meetings progressed like a cancer of the spirit and another of the multitudinous Educational

Advisers – of the increase of their governance there is no end – persuaded the geography teacher and me to start an Asian Studies course. Bolton was full of Asians – Indians, mainly – chucked out of Uganda by the malevolent idiot Amin. They were of the educated middle class and they took to Bolton like Roman administrators colonising some barbaric outpost. They rose in local government and politics, to the massive benefit of the borough. The children were attentive, biddable and hardworking. The boys chubby and round-faced. The slim girls all silky elegance. The Hindu weddings and Diwali celebrations lit up Bolton like a starburst.

The seminars appointed to set up the Asian Studies course gathered none of this verve and glamour. They were all memos and draft syllabuses, but when the Community Relations Officer – a dapper little Anglo-Indian agitprop Trotskyist - was roped in, The Bolton Evening News sniffed a nice, juicy racism story and asked the Senior Education Officer for a statement. He told them that multiracial education was a necessity,

"....because so many Ugandan Asians had come to live in the town."

The paper printed his remarks with the result that Advisers, teachers, parents, religious leaders and anyone else who could be clubbed on to a committee got together to form The Bolton Association for Multiracial Education and I was singled out to be its first chairman. I had no idea a committee could be so exciting. We held our inaugural meeting in the Town Hall and the National Front arrived to spit and snarl. Interestingly, the NF divided themselves into two groups. There was the intellectual section which numbered about six people in jeans or battle dress who sat on the front row and observed from time that they wanted

"...no niggers in Bolton."

An effervescent little Indian off licence manager provoked cheers and hilarity when he cried out melodiously,

"But Mr Chairman, I'm not a nigger; I'm a wog!"

And then there was the less polite section of the NF who rumbled around the back of the hall, disrupting the meeting and lurking in the exits to beat up its members on their way home. The local Trotskyists, who numbered quite a few schoolteachers in their company, turned up in the hope of a fight. They combined in a slovenly heap to exchange socio-political clichés such as consciousness-raising and alienation and the occasional cultural interjection fascist scum!

Undiscouraged, a cheerful Indian doctor, Asim Chakrabarti from Oldham, made a friendship and co-operation speech which was responded to in impenetrable jargon by the Chief Educational Adviser. At half past nine I declared the meeting closed, took out my handkerchief and wiped the NF spit off my lapels and sleeves. Getting out safely was not going to be easy. The NF and the Trots circled the hall and each other as if in some nasty version of the children's party game, The Stars Go Round and Around. And we would not have got out without a fight, had it not been for the prompt appearance of half a dozen burly men who took control of the porch and the exit. They never spoke, but just shooed us out – by us I mean the platform party: Chakrabarti, the Chief Adviser and me.

Uniformed policemen held doors open and wished us Goodnight as we left. The burly men – I discovered later they were Special Branch – were no longer to be seen. Next day the Bolton Evening News reported that our meeting had passed off without major disturbance. As it happened, the newspaper had got it about right.

Around this time, Nicolas McDowell wrote me a serendipitous letter: would I be interested in/had I ever had any experience of producing material for school assemblies? Had I had any experience? Had I not stood up every morning before the drowsy multitude for as long as anyone could remember! Nicolas wanted a book of short, hand-me-down talks for busy teachers.

"How many talks do you need, Nicolas?"

"About a hundred."

Whimsical, laconic pieces with titles such as The Head of Peter Tchaikovsky, Stripey White Lines Don't Hurt as Much as Buses and Christmas Humphreys Uses Brass Door Knobs. We called the book Assembling and Nicolas published it within a couple of months of my submitting the manuscript. The busy teachers took to it and there was demand for a sequel.

"Shall we call it More Talks for School Assemblies?" said Nicolas.

"Why not Carry On Assembling with a picture of Barbara Windsor topless on the front?"

It got called Assembling Again. Headteachers in Bolton, Rochdale and Accrington – and one in Keswick – invited me to visit their schools and introduce my books to the teachers. Well – blazes! – how much spoon-feeding to these pedagogues require? Those two books contained a hundred talks apiece, the text of each talk taking up a single page and containing few words that your averagely dull thirteen- year-old just might fail to understand. Still, I did accept the invitation to Keswick which gave me a day in the Lakes.

The Magic Flute was enchanting. Gorgeous, delinquent Fifth year girls took turns at miming The Queen of the Night to the hi tech bought-in sound system, and plump Indian lads played the Three Boys;

Drei Knabchen jung, schon, hold und weise... Except they sang it in English, a lilting sort of chapatti English. All Wohltatigheit and the aroma of curry. For weeks the corridors were full of kids' whistling of Papageno's arias and the Educational Advisers attended performances and made noises of theoretical approbation. Barnes said,

"What will you do to follow this next year, Peter?"

"The Ring of the Nibelungen"

Not even he could have thought I was serious.

He took me into his office towards the year's end and sneaked me a whisky out of his secret drawer.

"You know, Peter, I can see a career developing for you."

So could I. It was marked ALSEB and Admin. Multicutural Studies Committee. Educational Theory. Possibly becoming a Deputy Head. Timetabling. Rosters. More Admin. Bigger ALSEB. I was already up to my neck in the quicksand of bureaucratic teacher-speak. A letter from Broadcasting House:

"Through your publishing of educational material, your name has come to the attention of the Schools Broadcasting Council of the United Kingdom...."

Another committee. It met three times a year in the conference room on the first floor of Broadcasting House. The oak panels. The oval table. The huge, disdaining portrait of Sir John Reith. The agenda papers were a foot thick. The delegates were thicker. Half the topics for discussion were ploughed through before the taking of lunch in the BBC canteen, then we returned sedated to plough through the other half. Nothing tangible was ever achieved. What did Eliot say? – Tumid apathy with no concentration;

men and bits of paper. They were all developing their careers – just as Billy Barnes had wanted me to develop mine. Well, the Schools Broadcasting Council gave me three days a year in London, paid for by the BBC. And I did once spend a fascinating twenty minutes with Robert Robinson in the canteen.

I tried to stay awake by actually raising a matter of practical policy. I said,

"The schools' music syllabus is a disgrace. Pupils hear nothing of the western classical tradition and instead they're just encouraged to use any bit of metal or wood they can lay their hands on and make a noise with it. I don't call that music. I call it Bang it and Listen."

They were not pleased:

"I thought your membership of this Council, Mr Mullen, was for your experience as an RE teacher?"

"O for God's sake, let no one step outside the tramlines!"

"In the music syllabus we are trying to cultivate creativity. Not passive listening, but getting the pupils to create music for themselves."

"But it isn't music. It's just haphazard. A cacophony. Anyhow, no one can create music until they know something about music. Give them digestible chunks of Handel, Purcell, Mozart and Haydn and you might hope to interest them."

The Chairman adjourned the meeting for lunch.

The philosophy book earned me a day trip to Skipton Grammar School and a refreshing couple of sessions with the Sixth Form, ruminating on what, for Aristotle, makes a good man.

"Or a good woman, Sir!"

"What are you doing for lunch, Sir? You don't want to go into school dinners. The Sixth are allowed into town. The best pork pie shop in the world, Sir. Come with us!"

And she was right. The ancient market town. The pastel green of the fields rising into the higher dale towards Grassington and Malham Cove. And the outcrops of limestone rock. New lambs. And away behind Settle, Mount Ingleborough in millstone grit, Pen-y-Ghent and Whernside. The Sixth Formers such cheerful company. It was better than ALSEB. It beat the Schools Council zombies any day.

So my dog collar had got me into the Multicultural Committee. The Multicultural Committee had got me further up the greasy pole in ALSEB. My philosophy book and my assembly talks had got me on to the Schools Broadcasting Council. I wanted none of it.

I decided to leave Whitecroft

XVI

So I wrote, with a hangover and at half past four in the morning, to Rt Rev'd Stuart Blanch, Archbishop of York. I reminded him of the time when, cricketing for my college, I had caught him (Principal of his college) for a duck at gully off the bowling of Mike Shearing. I hoped the Archbishop wouldn't hold this against me as I asked him if he would appoint me to a parish in the York Archdiocese. He wrote back:

"I remember the catch and Shearing. Didn't you used to call him Regius Professor of Indecision?"

Dr Blanch put me in touch with my old college Principal, daft old Arthur Widdess – the one with the young son and his Greek verbs. Arthur at that time was Canon Treasurer of York Minster. All compulsive rapid blinking and evangelical smiles. When he was thinking hard about anything, he really did scratch the back of his head – and so vigorously you thought it would bring all the sawdust out. Arthur introduced me to his boss, The Very Rev'd Dr Ronald Claude Dudley Jasper, Dean of York and Chairman of the Liturgical Commission which spent its time sidelining The Book of Common Prayer and producing substitutes in the form of sub-literary liturgical booklets.

"Dr Jasper do not touch it!"

But I said no such thing as I reclined on a vast sofa in the Deanery. They would need a sofa like that, given the size of Mrs Jasper who just then arrived on the scene in a dress that made her look like a decorated barrel of flowers.

RGDJ's face and pate were like waxed plastic. He went about with his mouth slightly open and his lips turned downwards, as if he was in constant pain. He wore his black clerical cloak. Tweedledum.

"Arthur tells me you did very well in Doctrine and Old Testament Theology."

"It's a long time ago, Dean."

"Nevertheless, nevertheless...Doctrine and Old Testament Theology."

"And Greek," chipped in Arthur, broadening that evangelical grin.

"And Greek...and Greek," said the Dean and I thought I could have had him for repetition.

In February 1977 a parish was offered to me under a red letterhead of the Very Rev'd. It was a plurality: two churches and three villages nine miles to the west of York on the B1224 Wetherby Road: Tockwith and Bilton with Bickerton. Tockwith was a village of some four hundred people and the church, dedicated to the Epiphany, was a large example of the Gothic Revival just prior to its final and phantasmagoric phase.

"Legend has it," the organist Tim Tunnard told me in The Chequers Inn "that the rich old lady who had paid for it to be built turned up in her coach on the day of its consecration in 1866, clapped eyes on the tower and said, 'Have I paid for that pepper pot?' turned round and never entered the place in her life."

Tockwith's wartime airstrip – Lancaster bombers – was the site for a new housing development adjacent the old village. The incomers – businessmen commuting to Leeds and their fastidious and bored to death wives – were known to the traditional farming folk as "...them as lives on't drome." The vicarage was a cavernous modern bungalow opposite the church. I often walked to my other church, sacred to St Helen in Bilton, two miles through the fields. Butterflies, skylarks, the mist melting into clear sunlight and country calm.

St Helen, who had embarked on a mission to discover the true Cross, was the mother of Constantine the Great who was proclaimed emperor at York in AD 306. The Vale of York is thick with Roman remains. There were Saxon crosses in St Helen's, proving that there had been a church on the site for more than a thousand years. And there were relics of the 1644 Civil War Battle of Marston Moor when the Royalist Rupert was crushed by the Ironsides. Cromwell's army kept prisoners in the church and on the door dating from 1633 – known as the new door – they had carved with their bayonets caricature figures of King Charles I

As the date for my leaving Whitecroft drew closer, I declined into a schizoid mood. I knew I needed to get out, but I didn't want to go. The friendly aspect of the school intensified. I became shockingly aware that I was leaving not just friends behind, but a whole routine

– assembly, register, dinner- money, the day sliced nicely into periods, sports, outings with the children – which had grown a personality of its own. Kids have a way of coming right out with it. So Susan Greensmith put up her hand in an English lesson and said,

"Why are you leaving us, Sir? Don't you like us anymore?"

Caught me on the raw, that did.

I drove out for the last time to Belmont Moor and climbed the springy turf of Winter Hill to the television mast which looked down from 1500 feet over all Bolton and away south to smoky Manchester. Turn to face north-east and you saw the witches' hill called Pendle and, on a fine day, the black anvil shape of Ingleborough. High, moist, windy Lancashire with the clouds making fast-changing patterns across the fells. I had come to love it, to feel at home there. Though it was a different world from the rolled-out flatness of the Vale of York, low-lying, conducive to chest complaints.

The wind hummed through the TV mast. The evening was cool, iridescent, like a water colour. The Blue Lagoon reservoir lay like a pool of black ink at the foot of the hill. The only unrounded shape for miles was the steeple of Belmont Parish Church, pointing like an umpire's finger. I knew suddenly I should not leave this county and this job. I knew also that I must get out and face something new. I shivered. I was crying.

"Don't be so soft!"

I set off down the hill for a pint or two in The Black Dog.

As the custom was, I took cream cakes to the Staff Room on the last day. Billy Barnes was all valedictory twinkle, but his rhetoric of nostalgia was only a veneer over layers of stoic triumph which very definitely proclaimed:

"Teachers come and teachers go, but I go on forever!"

There was an antic cockiness in the way he walked. Soon after four o'clock the place emptied and I sat alone in that silent, sweaty atmosphere for the last time. It was only another Friday to everyone else. I opened the Staff Room door and walked out on to the landing. I listened to their footsteps clattering in the well of the stairs and watched from the window as they carried briefcases and piles of exercise books towards parked cars. Someone had left his school blazer in the dust by the gate. I remembered John Davies' words from years back:

"Kids can lose any item of clothing. Mine forget their trousers – honestly!"

Then there was only the sound of the cleaners' brooms knocking against the walls of the corridors below. A few grunts and shouts from Roy Platt's PE Club in the hall. The geography teacher kissed me on the cheek and said,

"You lucky sod, Mullen – getting out!"

I didn't feel like a lucky sod as I drove home along Moss Bank Way to complete my packing.

The removal men managed not to drop my piano but they did let the antique fridge roll off the back of the van and hold up traffic in the middle of Bolton. I saw everything on to the van and then set off for Yorkshire. Would I see the centre of Bolton again? There was the town hall, a lookalike for Leeds town hall. The Octagon Theatre. The Parish Church in golden stone. The Indian grocers' shops on every corner. Soon I was on the M62 and ahead the Pennines were saturated, lost in mist.

The appointment of Anglican clergymen to their parishes is a fearful muddle and a mystery. I knew an old lady who believed that God's finger wrote by night the names of those he had chosen on the notice-boards in the universities of Oxford and Cambridge. The reality is more mundane and more complicated. Parish churches were historically provided by the local landed gentry who were thus called Patrons of the various livings into which parsons were inducted and, as they say, beneficed. There is not much private patronage of this sort left in today's Church of England. The bishops fancy themselves as sole rulers of the whole church and so they have relentlessly coveted patronage of the livings and contrived, sometimes by fair means but usually foul, to acquire it. The appointments issue is further complicated by the fact that each parish has its churchwardens – men and women whose office dates from medieval times – who must agree with the Patron on the choice of candidate, who is then presented to the diocesan bishop for his spiritual approval. The bishop then fixes the date for the Induction of the parish priest into the living – very likely the only time in his incumbency that the priest will see his church full.

The priest kneels before the bishop who intones,

"Receive ye the cure of souls which is both thine and mine."

Well, in my day this form from The Book of Common Prayer was still in use in a few parishes. God knows what form of atrocity has replaced those words in the thoroughly modernised C. of E.

Among the two hundred or so who crammed into the little church, there came from Crossgates Broadstairs himself, looking more frail, as if he had been worn threadbare by all those thousands of lookings in on the Young Wives and the Girl Guides. Afterwards at the bun fight, he muttered laconically with his mouth full of sponge cake:

"The cure that is thine and mine, eh? Well, once tonight's over, you'll find it's well and truly thine!"

I had of course previously met the people – or at least that representation of them who turned up at the churchwardens' invitation to meet the new Vicar. This was in The Grange which belonged to Mrs Smith of Samuel Smith's Brewery (Tadcaster) Ltd. She lived elsewhere and the house was let to Tom and Pat Lovell who had taken in refugees from Eastern Europe after the war as part of a scheme called The Ockenden Venture.

We were in a large room with a billiards table and a broad, high window looking out into the trees. As soon as I sat down, the sun came out and dazzled me so that the faces of my interrogators could hardly be discerned through the dusty beams of light. About thirty locals sat there staring at me as if I had been some exotic fish caught in alien waters. I remembered Geoff Allen saying a long time ago:

"Parishes are all the same when it comes to appointing a new Vicar: they all want a married archangel with four children."

Farmer William Pick, a patriarch with a wooden leg, spoke out of the effulgence. He sounded distressed:

"But, Vicar, we hear you've lived in Oldham. Won't you miss the bright lights?"

No one laughed. I remembered the gloomy dampness of St Mary's estate:

"Bright lights? They've barely got street lights in Oldham."

Then they laughed.

Tom Pick – William's brother – spoke in a melodious baritone:

"But they know how to make black pudding in Oldham!"

There was a disquisition on this delicacy and other sweetmeats which lasted a quarter of an hour and even then was only concluded by an aleatoric interruption from Hilda Nicholson:

"Are you against cards, Vicar? D'you think whist is sinful?"

"Can be. Depends who your partner is!"

No laughter this time. It turned out that my predecessor had been an extreme Conservative Evangelical – or, in ordinary English, a religious nutter.

"He banned whist drives from the village. Wouldn't let us have 'em. Not no way. One day he came into the hall and shouted at a lady in front of everyone for bringing a bottle of sherry as a raffle prize."

"Did he disapprove of the sherry or the raffle?"

"Both. Anyhow, she threw the bottle at him. It missed and splattered all over the wall."

There was a sudden upturn in the quality of the conversation as Tim Tunnard, former Master of the Music at Birmingham cathedral and recently retired Her Majesty's Inspector of Schools, said:

"What you do in church won't matter half as much as what you do in the village, Peter. Country folk are pagans, you know. It's the same all down the eastern side of England."

All said with the combined mischievousness of Emanuel Schikaneder and Mr Punch. And what he said is true. Lancashire, with its Irish connections, has always been more Catholic than Yorkshire which owes much of its character to dour invaders from northern Europe. And Lancashire was not just Roman Catholic, but Anglo-catholic too: what they call High Church. At Pat Lovell's there followed tea and too many country pastries. It was raining when I left. All Wetherby racecourse steaming in the dampness.

"Very low lying," as Tom Pick had said. His wife Margaret from Devon added,

"Bad for coughs and colds. Chestiness."

Margaret had the same intonation for everything. A post-matriarchal Methodist who could read a shopping list as if it were a solemn warning. You felt a nameless guiltiness if you merely looked at her. There was always a remonstrative note in her voice. She had been my predecessor's biggest fan.

The farms of William and Tom Pick lay adjacent. They had been one farm until their father had died in the 1930s and split the property between the brothers in his will. There persisted a low key feud between them – though it was not so much the men as their wives who were at each other's throat. William's wife Jean was an iron-willed country woman: the sort who, if she had lived in Canada, would have cultivated the hobby of strangling grizzlies with her bare hands. Her flintiness had saved her husband's life. William – Bill – had been in the habit of carrying his gun when he went out on the tractor. One day he accidentally shot himself in the leg and lost nearly all his blood. In hospital they took his leg off but said there was not much they could do for him. He was expected to die. Whereupon, Jean took him home in a taxi and nursed him back to health. Within six months he was out on his land again.

I have an odd tale to tell connected with Bill Pick. The night before I first went to Bilton to meet the people, I dreamt I was being shown round an L-shaped village by a man with a limp. I discovered that was indeed the shape of the place – and my guide between church and The Chequers pub turned out to be Bill Pick.

Next morning I drove to the nearby village of Long Marston to meet the Rural Dean. Rev'd Arthur Mace, a dapper seventy-year-old with the sort of clipped nasal accent that goes with Spitfires and Brylcreem. He made instant coffee and brought in the cups rattling in their saucers. Arthur was trainspotter first and Rural Dean second. He called me Mullen, which made me feel I was back at school.

"Your biggest job in Tockwith, Mullen, will be to get the Watts family back. An excellent fellow, Jim Watts. Fell out with your predecessor though. An ugly scene in church by all accounts. One of Mr Watkins' hell fire sermons, I believe, and they ended up shouting and screaming at each other across the nave. Watts took the whole family to worship elsewhere – Green Hammerton, I think. Get them back, there's a good man."

I drove back across Marston Moor and past the monument to the 1644 battle. In Tockwith, I called in The Boot and Shoe for a pint of Sam Smith's. The wiry, sallow landlord, Robin Firth, shouted into his living quarters:

"Marj – it's the new Vicar!"

Then he looked at me as if he suspected I was about to commit a felony:

"So you like a pint eh, Vicar? Not like the previous fellow."

I wondered just how long the shadow of my predecessor was going to turn out to be. Marjorie came in, gingering up her hairstyle with the tips of her fingers as she walked. She was in her late forties, the motherly sort and wearing the look of hunted withdrawal symptoms.

"Have this one on us. So you're from Leeds as well, are you? We kept The Gipton pub a long time."

"I know it – just down the road from Crossgates."

"Aye, but Crossgates is posh. Gipton is a shit heap – pardon my French – like an open air prison for all the trash and low life in Leeds. We enjoyed it there though, didn't we Robin. Got on very well with the local police. They were all regulars – especially the Chief Super.... Robin, did you order more spirits? You know what the pipe-liners are..."

All this without a pause. Marjorie stood with her back to the optics and used her left arm like a section of the Indian Rope Trick to squeeze out a triple gin for herself while talking avidly across the bar. The pipe-liners were employees of Laing Construction Co and they were laying a water pipe in the area – to provide that essential for them as lived on't drome. The pipe-liners' mobile homes and temporary office buildings littered the derelict aerodrome like the aftermath of a visiting fair. I got to meet them in due course and to learn their names – names like Stan Ironside and Glasgow Willis. They came in The Boot about six o'clock and drank until, the early hours – spirits by the bottle. Two of them rented a caravan in Robin and Marjorie's garden and she would take them their breakfast each morning: three pints each of draught lager to assuage the spirit-fuelled dehydration.

"Well," said Marj "have another. You're a change from that Reverend Watkins."

XVII

I had an appointment to see the Bishop of Selby at half past three. He lived at the sonorously named Tollgarth, 100 Tadcaster Road, York, opposite the Knavesmire racecourse. My impression was of a large detached house which had acquired the character of a vicarage by osmosis. Compare and contrast houses of the same age and size and you can always tell which one is the vicarage. The paintwork will be less bright. If there is a lawn, it will need cutting. Even the crockery will have a vaguely ecclesiastical look. An open fireplace with an electric fire in it, burning one bar. Dark curtains half-closed and damp, noisy dogs called Priscilla or and Ichabod. Other incontrovertible yet indefinable signs.

The bishop was the suffragan, or assistant, to the Archbishop of York. He looked too healthy. The Rt Rev'd Morris Maddocks (Mad Ox to his clergy). Fiftyish with a highly polished face and a grin that moved like elastic. His voice was of the unmistakeably evangelical-joyous sort, loud, almost a parody of the mid-Atlantic twang. As if he was Chief Public Relations Executive for an advertising company called God Unlimited Inc. He reminded me of the man in the newspaper advertisement from the days of my boyhood – the one who was after in the chocolate laxatives promotion. I had never seen anyone look so transcendentally gleeful.

"What the fuck are you grinning about?"

I didn't say this of course but my civil "Good afternoon" seemed endogenously depressed by the side of such wild happiness.

"Hello!" His "hell" was a lot shorter than his "o."

His arms wider than a shirt in a gale. He welcomed me to Tollgarth, to the Diocese of York and to the Kingdom of Heaven (Charismatic Christian Branch). It was the first time I had met one of these enthusiasts, though I had read about their growing influence – some sort of backlash against the sceptical, secularising trend of the 1960s, I was told. Fundamentalism and fun. Aisle-dancing to the twang of the liturgical guitar. There was a sort of mandatory optimism about this sort, recalling homilies such as Laughter Is The Best Medicine in Reader's Digest. I felt embarrassed for not being able to smile at the same intensity of the bishop on the Richter Scale.

He sat cross-legged, swinging his foot.

"Bless you! Bless you! Sit down! Bless you! So, my dear Peter, you've come to do the Lord's work in Tockwith. Bless you! Bless you!"

There were too many exclamation marks. I suppose I had come to do the Lord's work, but it sounded awkward to have it spelt out like that – as if giving oneself airs. His talk was the syntactical form of the steamroller. It made me feel guilty for not being able to join in and it took me back to dark sermons I had heard preached in the Methodist Chapel when I was a boy – sermons directed against those who denied the Lord. There was that picture of Jesus on the Chapel wall – the one in which the eyes followed you. Creepy. The zealous language was an emotional trap, a sort of rose-tinted auto da fe. A different world from Arthur Mace's gentlemanly Christian chat. In a word it was un-English. Well the aisle-dancing movement had started in the USA, and now it had stretched itself as far as the Tadcaster Road where it seemed ridiculous. But I was going to hear a lot more about it.

It was Mad Ox who had inducted me into the living. He was like a streak of neon. Such bright beams decorating his face you needed dark glasses. Is this what heaven's going to be like? I'm not sure I could stand too much of it. He recited the service in a prestissimo exclamatory style. Really, it was as if the words could not stand on their own feet and required to have meaning put into them. The sermon made up in length what it lacked in sanity and bored everyone silly and uncomfortable – especially those who, in the packed church, had to sit on the stone floor or stood hunched against pillars. The bishop's performance was like a Rossini overture – all froth and dash and postponed penultimate climax. He seized on the fact that the new President of the USA, the peanut farmer Jimmy Carter, was a born-again Christian. The lies and sleaze of the Nixon years would now be done away with and a new bright epoch would dawn in world affairs. The arrival of Maddocks and Carter was like a dress rehearsal for the Second Coming. The picture was of the whole world setting aside the superfluity of its naughtiness and raising its multiracial arms in a Charismatic wave. He stopped short (just) of announcing that the lion was about to lie down with the lamb. But born again only made me think of born yesterday. It seemed appropriate that the Induction was on 12th May – Tony Hancock's birthday.

The bun fight was in the new school at Tockwith. More late evening sunshine through the wide windows. An ample sports field with agreeable tokens of cricket. More booze back at the vicarage and the last guests departing at about 3am. It had begun to rain, aromatic, drenching rain through the still air. It rained and rained.

Parishioners turn out in their millions to attend the new vicar's Induction Service and the supper afterwards. This only serves to give the vicar false hopes. My first regular Sunday service at Tockwith was a nine o'clock celebration of Holy Communion – without music. I opened the church at half past eight, first unlocking the wire grille that had been put there to prevent birds fouling the porch. I set out the altar and sat in my stall listening to those very birds. Light streaming through the east window and making rainbow patterns on the floor of the chancel. The air was cool and fragrant. No traffic. Bucolic bliss. I was still on my own when the clock chimed the hour. At a minute past nine, two old ladies waddled up the aisle and sat together on the front row. They chattered throughout the service. It was surreal. I would say such as,

"...thy manifold and great mercies."

And one of the old girls, in a crisp echoing whisper, would respond with.

"Them flowers 'ave lasted well from Cartwrights' wedding."

"Forasmuch as without thee, we are not able to please thee..."

"Don't you think Steve Cartwright 's nose is too big for his face?

"...grant that thy Holy Spirit..."

"Dolly Entwistle's husband is messin' around with that Sheila Tracy"

"May in all things direct and rule our hearts."

Their chatter never stopped. It was as if half the liturgy had been written by Alan Bennett

Still, they were friendly enough to smile and squeeze my hand on the way out.

I had time for a slice of toast before driving to traditional rural Matins at St Helen's, Bilton at eleven o'clock where the nearest thing to a sacramental gesture was the solemn elevation of the collecting plate. The organist was Barry Carlill, village newsagent, and his playing was immaculate – but half speed. It took an age to get through the Psalm. And the Te Deum was tedium, with the chant doubled in length so, for instance, instead of "Thou art the King of Glory, O Christ", we got:

"Thou art the King of Glory: O...O...O...O....O CHRIST!"

The congregation fainting through hyper-ventiliation.

Evensong at Tockwith was a treat. Tim Tunnard played magnificently and I counted myself fortunate indeed that he had left Birmingham cathedral in the early 1970s, disgusted at the imposition of the awful modern services:

"The new words didn't fit the old tunes, so I left."

Tim played with panache and dazzling mischievousness.

But parish life in the country was not all birdsong and Bach and the evening sun lighting the great circle of the high west window. There was money to be raised - and forked out. In the days when the Church Commissioners were efficient, they had paid the stipends and pensions of all the clergy. But they developed the knack of making bad investments and so the parishes were invited to contribute to central funds. It was not an invitation you could decline. In a word, it was a tax and, as taxes generally do, it kept going up. It was called the Diocesan Quota.

It's staggering to recall that the Church Commissioners, on behalf of The Church of England, were one of the richest corporations in the country. They were also large landowners – second only to the Queen in fact. But they aspired to a towering incompetence in financial affairs, not only losing more than £1000,000,000 on the stock market, but also contriving to sell off most of the ancient vicarages at the bottom of the property market. So now when you see, beside countless numbers of 18th and 19th century houses, a sign saying The Old Vicarage, you must not expect to discover an old vicar inside: but rather a prosperous dentist or, very likely, a church architect. What truly beggars belief is that the Church Commissioners thus ruined the Church of which they were appointed custodians during the period when the stock market enjoyed its longest bull run of the 20th century. The directors of any secular corporation failing to capitalise on such favourable conditions would have been sacked. As it was the church authorities merely took advantage of its ruin to blackmail the parishes into supplying what the Commissioners had failed to provide.

I was summoned, with Tockwith churchwardens Jack Walker and Margaret Jones, to Bilborough Church Hall to meet the Quota Assessors. Middle aged men in suits. One bald and clutching a clipboard so closely to his chest that I was sure he took it to bed with him. The other dark, with an oily look about him and bizarre arm gestures which made you think of strange sea creatures. These church bureaucrats had perfected the art of proclaiming failure and criminal incompetence as heaven-sent opportunities – a challenge, as they described it, so disguising their taxation mania as a theological principle. They even quoted Ananias and Sapphira in The Acts of the Apostles who were struck dead for holding back part of their subs. In keeping with this bureaucracy, the Christian souls in the parishes were redefined as giving units – but why not milch cows? - and each church had to find its annual quota assessment. Over the years the quota became by far the biggest item in every parish's budget:

Tockwith 1977 £340. 1990 £3700

Bilton 1977 £250 1990 £3100

The parson was in effect put in the invidious position of having to raise his own stipend – the church bureaucrats insensitive of the damage this did to pastoral relations between the shepherd and his flock. Naturally, the locals resent this tax imposed by a distant bureaucracy - them at York. Only too keenly aware of the pressure on his parishioners, many a rural priest tried to relive them by not claiming his legitimate working expenses. He can't afford to do this. The diocesan quota – that product of central incompetence – is more than anything else responsible for the decline of the country parishes these last forty years.

Diocesan Christian officialdom became adept at turning the screw. I often think that the Soviet Union would have endured many more years if, instead of capitulating to the forces of reason, they had employed the Anglican bureaucracy in place of the Politburo. The nastiness, the cruelty, was unconfined. The parish priest who fails to meet his quota must be made to suffer. And so the Archdeacon of York, the Venerable Leslie Stanbridge, used to read out the names of those churches which had not paid in full at the annual solemn assembly known as the Visitation. Recurring default would mean that a church had to amalgamate with another, or others, and so, perhaps, not retain its own resident vicar – a defeat and a mockery of the Established Church of the land in which the parson was historically the person of the parish.

Proud at his lectern
Like a crow by the bird-table,
The Archdeacon hectoring
About worn electric cable
Before churchwardens on their outing
(A cold May evening's Visitation)
The rota for the quota,
Spouting about spouting,
Lead, roofs, drains,
Administration:
But what's this newest, grandiose whim?
He speaks of "God, as I understand him."
So now eternal numinous theocracy
Is comprehended by diocesan bureaucracy.

My colleague next door in Long Marston was given four parishes to tend. In East Anglia there are clergy who have to look after a dozen or more churches. But when the vicar is always on the hoof, the result is always a sharp decline in both the quality and quantity of pastoral care – to say nothing of what this cruelty does for the health and sanity of the parish priest. The human touch, the personal hand of the person, is replaced by the rota, the bulletin and endless hours on the telephone trying to arrange coverage for the various services. The bureaucracy brazenly seizes upon even this deficit as if it were a surplus and talks brightly about opportunities for lay ministry.

Cynically indifferent towards historical realities and the relative dissimilarities between one epoch and another, the authorities pretend theological justification for their destruction of the clergyman's function by such spurious claims as None of the Apostles possessed the Parson's Freehold – as if anyone imagined that St Peter was once Rector of Upper Antioch-with-Damascus-on-the-Wolds. And that is not the end of it. If any lay person is thought suitable and qualified to do the parson's job, then the value put on clerical training and ultimately on Holy Orders themselves is bound to be diminished. I know dozens of churches where the conduct of services – including preaching – has fallen into the hands of unschooled and crackpot enthusiasts who don't know their Ave's from their breakfast but who claim a hot line to the Lord. Of course, the preferred clergy in the cathedrals are not required to pay the Quota. These places do not even earn their keep but instead are the privileged recipients of substantial grants from central funds – funds which are themselves obtained from the financially squeezed parishes.

So all over England the brightness of God's presence as mediated by Word and Sacrament is dulled. Historical lessons have been ignored: particularly that of the Methodist Church which by years of following similar policies, has been all but wiped out in the countryside. If it is alleged that any ignorant volunteer can preach, so long as he is inspired by the Holy Ghost, then we must accept that our estimation of the Holy Ghost will be conditioned by what we hear in such sermons.

I said some of this to the diocesan smart suits at the Bilborough meeting and observed at once that Tockwith and Bilton with Bickerton was being assessed as difficult. My comments were described as negative. Good God! – if drawing attention to a colossal deficit is regarded as negative, what degrees of negativity are required to speak of the monumental deficit itself?

But what is the parish priest for? Certainly none of roster-obsessed utilitarianism of the diocesan bureaucracy have a clue about this. I came to learn the truth of what retired Judge Sir Dermott McKee told me over the gin bottle with his foul-mouthed parrot chuntering in my ear:

"When these bastards ask you what you're doing, say, 'I haven't time to be doing. I'm too busy being.'"

Being: the parson simply there and to be about what everyone knows is his business. Tim Tunnard said – and his own father had been a country parson –

"Be the Incumbent, not the Encumbrance."

But the Church of England in the 1970s was being taken over by influences which were alien to its true nature. I have mentioned the soulless, conniving bureaucrats. There were also the insane enthusiasts, the emotionally- incontinent cheerleaders of the Charismatic movement – the scores of Reverends G. Smiley Aisle-Dancer at St Knees Up and All Change. The Kingdom of Heaven was being promoted as if it were a foreign holiday package by excitable PR men with flashy teeth and accents of mid-Atlantic triumphalism.

On the Tuesday after my first Sunday in the parish, I called on Sir Dermott in order to investigate his claim, telephoned to me late on the Monday evening, that,

"I'm bored, I'm dying, and I've drunk too much gin."

Drowsy flies buzzed around the shrivelled heads of the daffodils. It was indolently warm as I walked up the village street. A dog's bark sounded a long way off. You could hear above the birdsong the school kids at their playtime. Sir Dermott lived in the only thatched house in the village. Lady McKee resembled a pipe-cleaner. Sparse, grey, chain-smoking, she hovered with her clippers by the rose trees:

"These should have been cut down on Good Friday" – all without removing the fag from between her lips.

"Dermott!" she called, and at once the house was filled with noises. A parrot chattered manically and there was a lot of coughing. I entered a cool room full of sunbeams and drapes.

"Rector, come in! Is it the bloody Rector or only the vicar? I can never remember."

"It's only the bloody vicar, Sir Dermott."

"Good." He subsided and I entered the fizzy, aqueous, aromatic afternoon.

"You're looking well," I said.

"I've every right to be. What can I give you?"

He was already giving it to me: almost a full tumbler out of the green bottle, then a splash of the fizzy stuff like an afterthought. He was frail. His eyes the most agile part of him. He wore a suit and waistcoat and a regimental tie. Suddenly, out of nowhere, a piping voice:

"Who the fuck's this?"

I looked round. It couldn't have been Lady McKee's enquiry, surely?

The parrot, green as Gilbey's and scarlet as a blood-letting.

"The bugger doesn't mind who he swears at," said the Judge. A smelly dog got up and left the room with a look of self-imposed disgrace.

"Are you one of those newfangled ecumenical Christians?"

It conjured pictures of Broadstairs' comic attrition with the Crossgates Methodist minister.

"Because," said Sir Dermott "I'll tell you a story about that lot. Balls, of course."

He added with judicial authority, "As a matter of fact, it's all balls."

His eyes seemed to be on hooks.

"All balls. Young farm labourer in Tockwith, years back when I first came, dashes into the pub one Sunday lunchtime and demands of one of our churchwardens how much was in the collecting plate at the morning's Harvest Festival. When he was told, he fell about with glee. The churchwarden said, 'What's it to you? You never go to church. Why are you so pleased?' The lad said, 'Cos it's twenty quid more than the bloody Methodists got!"

There was no chortling, only another sip. Then:

"I had to be at a banquet in York and found myself opposite the old Archbishop – the one who talks like a twerp and farts like an alsatian – the one with the eyebrows. Ramsey. Naturally, I told him this tale as a sort of parable of all religious sects. He looked dismayed. He said in that voice – you know, it sounds like someone having a hard time on the lavatory – 'Here I am in York, trying my best for the message of unity among all the denominations and you tell such discouraging stories...'

"Well," I said "I'm talking about Tockwith – and that's a full nine miles from York."

The optimistic lapping of gin against tall, iced glasses and the solipsistic ticking of the grandfather clock. The great raconteur ran on allegro vivace:

"The red light girls in Leeds come up before me. I'm always as lenient as I possibly can be. Original Sin isn't very original, when all's said and done. Anyway, I let one of them off scot free. Amanda, it was. I was in town next day with Lady McKee and I saw the girl. Well naturally, I stepped off the pavement to let her pass, raised my hat and wished her a good morning. No response. Next time she came up before me, I let her off again, but I took her on one side afterwards:

"'Amanda, I wished you good morning the other week in the middle of Leeds, and you cut me dead What have I done wrong?'

""Nothing, Sir Dermott, but you were with a lady – and for all I know, she might have been your wife!' More gin?"

The parrot laughed and swore again. Dermot coughed and called out for his wife. She came in cigarette in her lips. A study in high-bred nonchalance, she placed another bottle of tonic water by the old man's right foot and went out into the garden again without a word. The two of them all unfussed. Indifference bordering on adoration.

"D'you drive, Rector? You don't mind if I call you Rector? At least it's better than Arsehole. I used to drive. Once I was on my way in the old Bentley to an RAF do at Linton-on-Ouse. Copper stopped me in the back lanes: 'Excuse me, Sir, but you're driving very slowly in such a powerful car.'

"'Yes, officer. I always drive slowly when I'm drunk.' I told him to hop in. Took him to Linton and he got pissed like the rest of us. Well, you know what the RAF are like..."

"What do you think I should do in Tockwith, Sir Dermott?"

He scowled and clasped his glass with both hands:

"Don't call me Sir. Dermott will do nicely. 'Do'? You should do nothing. Too many people are doing things. Too much motion and too much fuss. The country's dying from it. Things will never get any better until people learn to sit down and shut up."

"Yes, Dermott!"

When I consider the gaudy freneticism that passes for public life, the cult of celebrity, the endless parade of media banality, because idiots are paid to talk, I think of the old man's words, spoken on a dusty summer's afternoon, and I reckon they were the sanest since BE STILL AND KNOW THAT I AM GOD.

Out in the street, a funeral car crept by – not one of ours. I saw through its rear window there was no display of flowers. Just a single orchid. The church clock struck four. The grandfather clock repeated the message two seconds behind. Time and the bell. And a pertinacious parrot calling a valedictory,

"Piss off!"

As his final contribution towards mystical idleness, the Judge died. I saw him not long before in the Purey Cust private hospital beside York Minster. Gin. The Times. And new slippers by the bed.

"Good to see you, Rectum. There's a bird outside whistles Mozart – the opening of the last movement of the K. 595. Have a drink."

They gave his liver the Victoria Cross and sent him home to die. He took his time. Every Thursday, Tim Tunnard took Lady McKee to Wetherby market.

"He died as he lived," said Tim.

"We came in. He was upstairs in bed by this time. He called down – the door was never on the lock: 'Is that you, darling? Is that you, Tim?'

"We went up. 'Pour yourself a drink, girl. Have one yourself, Tim. You see I've got mine already.'

"He raised his glass: 'Last orders!' he said – and died."

XVIII

Do nothing. But the village did something fine for the Queen's Silver Jubilee. A Service of music and readings in early July. The church was full of farmers in their shirtsleeves and sunburnt wives in their leisurewear, like boiled sweets half-unwrapped. Tim Tunnard played Handel's The Cuckoo and the Nightingale and a little girl in a red, white and blue outfit sang:

This royal throne of kings, this sceptre isle,

This earth of majesty, this seat of Mars...

Virginia Wade, an archdeacon's daughter, won the ladies' singles at Wimbledon. The romantic heavy boozers – sorry, historical re-enactment society – The Sealed Knot invaded Marston Moor to commemorate the 1644 battle, before drinking both The Boot and Shoe and The Spotted Ox dry. We sang I Vow to Thee My Country then walked through the graveyard to our own refreshments.

Next evening Tockwith Parochial Church Council met in the vicarage. I turned up feeling in credit after the previous day's full church and the outbreak of bucolic happiness. But this was Yorkshire and so I was met first with a complaint. Jack Walker – his wife all chewed fingernails and hating Jim Watts – stood up and said,

"'ere Vicar, I'll tell you what was wrong with last night's service: we ran out of 'ymnbooks 'an I 'ad ter run over to 't'Methodists' and fetch more. But them 'as different numbers than ours!"

It took me back to the self-satisfied curmudgeons of Leeds:

"It were all right. It weren't bad..."

For God's sake, smile for once: it won't crack yer face!

Nothing happened. Nobody hit anybody. It was just the usual litany of complaint. And then speaker after speaker came up with ideas for new tasks to be performed by the Vicar. The boiler wasn't working...

"It never has!"

It was, of course, the vicar's job to go down to the boiler house late on Saturday night and turn it on. You had to balance on a pile of stones to keep your feet out of the standing water. Two out of three times it would light but go out in the early hours. Then the church was cold on Sunday morning – and naturally that was the Vicar's fault too.

There was a new damp patch on the south wall. When this was announced, with a solemnity fitting for the death of the Monarch, all eyes looked to see what the Vicar was going to do about it. Meg Stanhope complained she couldn't hear the Vicar's sermon

"Well tha's allus been deaf as a post."

Cheery old Jack Walker again.

Then there was Pauline Sorrell – I longed to call her Hetty – who boomed acrimony throughout. There was a real Hetty – Hetty Maltby all aerobics and sixty-one years slim and her husband, mild as Wensleydale. He was called Dick. I could think only in the absence of – with Hetty fidgeting lubriciously like that.

Just before midnight I sat with a large Scotch, listening to the Symphony number 35 in D –The Haffner when the phone rang. It was Joan Perry in Bickerton to tell me her seventeen year old daughter Alison was going in for a kidney transplant. Would I pray for her? I went to Leeds to see the girl a couple of days later. St James' Hospital – "Jimmy's" – with its own chapel in the grounds, brash as any 19th century parish church. The ward was all contraptions, wires and disinfectant. Alison, under a tent of bed clothes, was on dialysis. She whispered something which I couldn't hear and smiled knowingly as a saint. Through the windows I could see the stream of silent traffic crawl along Beckett Street. Opposite was a cemetery – as if the hospital were only its anteroom - and a pub imaginatively called The Cemetery. (That Leeds demeanour again!) Later they changed its name to The Florence Nightingale. (ie That Leeds demeanour again – plus sentimentality). A Jesuitical little consultant whatsitologist told me Alison would pull through.

Alison did pull through and she came home to the cottage in Bickerton. I would go and sit with her and her mother in the garden. There was a quality about Alison that you could call spiritual – but not in the mawkish sense to which that word has attained thanks to the Body, Mind and Spirit section in the chain bookstores. She was at once innocence and experience. She would smile as if she knew what you were going to say before you said it. Time seemed to slow down in her presence. Strange thing to say of a young woman who was dying: she herself appeared to dictate the speed at which time passed. That is how it felt on the patio behind the little house in Bickerton.

She was not a churchgoer, and we rarely talked about God by name, so to speak. She had been in and out of hospital all her life. She was calm.

"There was a fox in the garden this morning."

Her words always fell out just right. You felt that just by her speaking she did the world good. And her eyes – she was attentive to the point of trancelike vigilance – seemed to create what they were looking at, so that you developed the ridiculous notion that, if she were to choose to stop looking at an object, it would cease to exist. Crazy. Not really describable. Not in words, anyway. And when she looked, she saw what was there of course, but you knew she saw something else, something you never spoke about. The form of the object, in the Platonic sense – I mean in his philosophical sense. There was this quality. She knew she was dying. There was this Mozartean quality.

There was an incident. We sat among the stone ornaments under the trees. You could see the windows – it was an unusual effect, reflections, puzzling movements in the glass. And sometimes the reflections of distant trees, moving like plants under water. Occasionally you caught sight of someone passing by – it might be with a tray of drinks or a garden tool – and you saw and saw again. Commonplace, but you never quite got used to it.

This day I sat opposite Alison and caught sight of her reflection as the glass doors swung this way and that. The day itself was all hot haze, indeterminate – the very scenario for an optical illusion. Just for a second, I was not sure which was the real Alison and which the reflection. We were talking about Beethoven's Fourth Piano Concerto – the first concerto to open with the piano solo… well, since Mozart's Number Nine in E-flat K.271. At four o'clock I set off home. The sneck on the gate clicked behind me and a huge interior voice said:

"You saw her twice. Doppelganger. Death."

She did die. I took the funeral on 16th September 1977, but I have promised not to say any more about it

One of the churchwardens in Bilton was called Crapp, Colonel Crapp. One pondered his rise through the ranks: Private Crapp. Major Crapp and perhaps as far as his shitty apotheosis as General Crapp. He was, according to opinion, eighty or eighty-five. Thin, straight and tall as De Gaulle. Chippy as Hitler. He commanded me to lunch with him at Bilton Hall where, in civilised acrimony with the owners, he tenanted the West Wing. Bilton Hall is an 18th century manor house set on the only hill around. Hill being a relative term: there is nowhere between Wetherby and York above a hundred feet from sea level and, going a little way south towards Selby, some villages are actually below sea level. The house is in wide acres of rolling parkland, garnished with its own lake designed by Inigo Jones. Rabbits hopped across my path all the way up the long drive. The Colonel, as everyone called him, served lunch precisely – his hearing aid whistling as he ran around the table.

"What sort of fella are you?" he asked in that tone which left you unsurprised when you learnt he had served as a Staff Officer in the Raj.

"Not like the last man, I hope. I fell out with him. In the vestry after the service one day, he came up to me and said, 'Look here, Colonel, I want you to understand that you don't run this parish: I do.'"

The mounds of potatoes were dry as chalk cliffs and the peas like bullets. I said,

"What did you do?"

"I just carried on running the parish as before. Your predecessor – he was a clown."

There was a twinkle of Harold Macmillan about the old boy. And, in the best sense, he had run the parish. While Watkins was banning whist drives, watching booze bottles smash into the wall and slavering over lugubrious conversations with Margaret Pick, Crapp had uncovered some ancestral connection with Bilton – military, naturally – and twisted the PCC's arms up their backs for £800. With this money, and for the Queen's Silver Jubilee, he re-hung the bells at Bilton church. I mean exactly what I say. Two angina tablets under his tongue and he went up the ladder like an explosion to check the contractors' workmanship. Like the testicles on my father's prize boxer dog, there was something amiss with the balance of the two bells. Crapp made a correction. Mischievous, he would cause his hearing aid to howl during any sermon he found uncongenial. De mortuis nihil nisi bonum. He was malicious and he was a bully, but he loved Bilton church. He died suddenly and the village was shocked when they discovered his will had left instructions that he was to be cremated without religious ceremony – without ceremony of any kind.

Bilton Hall was owned by Geoffrey and Sally Rayner and they occupied the main part of the place. I married them: the first marriage I conducted in the parish. October 1977. She was forty-two. Exquisite. Refined. She spoke like the Queen. He was fifty-nine, unearthlily good-looking, like a portrait of the Transfiguration. I first met him in York District Hospital where he was being treated for cancer.

Sally's first husband had died the sort of death Colonel Crapp would have dreamt of, longingly. He was an explorer. One night in a desert encampment in the Middle East, he took his supper with some tribesmen. They gave him a portion of meat that was so highly-spiced that it tore his throat apart and he died on the spot.

Geoffrey was divorced.

They asked me to drinks after the service one Sunday and wondered if I would perform a service of blessing over their union.

"No."

"Oh, Peter, we were so hoping you would!"

Sally's dulcet tintinnabulation.

"But we do understand you have misgivings about blessings for divorcees in church."

"I have no such misgivings. I will marry you, if you like."

Geoffrey was already opening another bottle of the heavenly White Burgundy:

"But I didn't know you were allowed to?"

"That's what the bishops would like you to think. Look, English law says divorcees may remarry, but the state exempts the church from the duty to remarry such persons. The bishops are squeamish. They won't do the honest thing and allow folk like you and Sally a proper wedding so, with bum-clenching hypocrisy, they tell the clergy to say, 'I am not permitted to marry you but, if you get married in the Register Office, you can come to church for a Service of Blessing. It will look just like the real thing.'"

I said it was a pity that the bishops are not the real thing. Geoffrey handed me another glass as I said,

"How can they bless something they disapprove – when a blessing is, among other things, a sign of approval?

"Services of Blessing are dishonest. Behold the spectre of the second-hand bride as the very image of post-coital virginity, turning up in horse and trap to meet the second time, or third time, shy groom in top hat, and for the two of them to be enjoined by some soapy reverend gent in a rite which beggars rationality, conscience and charity!"

I explained how the church's policy was excessively bureaucratic:

"In a policy revision, the General Synod has invented a sort of General Committee for Sanctimoniousness which decrees that some couples may be married in church but not others. They set up a moral questionnaire consisting of religious tests by which couples and the priest might determine whether remarriage should be allowed or not. One of the questions is, 'Do the couple show signs of penitence for the failure of their first marriage?'"

I thus explained that church authorities were working towards a policy of marrying so called innocent parties at the same moment that pastoral psychologists – and even priests, for God's sake – were coming to understand that in marital breakdown there are no innocent parties. It is no business of the Vicar's to watch couples as they wash their dirty underwear in front of him in the vestry, so to speak, and then make some quasi-judicial-moral decision which allows Ron and Eth but not Ted and Sheila. The Synod even produced a bilious green document, entitled GS 38, on which the case notes were to be recorded.

"What's GS 38?"

"General Sodyn's documentary form of sanctimoniousness!"

"So we can be married! And in Bilton church too! How absolutely glorious!"

Geoffrey loved that girl. And...well, you only had to look into her face. No need for GS 38. The wedding came and the church was full of lilies and smiles. Back at the Hall, kindly, genial friends, a man in a white blazer spreading old fingers over the Bechstein, and children spilling about the place

We did not stand idly in the fields that year. I wrote a play about Gustav Mahler which was performed in the parish church with children from Tockwith Junior School dancing to the slow movement from his Resurrection Symphony. We set up a literary society at The Royal Oak pub in Wetherby. When my philosophy book came out, The Yorkshire Evening Press regarded me as famous as Terry Wogan but spelt ontological wrongly next to a picture of my fat face on page three. That book got me back into school again, but not to the mild delinquency of such as Whitecroft. No, to The Mount School in York, a Quaker foundation full of expensive girls who, by the time they were long-legged enough to get into the Sixth Form, knew just which bits of intellectual gossip to write home to daddy about.

I was asked by the headmistress – a sort of Bloomsbury relic who actually did wear blue stockings – to talk to her young ladies.

"Well, yaffat know about epistemology."

Recollections of Bolton and boggling lessons. But somehow not as interesting. There were the young ladies stretched out against the afternoon in the main hall, with only the faintest whiff of the morning's PE lesson. Girls enquiring about Kant and the Categorical Imperative, but you knew their criteria came not from Konigsberg but Carnaby Street. Luscious little bits of pampered empty-headedness, talking nonsense poshly. They felt they had a right to their opinions about the pre-Socratic philosophers – mainly that they were stupid – and no doubt they had. Daddy was paying for their education, after all. In a very short while, they came to resemble cardboard.

The Archdeacon of York, Leslie Stanbridge, phoned to say he had read about my philosophy book and he invited me to tea in his damp, echoing sitting room in St George's place. A bachelor, nasal and niggardly.

"How long did it take you to write it?"

The inference was that it couldn't be much good.

"I'm looking for someone for our press team. Perhaps you'd like to come and help out?"

His intonation suggested he didn't expect me to help at all. In fact, all his conversation dripped disappointment and the sense that dreariness – so long as it was pleasingly uneventful – was all anyone could hope for.

He was offering me a job, one Saturday out of six, to write a seven-hundred-and-fifty words piece for The Yorkshire Evening Press on some religious topic determined by himself. He made it sound as if he were offering me the Nobel Prize for Literature. The press team met in the library of The Bar Convent on the corner of Micklegate and included the Diocesan Communications Officer – who found communication difficult – a thunderstruck Roman priest, four local clergymen who looked fit, almost, for a course on Writing and Style, and couple of holy middle aged women, all thick lenses and lechery.

The Venerable Leslie began by saying,

"Religion need not be boring. We have to find new ways to communicate old truths."

The usual fraudulent propaganda of the modern church. It was about this time that the Church of England began to copy similar superstitions as those found in ALSEB, the education industry and management studies. That combination of slogans, clichés and the bureaucratic stranglehold. Indeed, the church was already recruiting its own corps of officers for this whole paraphernalia of pseudo-enlightenment. But then the modern church always follows secular fashion – but just like the Prince Consort, one dutiful step behind. Like the trendy parish priest advertising his cultural credentials from the pulpit by saying square, cool and with it at precisely the moment when these phrases had become un-square, lukewarm and decidedly without it.

My own deficiencies in these areas was quickly exposed when I asked what was wrong with communicating the old truths in the old ways. The press team were kind enough to tolerate me, but it was soon apparent that they could expect nothing much from a mere newcomer to their circle – and especially not from a man who had just published a book about philosophy.

We planned the weekly column for six months ahead – which was methodology a little odd from a group who were looking to be spontaneous, relevant and exciting. But at that time I knew nothing of journalism and laboured under the supposition that it had something to do with writing English prose. Leslie thought I was arrogant, and he said so. But this opinion did not prejudice him against me to the extent that he neglected my contributions to the relevant and exciting team. In fact he got into the habit of calling on me frequently and at the last minute to supply him with an extra article when one or other member of the team had been, for whatever pressing reason, unable to turn in his copy.

Nicolas Mc Dowell phoned one morning and cheerfully asked me if I would write a book for schools about death. It was a subject I was beginning to learn al lot about. Christenings and weddings are only for the photographs and the booze up these days, but a funeral in a country church, followed by the burial in the churchyard, still convects the mystery of ancestral rites. I mean of course the service in The Book of Common Prayer not the euphemistic modern versions which dare not mention worms and omit that apt description vile body.

I don't know why, but what I always remember about a particular funeral is what the weather was doing. You stand in the church porch as the people, boots polished, drift up the drive to be counted my Muriel Thurston who writes down all their names as if she were the Recording Angel. This list of names appears a few days later in The Wetherby News and it is picked over with pernickety satisfaction by the villagers. It also provides ammunition for mildly acrimonious wrangles:

"It says here Jack Walker was there. He never was!"

"He did go, but he sat at t'other side. There was that frosty woman in the purple coat in Jack's usual seat."

"Oh aye!"

You go down to the lychgate and see the pall-bearers – village lads on a small retainer from the undertaker who have shined themselves up for the day and put on their caps, which they remove as the gleaming hearse rolls silently up the main street. Denis Backhouse, undertaker of undertakers, gentleman of gentlemen, gets out. Slim.

Upright. White hair. Smooth and elegant as the hearse. In all his work most wonderful, most sure in all his ways. I wrote about him once:

I know this cheerful thing,
That death has got no sting:
The grave, it holds no menace
While ever we've got Denis.

You wouldn't mind dying if you knew Mr Denis Backhouse was to be in charge of the arrangements. It would be a pleasure: something like a grand day out.

In the porch you can hear the organ music. If Tim Tunnard is playing, it will be something by Bach. When Barry Carlill plays, it is diminished chords Edwardianiana: Come into the garden Lord music. The musical counterpart to ostrich feathers.

"I am the resurrection and the life" is what you say first. There is a frisson and a holy shuffle as they all stand up.

The words are shocking. They are the defining genius of traditional English Christianity at its most daring. Here is a dead body and a cloud of grief and sorrow. Black abounds. Even the sweetness of the flowers seems part of the musty stench of corpses and corruption. And what does the priest say?

"I am the resurrection and the life."

It's some sort of joke. In fact it's God's joke. In the midst of death, he says, you are in life. It is the apotheosis of the drama. It is the truth.

The organ music has stopped.

Unlike the anonymous disposals at the urban crematorium, the village funeral is a personal affair. The deceased was known to the parson. The congregation knew him. They know that the parson knows that they knew him. This makes it both easier and harder for the parson.

They wonder what he is going to say.

And what does he say? That John was a good man and now he is at rest. Our prayers are with his family. We will remember him. Of course he says more than that, but the rest is all intuition and fumble, irony to lay bare the bones of the man. All out of affection, supported by the affection of the villagers who, in this rare moment, for once shelve their pettiness and betray something which looks suspiciously like gentleness. That's what the Bible means by charity.

Even on hot days, when the air is thick with remembrance and the flowers in the churchyard are still, it is always cool in church. The sun falls here and there on the stone and the light seems as if it has always been exactly of that reverent hue. There are moments in the village funeral when the only movement in the place is the slow depreciation of the candles. Death is timeless.

When our language has to manage the unmanageable, it looks for a life raft. This life raft is the monosyllable:

"With this ring, I thee wed..."

"This is my Body...this is my Blood..."

And here: "Man that is born of a woman hath but a short time to live....In the midst of life we are in death."

There is awful comfort in this rhythm, for it is the best of human rhythms. And, since the Word is made flesh, it is the divine rhythm too. Our brother here departed now delivers his flesh back to the Eternal Word. And Christ with his open arms says,

"Come ye blessed children of my Father, receive the kingdom prepared for you from the beginning of the world..."

The close family stand near you by the grave. Others prefer to behold these things from afar. The straps are loosened under the coffin and there is a scratchy, wooden sound as it is lowered.

"Earth to earth, ashes to ashes, dust to dust."

You look up and there are always crows in the tall trees.

They all dawdle off in the sunshine to their ham and tea and beer and whisky – for father, I got a drop in specially – and pies and sausage rolls. Or when it rains, coats are stretched out over the radiators, umbrellas get left behind and Anne Milner says,

"The porch is a mess!"

All that is left to do is to stack away the hymnbooks and put the candles out. Silence except for the churchwarden counting the collection. Silence. The church is silent - not in the sense that it has emptied itself of sound, but as if it has absorbed the sound – like the first second of quiet after the last line of a hymn. And after the rain, in the evening, you can walk round the south side, over the sweet-smelling grass, and talk to the gravedigger as he fills in.

The country parson is sustained by his people whether he likes it or not. There is a mental map on which he locates them, and sometimes this map resembles a minefield. Intuiting where an explosion is likely to occur is part of his job. You go out visiting in the afternoons, having put on the whole armour of God which enables you to eat the inedible and mix your drinks. Try a cup of milky, sugary instant coffee, nearly cold, after half a bottle of gin at Sir Dermott's place. Suddenly the mental map can change and start to look like the blueprint for an asylum.

I had to call on Rita Threapleton who lived in one of the dozen or so houses owned by the Council across the road from Bilton Church. This was to deliver her son Gary's baptism certificate. Rita was out at work but her mother Connie was in.

"Come in. That's right, come on in, Vicar. It's gone so overcast. I can't abide it when it's like this. Rita's at work. Gary's asleep – touch wood."

She raised her hand to her mouth and called out into the back garden. There was a clanking of spade on path.

"Who? Who is it, Connie?"

"Mr Mullen. You know Mr Mullen – the Vicar. Lay off for a minute Harry and come and have a cuppa."

She put out three blue and white mugs on the draining board.

Harry, squat and red like the mock Georgian houses on the drome in Tockwith – though not as trim – lumbered in from his digging. His boots creaked over the bare boards. He breathed heavily as he wiped his feet on an old mat and flung his dilapidated gardening gloves into a wicker chair. He lit his pipe and sat looking sanguine on the doorstep under the blue haze of tobacco smoke.

"And you take too much of that 'an all," said Connie, pointing towards the pipe and spitting as she spoke.

"Every morning when I come down, I can't get rid of the stink no how. You can't have the windows open all weathers. Gary'll catch his death. If there's one thing I can't stand, it's stale tobacco smoke. It gets into your clothes."

Breathless, Mrs Threapleton had been shuffling between the draining board and the top step, but now Harry said,

"Come on, let's go into the parlour for five minutes. Tek weight off yer legs."

We sat down in the front room which smelt of mothballs and Harry's feet. On every flat surface – the window ledge, the small table, the large table with the velvet cover, the fireplace, the old sideboard, were hundreds of small glass animals of the sort children buy at the seaside and break on their way home to tea. And on every wall, varieties of clocks – antique, digital and cuckoo. Among the animals and clocks were family photographs in fine historical continuity from sepia to Polaroid.

"That's Gary with Rita," said Connie Threapleton, showing me a picture of Gary with Rita.

"And that's Sheila, as has gone to Australia. That's her husband Brian with the tankard Jackie bought him for his twenty-first. Likes a drink or two does Brian. There, look, they're on the beach. That's Blackpool. There's nothing wrong with that, having a drink. In moderation, that's what I say, don't I, father ?"

His face took on a gaze of fond reminiscence:

"And there's nothing wrong with Blackpool, neither. We 'ad some fun at Blackpool when we were a bit more sprightly, didn't we luv!"

And he winked laboriously

"Nah then, don't you be getting so much off yer chest Harry Threapleton. Mr Mullen doesn't want to know what you used ter get up to!"

He opened his mouth to answer, but the clocks spoke first. They were all out of time with one another, so the interruption was prolonged while Connie's face took on a dazed, contemplative aspect and she was, as it were, struck unusually silent. After the chimes, tinkles and jingles had finished and one tardy cuckoo had finally returned to its or some other creature's nest, another untimely pseudo-cuckoo, whose spring was not all it had once been, set about a sluggish and unilateral declaration of the late fact that it was four o'clock.

The strangeness of the surroundings, the surreality of events and the acridity of Harry's pipe combined to produce in me a sudden mood of incipient hysteria. I knew I should have to leave before I disgraced myself. Standing up, I momentarily lost my balance, tripped over the hem of my cassock and sent a large green glass canary, with only one eye, shattering on the edge of the tiled hearth. There was no sound except Harry's strained breathing and the contrapuntal ticking of the clocks. What could I say? What could anyone in my position have said? I was dreadfully sorry. Could I buy a replacement? Where were they sold? But in the matter of little birds, Connie Threapleton resembled God. She bent reverently to gather the pieces of the tragic bird and cut her finger on a jagged feather. The comedy of the bizarre room turned to a sort of Pinteresque menace. The atmosphere was not improved by Harry himself who stood knocking out his pipe rhythmically on the chimney breast. Connie was sucking her bloody finger. Tears rolled down her face. Harry stared at me with hypertensive hostility:

"Now you've gone and upset missus!"

Gary started to cry.

"Baby an' all!"

I said I was really sorry. It was all my fault. Of course I would replace the broken ornament. And shouldn't we do something about Mrs Threapleton's finger? But she rushed off into the kitchen to do something about her own finger.

Harry's face wore a look of abject melancholy:

"You can't replace it. They don't make 'em any more. Not like that they don't. It's just rubbish these days. No, you've put t'cap on it now, Vicar. It's done wi'."

I stared down at the fragmented bird of quality. It stared back out of its one red eye.

"Connie!"

Connie came back with a band aid around her finger.

"Connie, who gave us t'canary? Alice, it were Alice, weren't it? That's who it was an' all, Alice. Brought it back from Morecambe. If ivverybody 'ad their own, it were our Rita's. Nah then, what we're going to do?"

"Nay Harry," said Connie, putting on a brave face despite the tragic events, don't tek on like. It doesn't matter. It'll be all right."

"Doesn't matter? Doesn't matter!" said Harry, like one of his repeating alarms. It does matter. It does matter. I'll say it damn well matters! Can't be careful, some folk. Comes in 'ere like Lord Muck, knocks all yer bits and pieces about..."

He was breathing like a steam engine and his face went the colour of his wife's apron.

"Leave be, Harry. I'll get us another. I know where you can get 'em. Just down behind – "

"I'm not interested where you can get 'em. I don't want to know. All I know is that bird belonged to our Rita and it 'ad sentimental value. It's thought that counts. You can't put thought back, Mr Mullen."

"I'm sure Mr Mullen didn't mean to break it. I said, I'm sure Mr Mullen didn't mean – "

Gary's screaming had achieved top gear.

"That's 'er baby. That's Rita's baby you've upset, "said Harry."

"I'll see to him!"

"You stop where you are, our Connie. 'E'll pack it in in a minute. I said, 'E'll pack it in in a minute. Now then Mr Clever Dick Mullen, you know what you can do. You can just get off back to that vicarage of your'n and don't come interrupting my gardening and pestering us no more..."

"Harry!"

"Don't you 'Harry' me!"

"Mr Mullen has said he's sorry."

"Sorry be buggered!"

"Harry!"

"You must look after that finger."

"Gerron wi' yer!"

I picked my way to the door in fear and trembling. Once outside. I allowed myself, like Lot's wife, one fatal glance backward. I noticed Harry Threapleton take a match to the baptism certificate and set fire to it. Then I heard the door slam behind and Harry's voice through the open window:

"I'll set fire to 'im an' all if 'e ivver dares come back 'ere!"

As I walked unsteadily towards the main York-Wetherby road, it was beginning to rain.

XIX

Speaking of Denis Backhouse... All the best stories originate at a funeral.

Amelia Lacey, spinster of my parish, died on Advent Sunday when the few leaves that remained on the trees in the churchyard shone like fire. There had been a frost and the path was white over as I walked among the graves to where Jack Martin was preparing Amelia's last resting place. Village gravediggers follow the inevitability of their trade. Son follows father down the years in a sort of dynastic nemesis which everyone respects because none can escape its ministrations. No doubt that was what lent big Jack's eye the cocky look as he sat on the steps by the south porch and slurped tea from his pint pot.

"Mornin' Vicar, what can I do for you?"

He stared at the half-dug hole in the ground as if he were thinking, "An' I'll do for you one day as well!"

I said, "I just came to make sure you knew it was a double."

A double, of course, is a grave dug extra deep in order to accommodate more than one corpse: husband and wife, brothers etc.

"O aye," said Jack "Pilin' 'em up like dominoes again, are you?"

An oily looking crow let out a huge guffaw, as if in appreciation of Jack's rustic wit. Jack finished his tea and turned reluctantly again to his shovel, smoothing the blade of it with his thick fingers, letting the wet crumbs of earth fall on to the path.

"I suppose you'd be visiting old Amelia many a time eh, Vicar?"

"Every Thursday. She used to give me tea and Eccles cakes and tell me how much better the parish was run before the war."

"Aye, she were a character an' all."

She was indeed. Thin, almost frail, she was a powerhouse of energy, always on the move, houseproud, green fingers and a consummate country cook. She eyed you across her crochet as if she thought you might be about to pilfer one of her china ornaments – her perfect guests, as she called them. She knew everything there was to know about the history of Tockwith and she would recite – it was as if she had memorised a script, now lost – huge chunks of it as we drank tea and ate those cakes. Occasionally, she would frown at her needlework and bite her lip. There would be a short silence and then her fingers would begin again, as if the crochet were a commentary on her conversation. She had departed this life after a brief bout of pneumonia, aged eighty-one. The funeral arrangements were in the hands of her younger sister, Elsie.

The village church is always full for funerals but the congregation, many of whom – like Housman in Bredon Hill - come only on these occasions, don't bear themselves like strangers, embarrassed sheep returning briefly to the fold. On the contrary, they look entirely at home in the place, as if it had been only on loan to the Christians and was now being reclaimed for more significant rites. At a quarter to two, Tim was quietly playing extracts from Edwardian oratorios of outstanding Schmaltziness, and the sidesman had lit the altar candles but had not switched on the lights. So the church looked even more eerily Gothic than usual, almost, you might say, like a funeral parlour. I flicked every switch on the switchboard. As the lights came on, the congregation began to cough and mutter among themselves like an audience just before curtain-up. The sidesman gave me an assured look:

"Is it wheels or bearers, Vicar?"

"Wheels, David."

I pulled on my surplice and walked off towards the lych-gate. The cortege arrived exactly on time and the old timers, who stood by the gate also wondering whether they would be required as bearers, stubbed out their cigarettes and stuffed their hands into their overcoat pockets. Denis Backhouse, latest in the long line of disposers supreme, stepped from the car to the pavement like an impresario.

"We can't grumble for December."

As he spoke, the sun came out. He caught sight of the would-be bearers:

"It's all right, lads," he said "I've got the wheels today."

Whereupon, three of the old men started their dawdle up the path and into church, while the fourth shuffled off towards The Boot and Shoe.

Backhouse let the chief mourners out of the first car while his assistants manhandled the coffin from the hearse. Elsie Lacey, in a great black hat which reminded me of a pulpit canopy I had once seen in Leicester, stepped out on to the path. What had been lacking in the flesh of her sister, she more than made up for. Her avoirdupois was legendary. She was the village metaphor for all things sizeable. But she shared her sister's liveliness – possessed it, you might say, more abundantly. There was a huge hatpin in the huge hat, so that she looked as if she had been arrowed in the head. Her face was red but it betrayed no obvious sign of grief: rather, it bore an expression of critical curiosity, as if suspecting trickery or foul play. Behind her were distant cousins from the East Coast.

I nodded gently and whispered, "Good afternoon!"

Elsie's forensic expression never wavered. When she saw the coffin, she applied a small white handkerchief to her face, then replaced it in the black and gold handbag. It was as if the movement had been a signal that the ceremonies could now begin.

I led off up the path and I could hear the wheels crunching over the gravel and the low murmuring of Backhouse's men. Backhouse himself made a further remark about the weather to the deceased's sister who gave no reply. As we entered the porch, I could hear more of the fin de siècle funeral music. The coffin on its aluminium trolley made me think suddenly of something I needed to pick up from the Harrogate supermarket.

"I am the resurrection and the life...."

My voice echoed throughout the interior and there was a clatter as they all rose to their feet. The service was straightforward. I told one or two anecdotes, gathered on my frequent visits to Amelia's cottage. I said that everyone in the village would have treasured memories of her. I said she had been a good woman and she had now gone to her reward. We sang Rock of Ages and, with Cup-Final gusto, Abide With Me. During the singing, it had become darker outside so that now, within, the dim lights of the nave glowed almost brightly. I stood for a minute by the chancel-step and stared at the reflected light on the coffin lid, at the small cross of red flowers and at the shining brass inscription:

Amelia Lacey RIP.

At such moments, one tends to notice things very efficiently and I saw that the candles were well burnt down. I made a note to replace them before Sunday. The organ struck up refreshingly with a march by Handel and I led the trolley back over the soft carpet to the west door which Jack Martin had flung open for me. More crows. Churchyard noises.

Outside it was dull, but it still seemed brighter than the inside of the church. The sunshine had been replaced by a thin drizzle. As I rounded the buttresses towards the south side, a crackle of plastic mackintoshes assured me that congregation were following. Backhouse held an umbrella over Elsie as the men made ready with the canvas ropes. There was the dull, solid sound of the coffin being lowered – exactly what is conveyed by the words earth to earth.

Backhouse ushered the mourners closer. The whole crowd of villagers stood still in the rain, as if posing for a photograph. Elsie needed no encouragement to come nearer to the grave. She was at my elbow and leaning forward, her face redder than usual and it had temporarily lost its critical expression. She seemed very distressed – and who, after all, could blame her for that, since she had lost her only relative, and she herself was approaching her departed sister's great age. Suddenly the warning chords of something Broadstairs had said all those years ago came rushing back:

"Always keep an eye on folks at the graveside – in case they do anything silly."

It turned out, he had once had someone throw himself on the coffin.

I looked down at the brass nameplate and the handful of earth which Backhouse had solemnly cast upon it. I looked back up at Elsie whose face had turned even more anxious, and who was leaning yet further over the edge. I stretched out my arm in what, in the nature of the case, would have been only token restraint:

"There, Elsie, she's at peace now."

It was hard to sound reassuring.

The big sister stared fiercely into the grave, then drew back and faced me. The forensic look had returned, intensified. The black hat had dislodged its monstrous pin and sat at a precarious angle at the side of her head. Elsie inhaled deeply and folded her arms across her chest:

"There's no need to stick your arm out like that – you're not on traffic duty! Now then, I'd just like to say one thing..."

She paused. Seventy mourners stood silently by, waiting upon her next words.

"She never ate a good dinner, our Amelia. I was thinking – that double grave's after being a tight fit when it's my turn to follow her in!"

I stuck my tongue in my cheek and pretended to stare at the tall and leafless willow tree. I could feel the force of Elsie's stare hot on my face. At last I recovered the presence to say,

"...for they rest from their labours."

And we all went home.

From the bizarre to the fundamental. Halfway between Tockwith and Bilton, was Bilton West Grange, a farmhouse sturdy as one of Oliver Cromwell's Ironsides and its inhabitants, Bob and Nancy Lofthouse, likewise. Bob, posing as a walrus, would have made a good subject for a Health Education Council commercial for high blood pressure. His cheeks gave a new definition to the description deep purple. I often sat with him over pints of tea in his wide kitchen. High beams and damp dogs. The lady who did for them singing Danny Boy in the front room. All the talk was of horses. Nancy with tremulous hands and black coffee was actually the strongest, gentlest woman I ever met. She spoke huskily and frequently excused Bob from misdemeanours actual or only potential. Tall windows. Three skyscapes to choose from – the one to the north revealing the distant hillside, scarred and primitive: carved into it The White Horse at Kilburn. Horse boxes, homely smells. There was often a cigar and always whisky. Nancy would reminisce about her time in the Air Ministry during the war, working as a meteorologist, plotting Atlantic fronts and violent storms. It seemed good training for her life with Bob. I was there one day to discuss the forthcoming Harvest Festival.

Harvest festivals come by the dozen in the country. The two parish churches, the Methodist chapel, and "them over t'bridge at Hunsingore" where Denis Backhouse went to church religiously rather than professionally: each had its own Harvest Festival and everyone dallied promiscuously with them all. The Tockwith Methodist celebration – if such a word may be used of Methodists – was weird. Their Minister was a Mr Jackson, a Welshman who looked as if in better days he might have played fly half for Swansea. Now, alas he looked battered and run down. Pale faced, always in and out of the Oxfam shop. The phlegm caught in his throat as he ranted.

Methodists often accuse Anglicans of idolatry or, at the very least, of vain repetition – because we take our prayers from a book. Methodists disdain books – except the tediously interminable Methodist Hymnbook. They prefer extempore prayers or, as they say, prayers from the heart. There is nothing more tedious. No one can sustain inventive liturgical brilliance week in, week out, so the Minister falls into a set pattern of speech, the same yesterday, today and tomorrow. Vain repetitions in fact. Then there was that other trademark of the chapel crowd I had first heard a long time before in Crossgates, one Holy Week: a very indirectness:

"We would thank thee, Lord.... We would praise thy holy name."

You feel the congregational response should be, "Well just bloody well get on and do it, then!"

It sounds even more implausible when the use of the second person singular lapses and gives way to whatever the God-awful Methodist equivalent to our Alternative Service Book prescribes. Try saying:

"We would beg you to look mercifully on our sins, O Lord."

As an exercise in corporate unctuousness, it beats a mass casting session for the part of Uriah Heep. And then they will insist on putting the pulpit, and hence the Minister, bang in the middle, high and lifted up – where God ought to be. At least God doesn't have to endure a crowd of fat women called the choir behind his back. At the Harvest Festival they placed on the ledge, between the throaty old women and the phlegmatic Welshman, a row of apples, calling back recollections of small boys and catapults. At least it took your mind off the praying. Never mind that the English fields, so recently golden, and but a few yards from the chapel door – and the vast orange moon smiling over the roof – were glorious evocations of village life, Mr Jackson would contrive something more remote. A litany of distant atrocities in, as it might be, South Africa or the Chinese People's Republic was preferred before anything homely and wholesome. It seemed to me invidious. I mean, if you're going to single out five impoverished countries in Africa for intercession, aren't you being rather neglectful and partisan when you leave out the other fourteen?

Old Jackson had a lurid preaching style which might have been of interest to the psychiatric profession. Once, illustrating a point about something or other – I forget – he said,

"Suppose the Vicar was counting the collection in his vestry and I came behind him with a knife..."

I don't recall how it went on, for his voice often got lost in a gargle as his thoughts flew back, no doubt, to fast times in Merioneth. At least historically, Methodism was spunkier. Anyone who could write a couple of hymn lines:

There let it for thy glory burn
With inextinguishable blaze

...as Charles Wesley did, must be, to paraphrase George Eliot, a Methodist of the ecstatic rather than the bilious sort. You get more of the bilious spirit in the Introduction to that Methodist Hymnbook – always good for a diversion during the sermon – where, for instance, John Wesley chastises those who copy out his hymns:

"...that my brother and I are not responsible for the nonsense or the doggerel of other men."

There was always plenty of both at the Chapel Harvest. And afterwards there was tea in the penitentiary of the schoolroom when, if you were especially out of luck, you would be regaled by Margaret Pick on the evils of drink – or on the evils of just about anything else.

There was something wrong with the water supply in Tockwith. The Council were supposed to supervise the putting in of some sterilising fluid from time to time. What they actually did was to add nothing for ages and then dump a whole truckful in. This gave rise to what was known locally as Tockwith Tummy. It was less like ordinary queasiness and more like heaven and earth being rent in twain, with the consequent, and painful, mingling of the waters that were above the firmament with the waters that were below the firmament. Although I was not a great drinker of Tockwith water, I was struck down on the Sunday after Harvest and so I was not fit to attend Evensong.

So I engaged Jim Watts, who I had persuaded to rejoin the congregation now that my predecessor had long gone to spread the good news of our damnation in Macclesfield. Jim had community spirit like the sea has fish, though he also had a ceaseless and insistent bureaucratic mind – like a continual dropping in a very rainy day, as The Book of Proverbs puts it. He also had a tendency to think that the most intelligent words he had ever heard were those just uttered by himself.

Tim played the organ, as usual, and Jim read Evensong. This is permitted by church rules which provide for any fit person to read the service in the absence of the parish priest. But, out of a supererogatory enthusiasm, Jim went further than he ought strictly to have done and gave them a little talk in lieu of the sermon. I was grateful to him.

But next morning there was an angry phone call from Archdeacon Stanbridge, who already thought I was several sizes too big for my boots:

"What you did was illegal. I'm giving you an official warning!"

The yellow card, then.

"Who's complained, Leslie?"

"That I'm not inclined to tell you."

"Then I'm not inclined to accept your official warning. Tell me who's speaking against me and I'll answer in full. If not, I've nowt to say."

I heard his plunge into the emotional vortex, then I put the phone down. Stanbridge had a reputation for being a martinet and he was used to clergy going in fear of him. Why were they so afraid? There was bugger all he could do except bluster. I wrote and told him it was singularly unchristian of him to bully a bloke who, though voluminously incapacitated, had made alternative arrangements for his flock. And I soon discovered the name of the person who had been so outraged at hearing a layman speak in church about God that she had immediately complained to higher authority, as it were. It was Dorothy Walker, churchwarden Jack's wife, that wizened acolyte of my lugubrious predecessor who had savoured a long feud with Jim Watts. Bony, nicotine-stained Dot Walker who scowled through every Parochial Church Council meeting, always in the rocking chair in the corner under a haze of cigarette smoke.

I went to see her. She would not discuss the affair but sat there sullenly, smoking of course, her violent nervous tic like an accusation. I said,

"The Vicar is always in no man's land in this sort of dispute, Dot. But I don't expect to be stabbed in the back by my own church officers."

I might have been talking to a waxwork.

I called on Jim and apologised for embarrassing him. He didn't have much to say either.

In The White Swan at Wighill, spending the bier money – our fees for officiating at a funeral – Tim said,

"I would have taken the service for you, but I'm no good in't duck. Not bad behind, tub."

This was gibberish to me and Tim had to explain that duck referred to the pulpit and tub to the lectern. Another pint. And another. The evening stole on by the log fire until we came home through fields which lay like white ash in the moonlight.

There is a great error which imagines that, if it's variety you're looking for, then you should live in the metropolis. But the metropolis is too huge to focus on the particular: and it is relevant particulars which define variety. So the village contains a whole world, a cosmos, a universe of differences. Differences of character, embodied in characters. Take Tockwith's Bill and Phyllis Cooper, for example. They lived next to the Judge's thatched cottage in the main street, in colossally amiable untidiness. An open fire with an old range oven in black lead. Phyllis cooked Bill's Yorkshire puddings in it and they were on the table every Sunday at noon – not a minute earlier, not a minute later.

Phyllis was, if I may lapse into the international style, of notable construction, grosse et grasse – so much so that, when I took the parish trip to the ancient crypt at Lastingham on the North Yorkshire Moors, Phyllis was too wide for the stone staircase and so, while we said Mass in St Cedric's white stone chapel, she had to remain in The Blacksmith's Arms where, thanks to the comforts of its copious repast, she grew wider still and wider. Once, getting out of a Morris Mini – how ever she had got in was a sublime mystery – she rolled over and couldn't right herself. So she just rolled around on the pavement like a Kelly, laughing like a child.

Bill lived among bottles of brown ale, fetched every lunchtime from The Spotted Ox and emptied by four o'clock, whereupon a deserved sleep until it was time to stroll though the late evening air, take the empties back to the pub and enjoy a couple of points of draught before closing time. When I first arrived in Tockwith, I asked Bill and Phyllis if they knew a decent place to eat in York:

"Aye, by the river. Lew's Place. We go whenever we can for our lunch, don't we Phyllis? Steak as big as the dictionary. And spuds – what spuds! – all the plate covered with 'em. Heaps of cabbage, nearly black. Trifle – they give you seconds if you ask. And the cheeseboard piled with Wensleydale and Blue Stilton. Milky coffee with brown sugar – they bring it to you in a basin. And mints. Didn't I say to you, Phyllis, them mints were t'best I've had since Mint Imperials? "

Phyllis savoured his anamnesis of lunch, then said:

"They give you such a good meal at Lew's Place that we can only manage a few scones with jam and cream at teatime."

Relevant particulars. Characters. Barrie the Bilton organist who kept the newsagent's shop in Tockwith, delivered papers every day morning and evening. And never gave you his bill until you'd asked half a dozen times. Then it would be written out in copper plate handwriting, exquisite as a museum exhibit. Barrie, shy to the point of being shell-shocked, because in the late 1940s he had lent his father his own attic bedroom and a plane, mistaking the main street for the runway, crash-landing, tore off the roofs and killed Barrie's dad. An awful irony: the plane mistakes the street for a runway, and now all the new streets in the village are built on former runways. Barrie never, in decades, threw out a single newspaper. They were all piled in bundles in every room in the house, turning the place into a tinderbox. Barrie, with only one lung, cycling to Bilton church every Sunday morning in all weathers, refusing lifts in parishioners' cars. Retiring. Scrupulous. Knowledgeable. Clean as a sixpence. Straight as a die. He lived with his sister, Dorothy, a dedicated spinster with hair like wire wool. She had taught at Tockwith school for thirty years and always had her salary paid directly into the bank. She never touched a penny of it. As far as I could tell, she and her brother lived on cans of Heinz beans and pots of mint tea. When she took ill, she was hospitalised in Northallerton General and Barrie cycled to visit every weekend – a round trip of forty miles. When Dorothy died she left three decades' salary – around £300,000 – a significant sum back in 1989.

Characters. That old Pauline Sorrell, widow with a wide waddle who could be such a trouble at PCC meetings – the one who had talked all through the service on my first Sunday. Always wore the same camel coat. Always shouted. Even her whispers were shouted. Fiercely kind.

The trade of the parish priest is in life and death. And, given enough practice, he learns to cope with these two impostors pretty well. But sometimes, only rarely, thank God, he gives way and weeps in anger and something approaching the sin of despair. There is no excuse for this. The remedy is fervent prayer. But I gave way now and again. For example, I had just watched a mother of two, aged twenty-eight, die of breast cancer in York District Hospital with her husband sitting there, shaking and sweating beside the maze of gadgets and tubes that had preserved in her the semblance of life for days on end. He held her hand. He never spoke. Just stared into his wife's face with a look that said Don't leave me!

I drove back home over Marston Moor, trancelike. What could one say or think?

The day was hot and relentless. I took the whisky bottle and sat on the vicarage wall watching the cars go by. When I had nearly finished the bottle, I went in search of utter seclusion – where better than the grave? So I crossed the road into the churchyard and, bottle in hand, propped myself against one of the 19th century gravestones and nodded under the tall trees. The sky was brilliant white and the church clock sang the hours drowsily. Next thing I knew, it was six o'clock and Pauline Sorrell was shaking me.

"Whatever's the matter, love? Come on, I'll take you home!"

And she never once mentioned my impropriety. Ten years later, she turned up to church as usual, read the Epistle with sonorous penetration, returned home to put the Yorkshire puddings in the oven and dropped dead in the kitchen. I buried her abetted by Carllill, Backhouse and the usual gang. I think for a long period I had been in love with the old girl.

For characters, read hieroglyphics. It's appropriate: they all had their names written in the temple book - well, the church registers anyway. There was Penny Cole and her horse, or the horse and its Penny Cole, whichever way you looked at them. Rustic Penny who knew her wild mushrooms, picked them and sold them at the village fete – or anytime if you called at Bluebell Cottage. Retired, twinkly, General Henry Woods who, it was rumoured, was building a nuclear bunker under Grafton House. His comprehension of military strategy verged on the supernatural. At the beginning of the Falklands War in 1982, I asked him what he thought would be the outcome:

"They've only got one significant ship – The Belgrano. We'll sink it and then we'll win."

His yappy wife walking her yappy dogs. But a woman with enough kindness for a regiment. Johnny Metcalfe who wound the church clock and regularly turned up at church with another man's wife. It was all understood. No aggro.

There was also a small convocation of strange folk who thought well of themselves and stood aloof. You felt they expected the ordinary villager to curtsey or touch the forelock. They would turn out and help on the annual Gift Day, though – even if they announced their charity from the housetop, like the Pharisees who loved their long phylacteries.

Marjorie Firth, landlady at The Boot & Shoe, was a saint, drunk or sober. She provided lunch for God knows how many aged, feckless, waifs and strays and she had a receptive ear for those who all but God had forgotten.

"Have a little drink, Peter, before you go into the service. Steady your nerves. There's no harm in it."

Marjorie herself knew just how much harm in it there could be. But it never blighted her generosity. Of such is the kingdom of heaven.

The nasty old innkeeper of The Chequers in Bilton was the shape of a barrel and he beat his wife. She exulted publicly when he died and that night in her pub was joyous as Christmas Eve. There was a Chequers gang of churchy boozers who met weekly and called themselves The Monday Club – though they were probably quite a bit further to the Right than their Westminster namesake. Alf – originally German and real name Hans – Schmidt with his wife whose intonation was unnervingly like that of Kenneth Williams. Roger Topliss, Treasurer of Bilton Church with his smoker's cough and excess of self-deprecation. Sheepish. Married to Rusty – an ordinary girl who took ordinariness to extraordinary lengths. Knowingly sexy too.

Deryck Wilson, young bachelor, only child of Ella and Dick, born when Ella was over forty because, as she said, they had been waiting. Deryck the young professional working for the Water Board and much obliging me by taking on the position of Churchwarden at Tockwith after Jack Walker, husband of the nerves and nicotine Scorpio Dorothy, had retired to the steep cliffs of Robin Hood's Bay to do his ailing heart good. Deryck with his highly pitched voice and a comradeliness so fierce he would have been the perfect companion in the trenches.

The usual quota of loonies. Two old ladies in Bilton, saturated with diamonds, who wanted to remove a cherry tree from the graveyard because,

"...it's bringing up father."

A bald woman on the drome who begged me to exorcise her new baby who, she said, had been

"...possessed by her teddy bear who's really the devil."

Mrs Penn who bred – not herself, you understand – Boxer dogs with hifalutin pedigree names such as Stainburn-Dorf but which tended to be born with a testicle missing.

I said, Good morning to her once before a service – so she complained to the Rural Dean that I had been frivolous.. She left the village shortly after that shock to set herself up as the Dowager Duchess of the nearby village of Nun Monkton:

"When the Vicar said Good morning I was so offended! In church one should speak only to The Almighty"

Not to the high and mighty, then?

What can you say?

XX

There was an encroaching darkness. In the 1970s a new fashion in religion swept eastwards across the Atlantic. It was called Charismatic Renewal. Arm-waving, guitars, daft choruses and dancing in the aisles with mild libidinosity. Smart, sex-sublimating young people, professional types expostulating about being born again. They also went in for another attention-seeking party trick which they called being slain in the Spirit. A whole gang of them would stand up in church wail, shriek, wave their arms about, weep, laugh and hyperventilate until they fainted to the ground like kids in those farty assemblies. The rest of us were expected to believe that this temporary departure from the vertical was a sign of a visitation by God's Holy Spirit. The parsons who practised Charismatic Renewal copied themselves on the gleeful moribundity of the transatlantic trash TV anchormen.

Charismatic Renewal was a bigger indulgence than soft soap and so, of course, it prospered wonderfully in the better-off suburbs where there was the consumerist palate for everything, including religion. They were all shiny faces and soft options. Their music the three chords of the liturgical pop guitar. Their theology wish-fulfilment. Their clergy combined the roles of chat show host and game show presenter and performed them in sacred space. The Rural Dean, Arthur West, was himself coloured this hue of cherryade. After the Deanery Synod meeting, he told me with a grin:

"I came back from holiday and, well, you know, I'd missed my people. So, at the start of my first Sunday back in harness, I stood on the chancel step, cocked my ear and called out, 'Nice to see you!' – just like Brucie. And the answer came back from them all, 'To see you, nice!'"

Charismatic Renewal is religion with the reality taken out. If true Christianity is substantial truth and its embodiment. Charismatic Renewal is a vacuous pseudo-spirituality, a sort of discarnation. Its adherents look for supernatural healing even for the most trivial ailments. Miracle cures. The maudlin exuberance of its twanging songs. The vacuity of sentiment in what I must call their lyrics:

"Bind us together, Lord...ya ya ya."

Its God-awful versions of Holy Scripture. Prayer reduced to banality. One day I cadged a lift into York from one of the Charismatic types and, as we drove over Lendal Bridge, she said,

"You do believe in the Holy Spirit, Peter, don't you?"

"Yes – that's what we say in the Creed."

Great! So let's send him a quick arrow prayer to ask for a parking space!"

"Why should God prefer us over all the other buggers looking for a spot?"

"Have you no faith, Peter?"

"Yes, but I don't think the Holy Ghost operates through the traffic department."

"Why not?"

About this time, I was on a course organised by the Social Affairs Unit – an outfit which the BBC describes as a right of centre think tank. Makes me want to describe the BBC as a left of centre no-think tank. Late one night in the bar I suggested to the Director of the SAU, Dr Digby Anderson, that we should produce a book of essays on the sentimentalisation of society which seemed to be proceeding apace – its religious wing being Charismatic Renewal .I volunteered to investigate the movement's activities at its shrine in York, the ancient church of St Michael-le-Belfrey, close by the Minster.

Only the Medieval stone walls and the 18th century religious portraits reassure the visitor that he has in fact entered a church. The milieu is that of the pop concert, as early-arriving members of the audience – the word congregation has no place here – stroll among the pews, calling out Hi! to friends and acquaintances and pausing now and then to emit whoops of delight and hug one another flamboyantly. All the body-language is over-inflected in a style which would be seen as insincere even on the theatrical stage. The supercharged emotionality can hardly be genuine. One would be ill from it, if it were – as from an excess of chocolates or a surfeit of lampreys.

No organ music for Introit. No robed clergy or choir. Nothing at all to let the alien know that the service has begun. The designer-scruffy impresario, who turns out to be lead singer in the rock band, bawls into the microphone in his transatlantic twang:

"I wanna teach you a new song!"

The overhead projector displays the doggerel of this first song and the noise starts. The impression is of audience participation at the Christmas pantomime at York's Theatre Royal. The audience sways from side to side and does its best to look like the audience at the BBC's Top of the Pops. Many take little notice of the proceedings at all, but continue to wander about the place, gesticulating to acquaintances, talking like Americans and stopping off here and there for another stylised hug. The mind – an unusual spectator at this feast – casts around for some vestige of form among the formlessness and finds itself at last falling into the recognisable rhythms only of its own recollections. And these turn out to be a definition of what is going on:

Shape without form, shade without colour,

Paralysed force, gesture without motion...

A second impresario in a pullover featuring a commercial design stands up to give out the notices and to publish the Banns of Marriage. It is all done hurriedly, as if the speaker is ashamed of this small interlude of unavoidable conventionality. This is the only vestige of structure in the whole show. The impresario prays that those to be married...

"...might know the joy and fullness of marriage from the very start."

The alien, the sceptic, asks himself,

"How could they – except by a sentimental reduction of the whole concept of matrimony and the causes for which it was ordained?"

A round, bearded man in a woolly jumper, which prompts recollections of circumnavigation, preaches the sermon. But this is not a sermon as we know sermons. It is a series of in-jokes to massage the egos of his audience, his coterie. Its utterance in an ancient church, a consecrated building, borders on obscenity, on what is blasphemous:

"Paul" – the woolly jumper means Saint Paul – "was against circumcision. The Judaisers said you had to be circumcised in order to be saved. That rules out half the human race. Think about it. Not for too long though – it could be sinful!"

The whole performance is characterised by this sort of desiccated sexual innuendo. They snigger and nudge one another in the pews. The alien wished he had prepared himself for this ordeal with a prophylactic dose of Imodium.

The slouching, beardy in the Magellan pullover – suddenly I realise he is the Vicar – interrupts himself:

"Let's have a break. You know, I see all sorts of things from up here. Burgeoning romances. Hands moving towards each other across the pew – not mentioning any names..."

Insofar as he had a theological theme, it was, self-defeatingly,

"The Gospel plus anything else is not the Gospel."

No? Not even the Gospel plus smutty jokes and spoilt music? He requires forty minutes to get across his point about spurious additions. The sermon is followed by more spoilt music and banal choruses repeated so many times that the alien is left feeling giddy. It is all content-free, insubstantial, and its evident purpose is to foster a rootless, nebulous togetherness.

I wrote an article in The Guardian about my experience in that York church and the smiley Bishop Maddox came round to tell me off. He found me in bed with a fluey cold and I spent a fevered twenty minutes racing around the bedroom trying to escape his attempts to administer the Laying on of Hands.

But now for the encroaching darkness...

In January 1981, Sally Raynar's husband died of his cancer. I had spent two afternoons each week with him for the duration of his final illness. He had been very afraid:

"What happens to us, Peter? And you know I can't bear to leave Sally. And what will she do without me?"

We sat in his bedroom, the pale blue curtains drawn back, and looked out over the lake towards the tall trees nudging the horizon. We talked of music and poetry – Donne's Death be not proud – and listened to Mozart. Gradually he grew into a kind of resignation, of acceptance even. The ache was still there but the sting had gone.

There was the dawning of hope – not wishful thinking, but hope in the theological sense: we dare to have hope because our hope is in God alone.

As a prominent local gentleman, Geoffrey was well known to the Yorkshire Evening Press, and so it was natural for the paper to carry a few respectful paragraphs about his condition. This encouraged two of the religious maniacs from St Michael-le-Belfrey to call on him, all uninvited and unannounced – grinning and praying, praying and grinning – to tell Geoffrey that, if only he would believe, God would restore him to full health.

Straw-clutching, he was seduced by the hype. He became exultant, manic even. He was now certain, in the light of these new and exciting ministrations, that God was going to make him well again. And what beside this promise was the unglamorous ministry of the boring Established Church and the insipid music of Mozart? Geoffrey died. But he died in confusion and torment. And haunted by guilt as well – for surely the reason God had not healed him was his own pernicious lack of faith!

I wrote about this too and earned another visit from the effulgent Bishop Morris Maddox:

"Why did you write as you did. Peter? It was mere bitterness."

"Because I was bitter. Still am."

"My poor boy!"

I did not welcome his hand on my shoulder.

"Sod off with your poor boy!"

"Oh my dear Peter, there is no need for such strong language!"

"There bloody well is!"

"Shall we have a word of prayer?"

"I'm at a loss."

"And what d'you think Geoffrey was, then? He was dying nicely, you know. Then a couple of your superstitious lunatics turn up and all the good I'd tried to do is undone. Geoffrey died in agony of soul. How do you like that on your conscience, you barmy bugger!"

"It is regrettable. But sometimes excesses occur. They are bound to."

"Excesses?"

"Yes, of course..." his eyes were like illuminated goldfish bowls –

"when people are possessed of God's Holy Spirit..."

He said Holy Spirit with the riotous intensity of a football hooligan cheering on his team.

"...they can get rather enthusiastic."

"Well, they killed Geoffrey with their enthusiasm."

"Let us pray."

"Why don't you sod off!"

He began to mouth a prayer at a gallop, on the verge of hysteria. I felt like grabbing him by the lapels or the ears. I was so purple in front of this episcopal clowning, I might have killed him. Then I suddenly lost all my energy and fell into a desperate calm. Speaking deliberately, on a monotone:

"Look Morris, if you get a bunch of loonies hyped up on repressed sex – blaming it, you know, on the Lord Jesus – and then you tell them they can work miracles, that the world is populated with angels and demons – a cartoon supernaturalism – that present day York is no different from first century Corinth, and that God will enable them to do anything, what do you expect except megalomania and barbarism?

"They killed Geoffrey as much as the liver cancer. I know because I saw it happen. Now why don't you stop trying to make yourself into a telly star and act like a bloody bishop instead? Stamp out this nonsense in the diocese."

He began to mouth a silent prayer of his own, his lips twisting, twitching. I should not have been surprised if he had started to foam at the mouth. Five minutes later, he had arisen from his prostration and taken his leave – throwing me a last look which told me how infinite was the sorrow caused to him by my unbelief.

God moves in a mysterious way. He slew his most prominent Charismatic servant with another cancer of the liver. I mean the grey-faced David Watson, members of whose congregation had so recently discomfited Geoffrey Raynar. Watson was urbane, sanctimonious. He knew exactly what to say to the middle class teenagers in his thrall – to legitimate their pale libidinousness and to get them to locate all their emotional spasms in the action of the Spirit.

When Watson was dying, he broadcast a half hour documentary on BBC Radio Four in which he said he knew that God was curing him. Then he died. His disciples wanted to have it both ways: here was a man possessed of the Holy Spirit who knew that God was healing him. He died. This was meant to be a sign of the infinite mercy of God who, as they said, healed him by his death. Not so much kill or cure as kill and cure. But this is only ordinary logic. And, as smiley Mad Ox, said,

"God makes foolish the wisdom of men."

I saw so much misery being caused by the Charismatics. There is already misery enough: birth and death and the interval between which may include marriage. But these mortal coils can be coiled more painfully, as I discovered, by the promises of false hope and the god of wishful thinking. I sometimes wonder whether, when poor old Watson was dying, any members of his exuberant congregation turned up to comfort him – as they had comforted Geoffrey Raynar. I wrote about that incident too in The Guardian and Church Times and received by reward an anonymous poison-pen letter postmarked York.

I was angry and totally baffled. I could understand the Charismatic Movement as a fashionable nonsense might appeal to under-educated and over-praised adolescents from the comfy suburbs, but how could a man like Maddox, ordained in the 1950s, acquainted with real life in the real world, be taken in by it? Was it just an escape – a happy deliverance from the ordinary drabness of hassocks and the Parochial Church Council into a supercharged world of glossy excitements? You no longer merely had to comfort the bereaved and pray with the dying, you could put a Jimmy Carter inflection into your voice, grab as much glee as you could and promise folk they would be healed of all their infirmities. This religion of false promises is an obscenity and its exponents do violence to the very people they pretend to be helping.

This sentimental, infantilised, Disneyfication of the faith has no roots in reality. It is like a tightrope walk – not just without the safety net, but without the tightrope. But if your grin was wide enough and you ended every sentence with the whooped words the Lord and the Holy Spirit, you could achieve a passable appearance. But then your parishioner died of cirrhosis or cancer of the lung: that was when the appearances were swallowed up by the painful reality. Why did they do it? Vanity. Conceit. The desire to build yourself a spurious small empire of credulous sycophants, as Watson had done in York.

There seemed to be no end to the atrocities.

For example, Sylvia and John were married. They went because, as Sylvia told me, they had seen a St Michael's service on TV, to Watson's church. John went along with it, but Sheila became avid. They started going to what he later described to me as seriously barmy house meetings where people

"...spoke in tongues and sang about Jesus in the same way Joan Baez used to sing about Vietnam."

After a few months of this, John withdrew from the meeting and Sylvia continued to attend by herself. She became unhappy because this meant she was spending evenings apart from John, so she gave it up as well. When she told them at St Knees Up, they said she would have to choose between Jesus and her husband. They told Sylvia that it was Satan who had got into her husband and lured him away from the group. She must resist any temptation to side with the devil against the house meeting.

This was England 1981. And these things were being done in the name of the Church of England. The church of Cranmer and Donne, Johnson and Samuel Coleridge had lost its marbles. Sylvia and John divorced the following year. A few months later John killed himself. A bottle of sleeping tablets and a bottle of whisky. Too much spirit. Another of Mad Ox's rare excesses.

As a result of my excursions on this topic in the national press, I began to receive letters from all over the country:

"Our daughter has fallen into the hands of these idiots..." – this from Bristol – "...and won't speak to us anymore. We were such a close-knit, happy family. Now I feel as if she's died. It's almost worse than if she'd died: she's become so alien."

"Tony..." – from Blackburn – "he's started going to this weird church at the other side of town. Now he says we're in Satan's thrall, his father and me. We've written to the bishop but he says he can't intervene."

Janice, from Cheltenham, renounced her unsaved family and six months later her mother died of cancer. Her father was convinced she had developed the disease out of her distress.

In 1979 a book had appeared: Healing by Francis MacNutt. (I am not making this up!) He said that there are eleven ways in which

God heals and one of these ways of healing is by death. So if you are cured, it's a miracle and if you die, it's still a miracle. If you press on stoically, that's also a miracle. So many miracles and so much misery. I asked Archdeacon Stanbridge what he thought of Healing and he replied,

"It's a very sane book."

So negligible was mind when measured against ratings in the contemporary English Church

The worst came in 1984. I was teaching philosophy every Tuesday evening for the University of York's extramural classes. A woman called Margaret turned up one night. She had been to one of David Watson's house groups. Why not? A widow, lonely, she had only recently moved to York. Where better than an Anglican church to look for friendship? Thirty years earlier, Margaret had gained a First Class Honours degree in philosophy – a mark of intelligence which would surely immunise anybody against the Charismatic trash? But loneliness is wearisome.

One evening in the house meeting, the group were discussing evil. Margaret told me:

"We were sitting around – some on settees, others on cushions on the floor. Someone was playing the guitar and there was singing – the choruses that go on and on. Then they started praying very loudly. They were very uninhibited. I felt nervous about it all and wished I hadn't come. Then they started talking about a personal devil and I said I didn't believe in a personal devil – you know, I could never go along with all that horns and a pitchfork stuff.

"Of course, I said, no one in his right mind could doubt for one minute that there is a great deal of evil in the world. I certainly believed in evil. I just didn't believe in the existence of that pantomime demon. This wouldn't do for them. They said the reason I denied the personal devil was obviously because the devil himself had put me up to it. I was possessed. Nothing for it then but to perform an exorcism.

"They lunged at me, pushing and shoving until I was flat on my back on the floor. Then a lot of them all at the same time tried to lay their hands on me and command the devil to come out. I was nearly crushed alive - terrified, shaking. I thought I was going to die."

Margaret ended up incarcerated in one of the many mental hospitals in which York specialises. I wrote about her case in a book Strange Gifts: A Guide to the Charismatic Movement in the Church of England which I co-edited with Professor David Martin of the LSE. A press agency picked up the story and it made front page every night for a whole week in The Yorkshire Evening Press. By this time Morris Maddox had left his post of suffragan Bishop of Selby to float off into some peripatetic Charismatic lunacy in which he toured the country propagandising the Movement. The new bishop, Clifford Barker, called on me to complain about my treatment of the Charismatics at St Michael-le-Belfrey.

He had the manner of a small town solicitor entering a plea for excuses:

"Well, Peter, I've done a lot of research and I find that this Margaret of yours has a history of mental instability. Perhaps you should not judge the good people of St Michael-le-Belfrey too harshly after all."

"Let me get this right, Clifford. What you're saying is that the treatment meted out by that house group is the sort of treatment appropriate to be dished out to a frail and distressed woman by Christian people?"

He was clearly irritated:

"I'm not saying that at all!"

"Then what are you saying?"

Not much, as it turned out. The bums put on seats – and the funds consequently contributed to diocesan funds – by such as St Michael-le-Belfrey put them beyond criticism and so members of the lesser hierarchy such as Barker were deployed to silence criticism, if necessary by issuing scarcely-veiled threats to the critics:

"The authorities may have to look much further into this matter, Peter."

"They can look into it till the cows come home: they won't find any way of defending the indefensible."

"Where there is so much spiritual vitality, there are bound to be excesses, mistakes made."

"That was your predecessor's line and it's bollocks. When you institutionalise emotional blackmail and brainwashing, as the charismatics do, your so called excesses are simply the naturally expected consequences."

"Do be careful, Peter! Do not set yourself against a good work being done by the Holy Spirit."

"This Movement has nothing to do with the Holy Spirit. Actions don't become good and acceptable just because some half-crazed enthusiast attributes them to God. At the bottom of all this stuff is vanity and the will to power – and it is always vulnerable and inadequate people who are hurt most."

"Well, I have said my piece. I think you are seriously misguided and you're making a big mistake."

"Yes, you've said your piece so you can go now. Report back to your friends at St Michael's that you have called on Peter Mullen and read him the Riot Act."

"It's not like that at all."

I said nothing. He stood up and we stared silently at each other for what seemed like half a minute.

"I am so sorry to hear you speak as you have done, Peter."

This as he turned and walked towards the door. Then he was climbing into his little white car and setting off down the drive.

For six or seven years I found myself engaged with the Charismatics. I had not looked for a fight, but the fight had come anyway, created out of the misery the Movement inflicted on those for whom I had pastoral care. Once I had criticised them publicly, I became their clearly-identified enemy and, by reason of the hundreds of letters I received from victims, something of an expert on their doings. It was an expertise I could have done without. I accumulated a file of reported cases, two feet thick. When I walked into my study where these letters and papers were locked up for safe-keeping, I often felt that the room itself shrieked its indignation against the horrors they contained. Wars of attrition are just that. I was being ground down, worn out.

What when you got an anguished phone call at midnight from a woman in Gravesend whose daughter, having fallen in with the Charismatic loonies at Exeter university, denounces her own family as children of Satan?

"Well, I'm sorry. I think I understand, but there's nothing much I can do at this distance. Go and tell your parish priest about it."

"But you don't understand. The Vicar is new here and he's up to the same tricks!"

There was nothing I could do. I had to admit I had bitten off more than I could chew and now I was beaten. I could no longer bear the strain of receiving dozens of letters each week: all that suffering in the face of which I was powerless. So I gave up writing about the Charismatic Movement. No doubt it was a cowardly thing to do. I felt guilty. But I had no energy left for a struggle I could not win. Nonsense – sometimes psychopathic nonsense – not infrequently attends religion. I simply had to accept that fact and give up. Before I did, I performed a sort of exorcism of my own – on the Movement itself. I wrote a novel Blessed Assurance, the title derived from the old revivalist hymn:

Blessed assurance, Jesus is mine!

O what a foretaste of glory divine!

It was published in 1990 by Robert Hale

I was writing other things too: picture strip stories of Jesus for Nicolas McDowell at Edward Arnold. I merely wrote the words – the libretto, you might say. The wonderfully evocative illustrations were the creation of Martin Pitts, my old college friend with the mellifluous voice and the yellow trousers. I also wrote a dramatic chorus based on the Passion narrative in St Mark's Gospel and went to the BBC studios in Manchester to hear it recorded. In it I had tried to represent the chaos and confusion of the arrest, show trial and Crucifixion of Christ by having the six voices in the chorus speak across one another and so subvert the ordinary prose of a narrative line. It was broadcast on Radio Three on Easter Eve and not well-received.

After the recording, I stayed with Eric Wright, an art teacher I had got to know at Whitecroft. He was fiftyish, lived with his wife in Horwich, under Belmont Moor, close by the Chinese gardens constructed by Lord Leverhulme, of Sunlight Soap fame. From these ornamental gardens high on the moor, Leverhulme could look down on his factory, forty miles away in Cheshire at Port Sunlight. Eric's baby granddaughter had just died – a cot death. Her cot was in the corner of my bedroom. Unnerving, because a cot death was the main feature of Blessed Assurance.

I hardly slept.

XXI

It was the Fourth Sunday in Lent, variously called Mothering Sunday – now of course collapsed and sentimentalised into Mother's Day – or Refreshment Sunday, so called because it came with provision for a break in the Lenten Fast. Actually, none of the Sundays in Lent is a Fast, since every Sunday is a commemoration of the resurrection and therefore a Feast. I usually gave up booze for Lent and I resisted the temptation to drink on Sundays, reasoning that it was less arduous to stop drinking once on Ash Wednesday, and leave the bottle alone until Easter, than to have to give it up all over again every Monday morning for six weeks.

I was preaching when I noticed a stranger in the congregation – a tall, languid sort, aged about thirty. He joined in the service vigorously, standing straight-backed for the hymns and the Creed, kneeling with lavish devotion for the prayers. I discovered later that he followed the Old Testament lesson in his own copy of the original Hebrew and the New Testament reading from the Greek. His stiff posture and exuberant singing – not always in agreement as to pitch and tempo with the rest of the congregation's interpretation of Hymns A.& M. (Revised). He politely resisted all invitations to stay behind for a drink after the service.

He attended every Sunday in Lent but steadfastly refused to socialise. Just that smile as he gathered his books and went his way. A few weeks after Easter, he remained in his place for a long time after the final hymn and, as I passed by the end of his pew, stood up and said,

"Father, may I introduce myself?"

His voice was deep, resonant, measured – the sort of voice you would expect Abraham to speak in. And scarcely anyone referred to the clergy as Father in the Puritan east side of England. I found myself alone with this devout, scholarly and diffident stranger.

"Christopher Boyd-Martin, Father."

And he gave my hand a potent squeeze.

"Come across to the vicarage and have a drink."

"I'm afraid I can't. Not now."

He looked at his feet and fingered the gold edging on his Greek New Testament:

I must go and prepare lunch for my mother. We live in York. She's an invalid. But I would like to talk with you urgently. Would after Evensong be a good time?"

As soon as I had said that would be fine, he smiled faintly and blushed then strode off, seeming to cover the distance from the chancel to the font in no more than three or four paces.

When I arrived in church at six o'clock, Boyd-Martin was already at his prayers and he remained kneeling until the first hymn when, as usual, he stood imperiously to attention and bellowed out the verses in his eccentric style. Throughout the service he maintained his customary, almost aggressive, piety and during the sermon he looked particularly agitated, preoccupied. Later, in my study, he was perfectly calm again as he began to tell me his story:

"After Cambridge, I went into the Civil Service, as a translator. I enjoyed that a lot at first. Anyhow, I had a bad patch with regard to my health. But I'm fine again now. Since my father died I've looked after my mother. She has a sort of nurse/visitor during the day and I cook the evening meal."

"Sherry? Orange juice, then?"

He wouldn't have anything. He never drank, he said with a particularly severe emphasis. It turned out that he now worked in the reference library at York University but he didn't enjoy that as much as the Foreign Office. As we talked, he stared up at my bookshelves and the look on his face suggested that he had noted all their titles and found nothing of conspicuous interest.

Suddenly he stood up:

"Father, I will come to the point. I hope you can help me. You see I want to offer myself for the priesthood."

That blush again. And his speech had become anxious, imploring, almost prayerful.

"Well, I'm delighted to hear it!"

My next question was awkward:

But look, what made you – how can I put it – what made you come to Tockwith, to me, rather than to your own parish priest or the university Chaplain?"

"Oh Father, I couldn't! You'll think me an awful church-taster and a snob but I stopped going to our local church – that's St Agnes – when the new Vicar came with his guitars, choruses and dancing in the aisle. Not my sort of thing at all."

"Not my sort of thing, either!"

"I know. I saw your articles about St Michael's in the Evening Press. That's why I came to you, actually."

I couldn't make him out. It was a long and at times an uncomfortable discussion and I felt that, for all his enthusiasm, he was holding something back – as if he was wanting to reveal his secret, but kept losing his nerve at the last minute. He would drum on the chair arm for a few seconds, then check himself, cross and uncross his legs, take out his pen and fidget with the screw cap. A March gale was getting up and the vicarage started to creak nervously.

Suddenly Boyd-Martin thrust his hands on to his knees vehemently, as if in performance of some strenuous physical exercise. He looked straight ahead. It was now dark outside and I became aware that I could see two Boyd-Martins: the stiff-looking fellow on the edge of his armchair and his equally stiff reflection looking through the window from among the tombstones and crosses in the graveyard opposite..

"The trouble is, Father, that I am not worthy of the priesthood!"

I shrugged:

"Is that all? None of us is worthy. Thank God the unworthiness of the priest does not affect the validity of the Sacraments – that's what the Prayer Book says. Else heaven help the lot of us, so to speak."

At once there was much more spirit in his conversation.

"Oh I know we're all unworthy in a general sort of way – but I'm particularly unworthy."

"Oh I see – like St Paul, eh? You're not content o be a common or garden sinner but you have to be the Chief of Sinners. Beware the sin of inverted pride!"

"Ah but in my case it's true."

"It always is. And what's so special about your sins eh? Have you murdered someone, or something?"

For a moment I thought he looked almost disappointed that he was unable to count this crime among his misdoings. Once the conversation had turned to sin, I could tell he felt himself to be on more secure ground. He didn't actually make a formal Confession, though given his very protruberant High Church proclivities, he would need little encouragement to do so. I threw another log on the fire and it blazed briefly, brightly. He said,

"But I am serious about the priesthood. And I have no illusions. My uncle was a priest and so I know what the job entails... the disappointments."

"Don't overdo the disappointments!"

My remark seemed to disappoint him. I said,

"Well, we must put the wheels in motion for you to try your vocation. I'll write to the bishop about you – and of course I'll have to get in touch with your parish priest and let him know what's going on. Perhaps you might call and see him yourself?"

"Perhaps."

There was a very loud silence. I went across to the desk to get pen and paper.

"Now I should take down a few details. Christopher Boyd-Martin, right? Date of birth, Christopher?"

He went and stood with his back to the window.

"Why d'you want to know that?"

"Just admin, you know. The diocesan office will have to have something to recognise your file by."

He looked distraught.

"File? Will I have a file?"

"We're all in the files somewhere – you must know that well enough with your Civil Service background."

He was almost in tears. He wouldn't say what was the matter. I tried the light-hearted approach:

"There's nothing to worry about. You did say you hadn't actually committed a murder, didn't you? Well, the office will have to have some way of referring to you – I mean, so far as they're concerned, you might be the uncrowned King of England!"

"I am!"

"You are what?"

"The uncrowned King of England. Now, if you will excuse me, I have important matters to attend to."

Attending the Privy Council, no doubt.

Having declared himself, as it were, he became very calm. He was courteous but insisted he had to be on his way and so I accompanied him to his car and watched him drive off immaculately towards York.

I phoned his Vicar, who did not sound in the least bit surprised:

"Yes, Peter, I knew he had been visiting you at Tockwith. I wondered how long it would be before he revealed his little obsession. He does the same thing wherever he goes, apparently, poor soul. I know his psychiatrist. There's no need for alarm. Mild schizophrenia. No danger to himself or anyone else – I've been assured of that. He copes wonderfully at work – and with his mother. Look, I'll let things ride for a couple of days, then I'll call round and see him."

I never saw Christopher Boyd-Martin again. And Tockwith is still waiting for its first candidate for Holy Orders.

At the end of May, that old college pal, the cricketing Mike Shearing – nephew of the late great blind pianist George Shearing – called in on his way to a conference in York. On his way back downstairs from the loo, he paused on the landing to look out over the churchyard:

"Ugh! I don't know how you can bring yourself to sleep in a house overlooking a graveyard!"

"Why not? You've been watching too many horror films. This is Tockwith, not Transylvania, you know. English graveyards are homely places – not at all sinister."

Mike stared out over the haphazard crosses half-hidden in the long grass and shook his head:

"No – not for me, thanks. But I must say, I like that."

He pointed to a large statue of an angel holding a scroll.

"Now that's the sort of memorial I'd like!"

"Yes, but at today's prices you'd need to raise a mortgage. Anyhow, the diocesan authorities wouldn't allow it."

As we were talking, I noticed a little girl in a bright yellow dress wandering about among the gravestones. She stood for a while by a neglected grave upon which stood a rusty, empty vase. Then she bent to pick up a handful of daisies and dandelions which she arranged neatly in the vase. She stood back with her arms folded and admired her handiwork.

"What d'you mean, the diocese wouldn't allow me my angel?"

I led him into the study and took down the Diocesan Handbook.

Page forty-seven. Regulation 16 (Churchyards):

"Only certain specifications of memorials are permitted. No kerbs. No extravagant figures. No open books."

"Spoilsports! Bloody bureaucrats!" said Mike

"That's nothing. Just turn over the page."

He read aloud:

"Crosses: these are to be discouraged as they represent undue repetition of the supreme Christian symbol..."

He paused: "No," he said "You're having me on. This isn't the – what is it? – the Diocesan Handbook. It's a spoof eh? Monty Python version of the C. of E."

I assured him it was not. He laughed:

"Undue repetition of the supreme Christian symbol! Ha! I can just see members of your diocesan committee descending in pinstripes and pique on the war cemeteries in France: 'Ah Monsieur L'Archdeacon, ne touchez pas le croix s'il vous plait...' '...Mais Je regretted, madame, la commission a dit...' Peter, you must cut it out and send it to Private Eye. Hey – what bureaucracy! It beats the Common Market. You could start an EEC crucifix mountain with all the unwanted crosses!"

He looked at the kitchen clock and said it was time he was off to his York conference.

When he had gone I strolled into the churchyard. It was all bright colours – a blazing start to the busy rural summer. The heat and the extravaganza of grass and the wild flowers set the churchyard aside as an indolent, timeless place. Old men would sit in the sun on the south side and talk over past times from now until the middle of September. The path from the lych-gate was speckled with blossom brought down in Wednesday night's heavy rain. It looked like confetti.

I found the little girl in the yellow dress sitting silently on one of the kerbstones that were officially disapproved of. She looked thoughtful.

"Good afternoon! Have you finished collecting flowers?"

She jumped up suddenly and overturned the rusty vase.

"Oh, I was only picking the wild flowers!"

"I know you were."

I helped her replace the daisies and dandelions in the vase.

"I often come in here when I want to think. It's so nice and quiet."

"And what do you think about?"

"I sometimes think about God and why he bothered to make everything."

"Why do you think he made everything?"

"Because if he hadn't made everything, there would have been nothing. Then God would be bored."

She was about seven. I was on the edge of repenting my view of youngsters as having nothing in their heads except pop music, when she said,

"What are graves really for?"

How to explain without giving her Mike Shearing's queasiness about cemeteries!

"They're for memorials. That grave you put flowers on – that's a memorial, in memory of someone who's died."

"And are they really in them, all the people – in the graves?"

The ribbons which held her plaits were shaped like the forbidden crosses. She sat down again and rubbed her fingers over the inscription on the edge of the kerb:

"Emily Hayes 1818-1893 RIP"

"Why does it say 'rip'?"

"it's not 'rip.' It's initials – short for 'rest in peace.'"

She asked several more questions while I was still struggling with the first one. I managed to explain that when people died and went to God they didn't need their old bodies anymore, so these were brought into church to a funeral where all the people could give thanks for the life of their friend. Afterwards – and only because the old bodies were no use any longer – the dead person was put in a grave.

"Some of the dead people do get forgotten though, don't they?"

She gazed at the grave she had been tending. There were bird droppings on the headstone and the marble chips – or what was left of them – were piled up unevenly between the shabby kerbs.

"Well, even the sons and daughters of very old people have to die sometime. Look at Emily Hayes here. I don't suppose there'll be anyone alive today who remembers her."

She did not seem at all upset by this and we had a long talk about other things. She told me her name was Lesley. When it was time to go, we walked across the middle of the graveyard to the little gate in the far corner near the yew tree. We passed a very superior Victorian grave with iron railings and an obelisk. Lesley wanted to know why it was bigger than all the others. I said it must mark the last resting place of someone reckoned to have been very important. She said,

"God is very important, isn't he?"

Naturally, the Vicar agreed.

Suddenly, she looked up, shielding her eyes against the sun, and pointed towards the church. She spoke very confidently:

"I know that's God's grave. But it doesn't say his name on it. Is that because no one remembers him?"

Out of the mouths of babes and sucklings...

XXII

I was beginning to enjoy my Yorkshire parish. Sunday services from The Book of Common Prayer with The King James Bible. Visit folk when they're sick and bury them when they need it. A flurry of weddings. Children at the font and in the school. The two village pubs. Fundraising and tombola.

The big event of the summer was the Garden Fete at Bilton, at Peter and Jennie Bissett's house, a grand Edwardian building with a tree-shaded lawn, perfect as a bowling green. It was set in the oldest part of Bilton, the part still called the village by the locals.

"Just look at the sunshine! You've done it again, Vicar. Someone up there really does like you."

Mrs Lacey and Mrs Threapleton and Mrs Lacey's niece Simone, were already positioned like wicketkeepers behind the cake stall at twenty minutes to two.

"It's starting to melt the icing."

I walked among the stalls, hands behind my back like an old-fashioned policeman. Nancy Lockwood and Enid Marsh conspired over a black silk blouse with sequins before the official opening. Blood had been shed over such bargains.

"Hello Enid!"

"The elastic's gone in everything, Vicar."

She made it sound as if the whole cosmos would run out of puff even before the Fancy dress had been judged and we should all be delivered into the chill of entropy. A small cloud, no bigger than a jar of pickled walnuts, edged across the sun. Suddenly there were crowds on the lawn. Angular, limping Michael Langton, new Churchwarden, came to tell me that the Guest Celebrity had arrived. This was Donna Lethbridge, nee Thirkettle, in Bilton about twenty-one years before, and baptised Maureen soon after. Enid whispered at Nancy:

"It's her stage name, you know!"

"I know – I knew her mother when she was alive. Elsie Thirkettle, Elsie Butterfield, as was."

The actress made a short speech, commenting on the weather, commending the Bissetts for their hospitality, commending the beautiful garden and recommending that everyone spend wildly in the cause of St Helen's church. Donna was slim, small, tightly-packed, vivacious, full of self-confidence which chiefly expressed itself in starbursts of wide smiles – her large, architectured, even teeth flashing white like the allotropes of icebergs.

"Nice Garden Party you've got here, Vic!"

Cream cakes now melted in their rapid purchasers' individual string bags, rather than federally on Aggie Lacey's stall. Peter Bissett doled out tea to old ladies who sat under parasols at small tables and complained amiably about the plastic cups.

"Never mind, it's all in a good cause."

"We don't mind. We were supporting St Helen's before you were thought of, young man!"

Peter Bissett was a kindly man, secure in the knowledge he had made good, on the small side but neat and self-possessed. He looked as if he had been born in his best suit. He was a solicitor. Jennie, with the high cheekbones and canorous accent, was an amateur painter.

"If you'd like to stay for drinks when this lot's over, Peter."

The crowds gave the impression they had seen everything. The raffle result, to be announced at four o'clock, deferred their boredom. Donna left off signing autographs and prepared to judge the Fancy Dress. Teeth flashing like whited sepulchres, she spoke softly and consolingly to all the entrants before announcing the winner: Marion Leyland, a cute little thing from Margaret Thompson's Sunday School class who had come as a hydrogen bomb.

The rather unreliable Celia Cook turned up flushed and dithering. She was at once surrounded by red-faced ladies, simmering, dishevelled, nursing tea-towels and used plastic table cloths from the endless stream of washing up. Pauline Miner, a demure and ruthless housewife in her early sixties with an unbeatable record for labouring for the church, said disconsolately:

"Oh Mrs Cook, weren't you supposed to be bringing the new table cloths?"

She was whining, distraught,

"We've had to manage with these!"

She held one aloft disdainfully, as if it had been a filthy rag:

"We've been washing them as we've gone on. It's been very difficult, hasn't it, Mrs May? You see, we were relying on you to bring us the fresh ones."

Her face wore the tortured expression as of one who has just looked out upon a field of many dead.

Emily May rubbed her hands vigorously on her apron and looked severely at Mrs Cook over her steamed-up spectacles. An immense rectangle of a woman, she looked as if she were about to defend Thermopylae.

"Oh yes, we've been busy! I'll say we've been busy. We've been busy all right. D'you know how many cups and saucers we've washed and dried this afternoon? Go on, tell me if you think you do – clever clogs!"

She paused clasping her wet hands in front of her and gazing numinously into the distance:

"Four hundred and sixty-eight – that's how many!"

"I thought you said you were going to use plastic cups?"

"Oh yes, some plastic cups, Mrs Cook. But not all. By no means all of them. Some folks don't like to take their tea out of plastic cups. That's why we thought you'd have been here before now with the clean cloths and towels."

Mrs Cook only smiled as if the matter had been of no importance. Emily May turned on me feverishly and declared:

"And if you ask me, Vicar, I didn't think the Fete was as good as it might have been. It was a lot better in Vicar Watkins' day when he used to invite the bishop to come and open it – not these young slips of things from off the telly."

Donna had been rescued from autographer's cramp and old ladies' questions about what was going to happen next in her TV soap opera. She was safely drinking, beyond afternoon opening hours, in The Boot and Shoe while I helped Roger Topliss carry some planks and trestles into the shed. Then we ambled across the lawn, knocking the dust off our feet, to a card table by the front door where our Hon Treas had just finished counting:

"£983 – and these!"

A palm full of foreign coins and an unsigned cheque for £295 which had been taken on the produce stall.

I was drinking in The White Swan at Wighill one night with Tim Tunnard. He said,

"The parson and the publican – they're the two key characters in every village. I've always had this yen to write an operetta on the theme, but I've never managed to get any further than. 'Good morning Mrs Statham...Good morning Major Bore...'"

"I'll have a go – but I'd be no good at the music."

And there it was – eventually:

"Good morning Mrs Statham...Good morning Major Bore...How are you Mrs Hetherington? I think it's going to pour...Don't forget the meeting, on Tuesday night at eight...with colour slides of Iceland – gosh I can hardly wait!"

All sung to The Church's One Foundation.

On to the lady owner of the brewery behind the landlord's pub:

"Bertha's beer is bitter and
Her precious stout is sweet;
Bertha's mild is not reviled,
Her strong ale is a treat."

An agreeably clichéd plot: the fictional Archdeacon's metaphorical bells re-hung; the parson's daughter married to the publican's son. Full audiences in the school hall for three nights of mirth and insubordination. Over the next couple of years we produced two more: an Irish scandal Paddy's Return and, just what it sounds like, Yorkshire Pudding.

"My father was a parson in Norfolk," said Tim over the Draught Bass. "He had this sexton, Jake. Well, the church boiler was always going out and Pa was getting it in the neck from God's frozen people. So he took Jake on one side: 'Now look, Jake, why's the damn boiler always going out?'

"'There ain't nothing we can do about it, Rector. It's what the coalman sends. It be that antichrist.'"

Our own boiler under Tockwith church continued to be a vast discouragement. One winter God caused a great flood and it was completely submerged. Then it froze, smashing every pipe and radiator in the system. After much haggling with the Ecclesiastical Insurance Company, we got the money to put overhead electric heaters in under the supervision of the stalwart Jim Watts. Then the whole congregation complained that their heads were too hot and their feet still too cold. They asked what could be done and I said,

"Run about a bit during the sermon!"

We never closed. The York Light Opera came and entertained us – proceeds to church funds. Fat white legs and the terpsichorean muse rowdy and sleazy enough to remind me of the 1950s and my sister's dancing classes in Madame Lilleman's Academy next to Meanwood Road gasworks.

I dramatised Oscar Wilde's short story The Selfish Giant and wrote some tunes to go with it. We put it on in the school. Bright-eyed urchins and little girls all nervous, pink and white. Parents charmed. I was accused of elitism for this production by Tockwith's token Marxist who said I should write a rock opera. I did, and called it Moses

One night, after a long discussion in the pub about the importance – or perhaps it was the self-importance – of Melvyn Bragg, we decided to move the literary society meetings from Wetherby to The Chequers in Bilton. A lot said it wouldn't work – not out here in the country where everybody went around with shit on their boots and straws hanging from their mouths. But it did.

"It's a nice change from the whist drive, Vicar," said Alf Schmidt.

We had Laurie Taylor on crime. R.J. Hollingdale on Nietzsche. The Archbishop of York himself came and talked about himself explicitly by reading out consecutive pages of his diary. Best of all the composer Robert Simpson, a genius, shamefully treated by the BBC Music Department. The Cambridge City Jazz band performed in church, having prepared by consuming a crate of whisky on their way up to Yorkshire from the Fens. The most surreal evening at the Lit Soc featured Rev'd Professor David Jenkins from Leeds University. I stood at the bar with him for ten minutes before his lecture and all he could say was,

"Guess what's happened to me? Guess what's happened to me? They've made me Bishop of Durham. You must come and stay: Auckland Castle has a hundred bedrooms."

He sat in the corner, his white hair brilliantly illuminated in the lamplight. The farmers were dazed and dumbfounded by his talk which was like a combination of the most impenetrable French Structuralism and the comic articulation of Stanley Unwin. This was the same Bishop of Durham who emerged every Christmas to tell us he didn't believe in the Virgin Birth of Christ and every Easter to confess he didn't believe in his Resurrection which, he said, was "... no conjuring trick with bones."

But why bother to deny what no sensible person ever asserted?

There was a sequel. One Sunday I took the evening off and went for a look around York Minster. There was a huge sign at the entrance to the precinct garden saying TRESPASSERS WILL BE PROSECUTED. I thought that even cathedral canons might have stretched their charity as far as TRESPASSERS WILL BE FORGIVEN. Another sign said NO CARS NO ENTRY NO DOGS NO BALLS You had to go inside to notice there was plenty of balls. The Minster authorities had lent it to the lunatics from St Michael-le-Belfrey, next door and they were practising some sort of hideous religious rock concert. Litter everywhere. An ice cream half eaten melting on a 14th century vestments chest. Men hammering away at a stage prop of Noah's Ark. Everyone shouting. A few youthful tourists were gazing at the glass and stone and playing their transistor radios full belt on Radio Awful. Others exercised recently-discovered lusts of the flesh under the scaffolding. Nothing too terrifying. An American tourist, the size of King Eglon, stood on a pile of 12th century copes to take a flash photograph of the reserved Sacrament. An Englishman gave us a commentary on an ancient statue:

"Ee looks as if 'ee 'as an 'ard on!"

Next day I wrote a caustic piece for The Guardian which I concluded with the line,

"Let's have a bit more reverence and respect – or else for God's sake burn it down."

The following week the Minster was struck by lightning. The popular press surmised that this Act of God was a punishment on the Bishop of Durham for his unbelief, The Bishop had just conducted an Ordination Service there. A few days later I received a postcard from the playwright John Osborne saying,

"So God reads The Guardian – how awful!"

The Archbishop of York had a letter published in The Guardian informing its readers that,

"God does not send down fire from heaven."

The Guardian had the decency to publish my one-line riposte:
"Tell it to Elijah!"

I was also called to exercise my privilege as Chairman of the Tockwith School Governors to appoint a new head-teacher. Jim Watts was a governor too and he drove us through the drenching rain to County Hall in Northallerton where we interviewed the four candidates. It brought back fading memories of ALSEB to savour once again the fetid phraseology of educational jargon: peer group identification... integrated day...semi-structured approaches to curriculum development. When people cannot think, it is a pity they retain their ability to talk. The best candidate was a forty-two year old exotic Methodist called Carmen who looked as if she had been playing with the face paints. Her dress was like something tossed off by Salvador Dali and her perfume strong enough to suggest she had commandeered the Chelsea Flower Show. God know what John Wesley would have said.

We appointed her.

Later that year I was summoned to the presence of Dr John Stapylton Habgood, Archbishop of York. The palace is out at Bishopthorpe, to the south of the city, an elegant residence in its own park and overlooking the river Ouse as it does, actually, ooze sluggishly towards Acaster Malbis and so on down to Selby before joining the great Humber. I had written an article in The Sunday Express criticising Habgood's support for research on human embryos. He kept me waiting below the stone stairs for a full six minutes before he beckoned me into his study and issued the one word:

"Sit."

If I had had a tail I would have wagged it.

His Grace wore thick black-rimmed spectacles and a dark lounge suit. His face was elongated, bony, pale and his tone acerbic. What, of all things – and not just a civil servant – did he remind me of? I know: a Deist – an 18th century agnostic primate performing churchly acts for only political motives. He wore expediency like a shroud. He crept about the place with a sort of agile indignation, interrupting his movements to show me press cuttings of what he had said and what I had written.

Strictly – or casuistically, according to the breadth of one's vocabulary – speaking, I was in the wrong. He had not specifically declared himself in favour of embryo research, not in as many words, but he had not condemned it.

He let me go with a reprimand.

There is a sequel to this tale for which I had to wait five years. In his Christmas message to the Archdiocese in 1989, Habgood wrote at length in favour of research on human embryos. I think it had become plain to him that the imminent vote in parliament was going to back this sort of research, and so the Archbishop thought it proper to position himself on the correct side – if he was to have any chance of making Archbishop of Canterbury. But of course he lost to George Carey. The story goes that Mrs Thatcher, presented with the customary two names prepared for her consideration by the Crown Appointments Commission, said,

"I've no idea who the other one is, but I'm not having Habgood!"

About this time I happened to be in the university in Cambridge where Habgood, post-grad, had been a Scientific Demonstrator, and I thought I would ask to take a look at his doctoral thesis. It was on the subject of animal pain. It was a shocking exposure of the standard required for the degree of Doctor of Philosophy in the Science Faculty at Cambridge. Just a small folder containing a few drawings to illustrate the Demonstrator's experiments. It was like nothing so much as the nature study notebook belonging to a child at junior school: think Janet and John look at frogs.

I wrote a piece in The Yorkshire Evening Press about the Archbishop's Christmas message. I referred to the way I had been carpeted back in 1985 and I thanked Dr Habgood for finally coming clean on the issue of embryo research. I bemoaned the fact that his Christmas letter had said nothing at all about the manger, the shepherds or the kings, but consoled myself in the knowledge that he had not neglected the Massacre of the Innocents.

Envoi

When you get into your fifth decade, time seems to speed up so that it can barely contain the events which compete to crowd into it. One of my best friends, Steve, died aged just thirty-one. He was a consummate actor and about to take the lead in my play The Chat Show. It was a sudden arrhythmia that killed him. Inexplicably, his heart went jumpy and he snuffed it. I conducted his funeral at the opulent church of St Wilfred's, Harrogate where my first Vicar Broadstairs was incumbent. He was now quite aged: so ludicrously pompous as to be beyond satire.

I published two volumes of short stories about the life of a country parson and directed my play about Mahler at The York Arts Theatre. I was writing regularly for the newspapers and I frequently drove up to the Tyne Tees TV studios in Newcastle to record The Epilogue. My producer was the elderly, elegant – though chillingly Christopher Lee like – Maxwell Deas who had played the part of a priest in Michael Caine's hit film Get Carter.

SCM Press published my Being Saved – a book which compared Christian doctrine with Jungian psychology – and a book of social criticism, The New Babel. My father died and I dedicated my next book to his memory, Death Be Not Proud.I really can't explain why I was doing all this stuff, except in terms of displacement activity: like some stupid bloody mouse insisting on washing itself even as it is about to be under the cat's paw.

I was no longer the new Vicar – in fact I was becoming – rapidly, it seemed to me – the old Vicar. I was presenting for Confirmation – and even marrying - children I had baptised. I might have remained at Tockwith and Bilton forever, baptising, marrying and burying folk wholesale, visiting them in their homes, eating and drinking anything and everything offered, hob-nobbing in the pubs, walking the fields in all seasons.

Suddenly, there was a woman who searched me out and knew me. I loved her, and love her. I wrote to her:

Your vivacious unease was the original stimulant:

The composure all costume and new-washed hair.
Behind the mask you eyes would move, provoked,
In that room above the curved stairs;
Framed by the window, the summer evening
An infinite, soluble blue. Your voice,
A delightful hiatus of articulation
Made self-forgetful by sharp recognition
Of some human truth you had known long before.
You catch yourself again in mid-astonishment,
And pink cheeks mock you under the Alice hair:
Discovery your undoing and how fresh;
For knowledge as we know belongs the flesh.

Then one morning I received an invitation from the Bishop of London...

It was nearly Christmas. And on the train I wrote to the woman another poem:

I wish you would enclose me in your breath
Which is my element,
And let me touch your thigh;
Pay fingertip obeisance to your neck,
Know your lips and tongue for sacraments,
And this night become incarnate in your flesh.

The New Year brought things I could not have imagined...